# CLEP Natural Sciences Exam Success

By Lewis Morris

Copyright © Network4Learning, Inc. 2018.

www.insiderswords.com/CLEPNatural

ISBN-13: 978-1983281273

## Table of Contents

| | |
|---|---|
| Introduction | 5 |
| Crossword Puzzles | 24 |
| Multiple Choice | 74 |
| Matching | 112 |
| Word Search | 152 |
| Glossary | 182 |

# What is "Insider Language"?

Recent research has confirmed what we have known for decades: The strongest students and leaders in industry have a mastered an Insider Language in their subject and field. This Insider language is made up of the technical terms and vocabulary necessary to communicate effectively in classes or the workplace. For those who master it, learning is easier, faster, and much more enjoyable.

Most students who are surveyed report that the greatest challenge to any course of study is learning the vocabulary. When we examine typical college courses, we discover that there is, on average, 250 Insider Terms a student must learn over the course of a semester. Further, most exams rely heavily on this set of words for assessment purposes. The structure of multiple choice exams lends itself perfectly to the testing of this Insider Language. Students who can differentiate between Insider Language terms can handle challenging exam questions with ease and confidence.

From recent research on learning and vocabulary we have learned:

- Your knowledge of any subject is contained in the content-specific words you know. The more of these terms that you know, the easier it is to understand and recall important information; the easier it will be to communicate your ideas to peers, professors, supervisors, and co-workers. The stronger your content-area vocabulary is, the higher your scores will be on your exams and written assignments.

- Students who develop a strong Insider Language perform better on tests, learn faster, retain more information, and express greater satisfaction in learning.

- Familiarizing yourself with subject-area vocabulary before formal study (pre-learning) is the most effective way to learn this language and reap the most benefit.

- The vocabulary on standardized exams come directly from the stated objectives of the test-makers. This means that the vocabulary found on standardized exams is predictable. Our books focus on this vocabulary.

- Most multiple-choice exams are glorified vocabulary quizzes. Think about the format of a multiple-choice question. The question stem is a definition of a term and the choices (known as distractors) are 4 or 5 similar words. Your task is to differentiate between the meanings of those terms and choose the correct word.

- It takes a person several exposures to a new word to be able to use it with confidence in conversation or in writing. You need to process these words several different ways to make them part of your long-term memory.

**The goals of this book are:**
- To give you an "Insider Language" for your subject.
- Pre-teach the most important words before you set out on a traditional course of review or study.
- Teach you the most important words in your subject area.
- Teach you strategies for learning subject-area words on your own.
- Boost your confidence in your ability to master this language and support you in your study.
- Reduce the stress of studying and provide you with fun activities that work.

**How it works:**
The secret to mastering Insider Language is through repetition and exposure. We have eleven steps for you to follow:

1. Read the word and definition in the glossary out loud. "See it, Say it"
2. Identify the part of speech the word belongs to such as noun, verb, adverb, or adjective. This will help you group the word and identify similar words.
3. Place the word in context by using it in a sentence. Write this sentence down and read it aloud.
4. Use "Chunking" to group the words. Make a diagram or word cloud using these groups.
5. Make connections to the words by creating analogies.
6. Create mnemonics that help you recognize patterns and orders of words by substituting the words for more memorable items or actions.
7. Examine the morphology of the word, that is, identify the root, prefix, and suffix that make up the word. Identify similar and related words.
8. Complete word games and puzzles such as crosswords and word searches.
9. Complete matching questions that require you to differentiate between related words.
10. Complete Multiple-choice questions containing the words.
11. Create a visual metaphor or "memory cartoon" to make a mental picture of the word and related processes.

By completing this word study process, you will be exposed to the terminology in various ways that will activate your memory and create a lasting understanding of this language.

The strategies in this book are designed to make you an independent expert at learning insider language. These strategies include:

- Verbalizing the word by reading it and its definition aloud ("See It, Say It"). This allows you to make visual, auditory, and speech connections with its meaning.

- Identifying the type of word (Noun, verb, adverb, and adjective). Making this distinction helps you understand how to visualize the word. It helps you "chunk" the words into groups, and gives you clues on how to use the word.

- Place the word in context by using it in a sentence. Write this sentence down and read it aloud. This will give you an example of how the word is used.

- "Chunking". By breaking down the word list into groups of closely related words, you will learn them better and be able to remember them faster. Once you have group the terms, you can then make word clouds using a free online service. These word clouds provide visual cues to remembering the words and their meanings.

- Analogies. By creating analogies for essential words, you will be making connections that you can see on paper. These connections can trigger your memory and activate your ability to use the word in your writing as you begin to use them. Many of these analogies also use visual cues. In a sense, you can make a mental picture from the analogy.

- Mnemonics. A device such as a pattern of letters, ideas, or associations that assists in remembering something. A mnemonic is especially useful for remembering the order of a set of words or the order of a process.

- Morphology. The study of word roots, prefixes, and suffixes. By examining the structure of the words, you will gain insight into other words that are closely related, and learn how to best use the word.

- Visual metaphors. This is the most sophisticated and entertaining strategy for learning vocabulary. Create a "memory cartoon" using one or more of the vocabulary terms. This activity triggers the visual part of your memory and makes fast, permanent, imprints of the word on your memory. By combining the terms in your visual metaphor, you can "chunk" the entire set of vocabulary terms into several visual metaphors and benefit from the brain's tendency to group these terms.

The activities in this book are designed to imprint the words and their meanings in your memory in different ways. By completing each activity, you will gain the necessary exposures to the word to make it a permanent part of your vocabulary. Each activity uses a different part of your memory. The result is that you will be comfortable using these words and be able to tell the difference between closely related words. The activities include:

A. Crossword Puzzles and Word Searches- These are proven to increase test scores and improve comprehension. Students frequently report that they are fun and engaging, while requiring them to analyze the structure and meaning of the words.

B. Matching- This activity is effective because it forces you to differentiate between many closely related terms.

C. Multiple Choice- This classic question format lends itself to vocabulary study perfectly. Most exams are in this format because they are simple to make, easy to score, and are a reliable type of assessment. (Perfect for the Vocabulary Master!) One strategy to use with multiple choice questions that enhance their effectiveness is to cover the answer choices while you read the question. After reading the question, see if you can answer it before looking at the choices. Then look at the choices to see if you match one of them.

Conducting a thorough "word study" of your insider language will take time and effort, but the rewards will be well worth it. By following this guide and completing the exercises thoughtfully, you will become a stronger, more effective, and satisfied student. Best of luck on your mastery of this Insider Language!

**Insider Language Strategies**

**"See It, Say It!" Reading your Insider Language set aloud**

*"IT IS BETTER TO FAIL IN ORIGINALITY THAN TO SUCCEED IN IMITATION."*
*-HERMAN MELVILLE*

Reading aloud is the foundation for the development of an Insider Language. It is the single most important thing you can do for vocabulary acquisition. Done correctly, it engages the visual, auditory, and speech centers of the brain and hastens its storage in your long-term memory.

Reading aloud demonstrates the relationship between the printed word and its meaning.

You can read aloud on a higher level than you can initially understand, so reading aloud makes complex ideas more accessible and exposes you to vocabulary and patterns that are not part of your typical speech. Reading aloud helps you understand the complicated text better and makes more challenging text easier to grasp and understand. Reading aloud helps you to develop the "habits of mind" the strongest students use.

Reading aloud will make connections to concepts in the reading that requires you to relate the new vocabulary to things you already know. Go to the glossary at the end of this book and for each word complete the five steps outlined below:

1. Read the word and its definition aloud. Focus on the sound of the word and how it looks on the paper.
2. Read the word aloud again try to say three or four similar words; this will help you build connections to closely related words.
3. Read the word aloud a third time. Try to make a connection to something you have read or heard.
4. Visualize the concept described in the term. Paint a mental picture of the word in use.
5. Try to think of the opposite of the word. Discovering a close antonym will help you place this word in context.

# Create a sentence using the word in its proper context

*"OPPORTUNITIES DON'T HAPPEN. YOU CREATE THEM." –CHRIS GROSSER*

Context means the circumstances that form the setting for an event, statement, or idea, and which it can be fully understood and assessed. Synonyms for context include conditions, factors, situation, background, and setting.
Place the word in context by using it in a sentence. Write this sentence down and read it aloud. By creating sentences, you are practicing using the word correctly. If you strive to make these sentences interesting and creative, they will become more memorable and effective in activating your long-term memory.

# Identify the Parts of Speech
*"SUCCESS IS NOT FINAL; FAILURE IS NOT FATAL: IT IS THE COURAGE TO CONTINUE THAT COUNTS." –WINSTON S. CHURCHILL*

Read through each term in the glossary and make a note of what part of speech each term is. Studying and identifying parts of speech shows us how the words relate to each other. It also helps you create a visualization of each term. Below are brief descriptions of the parts of speech for you to use as a guide.

VERB: A word denoting action, occurrence, or existence. Examples: walk, hop, whisper, sweat, dribbles, feels, sleeps, drink, smile, are, is, was, has.

NOUN: A word that names a person, place, thing, idea, animal, quality, or action. Nouns are the subject of the sentence. Examples: dog, Tom, Florida, CD, pasta, hate, tiger.

ADJECTIVE: A word that modifies, qualifies, or describes nouns and pronouns. Generally, adjectives appear immediately before the words they modify. Examples: smart girl, gifted teacher, old car, red door.

ADVERB: A word that modifies verbs, adjectives and other adverbs. An "ly" ending almost always changes an adjective to an adverb. Examples: ran swiftly, worked slowly, and drifted aimlessly. Many adverbs do not end in "ly." However, all adverbs identify when, where, how, how far, how much, etc. Examples: run hot, lived hard, moved right, study smart.

# Chunking

"YOUR POSITIVE ACTION COMBINED WITH POSITIVE THINKING RESULTS IN SUCCESS." SHIV KHERA

Chunking is when you take a set of words and break it down into groups based on a common relationship. Research has shown that our brains learn by chunking information. By grouping your terms, you will be able to recall large sets of these words easily. To help make your chunking go easily use an online word cloud generator to make a set of word clouds representing your chunks.

1. Study the glossary and decide how you want to chunk the set of words. You can group by part of speech, topic, letter of the alphabet, word length, etc. Try to find an easy way to group each term.
2. Once you have your different groups, visit www.wordclouds.com to create a custom word cloud for each group. Print each one of these clouds and post it in a prominent place to serve as constant visual aids for your learning.

# Analogies

"CHOOSE THE POSITIVE. YOU HAVE CHOICE, YOU ARE MASTER OF YOUR ATTITUDE, CHOOSE THE POSITIVE, THE CONSTRUCTIVE. OPTIMISM IS A FAITH THAT LEADS TO SUCCESS."– BRUCE LEE

An analogy is a comparison in which an idea or a thing is compared to another thing that is quite different from it. Analogies aim at explaining an idea by comparing it to something that is familiar. Metaphors and similes are tools used to create analogies.

Analogies are useful for learning vocabulary because they require you to analyze a word (or words), and then transfer that analysis to another word. This transfer reinforces the understanding of all the words.

As you analyze the relationships between the analogies you are creating, you will begin to understand the complex relationships between the seemingly unrelated words.

 A  is to  B  as  C  is to  D 

This can be written using colons in place of the terms "is to" and "as."

A:B::C:D

The two items on the left (items A & B) describe a relationship and are separated by a single colon. The two items on the right (items C & D) are shown on the right and are also separated by a colon. Together, both sides are then separated by two colons in the middle, as shown here: Tall: Short :: Skinny: Fat. The relationship used in this analogy is the antonym.

**How to create an analogy**

Start with the basic formula for an analogy:

____ : ____ :: ____ : ____

Next, we will examine a simple synonym analogy:

automobile : car :: box : crate

The key to figuring out a set of word analogies is determining the relationship between the paired set of words.

**Here is a list of the most common types of Analogies and examples**

| | |
|---|---|
| Synonym | Scream : Yell :: Push : Shove |
| Antonym | Rich : Poor :: Empty : Full |
| Cause is to Effect | Prosperity : Happiness :: Success : Joy |
| A Part is to its Whole | Toe : Foot :: Piece : Set |
| An Object to its Function | Car : Travel :: Read : Learn |
| A Item is to its Category | Tabby : House Cat :: Doberman : Dog |
| Word is a symptom of the other | Pain : Fracture :: Wheezing : Allergy |
| An object and it's description | Glass : Brittle :: Lead : Dense |
| The word is lacking the second word | Amputee : Limb :: Deaf : Hearing |
| The first word Hinders the second word | Shackles : Movement :: Stagger : Walk |
| The first word helps the action of the second | Knife : Bread :: Screwdriver : Screw |
| This word is made up of the second word | Sweater : Wool :: Jeans : Denim |
| A word and it's definition | Cede: Break Away :: Abolish : To get rid of |

Using words from the glossary, make a set of analogies using each one. As a bonus, use more than one glossary term in a single analogy.

_____ : _____ :: _____ : _____

Name the relationship between the words in your analogy:_____

_____ : _____ :: _____ : _____

Name the relationship between the words in your analogy:_____

_____ : _____ :: _____ : _____

Name the relationship between the words in your analogy:_____

# Mnemonics

> "IT ISN'T THE MOUNTAINS AHEAD TO CLIMB THAT WEAR YOU OUT; IT'S THE PEBBLE IN YOUR SHOE."  —MUHAMMAD ALI

A mnemonic is a learning technique that helps you retain and remember information. Mnemonics are one of the best learning methods for remembering lists or processes in order. Mnemonics make the material more meaningful by adding associations and creating patterns. Interestingly, mnemonics may work better when they utilize absurd, startling, or shocking examples and references. Mnemonics help organize the information so that you can easily retrieve it later. By giving you associations and cues, mnemonics allow you to form a mental structure ordering a list or process to help you remember it better. This mental structure allows you to create a structure of association between items that may not appear to have any relationship. Mnemonics typically use references that are easy to visualize and thus easier to remember. Through visualization of vivid images and references, the information is much easier to imprint into long-term memory. The power of making mnemonics lies in converting dull, inert and uninspiring information into something vibrant and memorable.

**How to make simple and effective mnemonics**
Some of the best mnemonics help us remember simple rules or lists in order.

Step 1. Take a list of terms you are trying to remember in order. For example, we will use the scientific method:

> observation, question, hypothesis, methods, results, and conclusion.

Next, we will replace each word on the list with a new word that starts with the same letter. These new words will together form a vivid sentence that is easy to remember:

> Objectionable Queens Haunted Macho Rednecks Creatively.

As silly as the above sentence seems, it is easy to remember, and now we can call on this sentence to remind us of the order of the scientific method.

Visit http://www.mnemonicgenerator.com/ and try typing in a list of words. It is fun to see the mnemonics that it makes and shows how easy it is to make great mnemonics to help your studying.

Using vivid words in your mnemonics allows you to see the sentence you are making. Words that are gross, scary, or name interesting animals are helpful. Profanity is also useful because the shock value can trigger memory. The following are lists of vivid words to use in your mnemonics:

**Gross words**
Moist, Gurgle, Phlegm, Fetus, Curd, Smear, Squirt, Chunky, Orifice, Maggots, Viscous, Queasy, Bulbous, Pustule, Putrid, Fester, Secrete, Munch, Vomit, Ooze, Dripping, Roaches, Mucus, Stink, Stank, Stunk, Slurp, Pus, Lick, Salty, Tongue, Fart, Flatulence, Hemorrhoid.

**Interesting Animals**
Aardvark, Baboon, Chicken, Chinchilla, Duck, Dragonfly, Emu, Electric Eel, Frog, Flamingo, Gecko, Hedgehog, Hyena, Iguana, Jackal, Jaguar, Leopard, Lynx, Minnow, Manatee, Mongoose, Neanderthal, Newt, Octopus, Oyster, Pelican, Penguin, Platypus, Quail, Racoon, Rattlesnake, Rhinoceros, Scorpion, Seahorse, Toucan, Turkey, Vulture, Weasel, Woodpecker, Yak, Zebra.

**Superhero Words**
Diabolical, Activate, Boom, Clutch, Dastardly, Dynamic, Dynamite, Shazam, Kaboom, Zip, Zap, Zoom, Zany, Crushing, Smashing, Exploding, Ripping, Tearing.

**Scary Words**
Apparition, Bat, Chill, Demon, Eerie, Fangs, Genie, Hell, Lantern, Macabre, Nightmare, Owl, Ogre, Phantasm, Repulsive, Scarecrow, Tarantula, Undead, Vampire, Wraith, Zombie.

There are several types of mnemonics that can help your memory.

**1. Images**
**Visual mnemonics** are a type of mnemonic that works by associating an image with characters or objects whose name sounds like the item that must be memorized. This is one of the easiest ways to create effective mnemonics. An example would be to use the shape of numbers to help memorize a long list of them. Numbers can be memorized by their shapes, so that: 0 -looks like an egg; 1 -a pencil, or a candle; 2 -a snake; 3 -an ear; 4 -a sailboat; 5 -a key; 6 -a comet; 7 -a knee; 8 -a snowman; 9 -a comma.

Another type of visual mnemonic is the word-length mnemonic in which the number of letters in each word corresponds to a digit. This simple mnemonic gives pi to seven decimal places:

3.141582 becomes "How I wish I could calculate pi."

Of course, you could use this type of mnemonic to create a longer sentence showing the digits of an important number. Some people have used this type of mnemonic to memorize thousands of digits.

Using the hands is also an important tool for creating visual objects. Making the hands into specific shapes can help us remember the pattern of things or the order of a list of things.

## 2. Rhyming

Rhyming mnemonics are quick ways to make things memorable. A classic example is a mnemonic for the number of days in each month:
"30 days hath September, April, June, and November.
All the rest have 31
Except February, my dear son.
It has 28, and that is fine
But in Leap Year it has 29."

Another example of a rhyming mnemonic is a common spelling rule:
"I before e except after c
or when sounding like a
in neighbor and weigh."

Use **rhymer.com** to get large lists of rhyming words.

## 3. Homonym

A homonym is one of a group of words that share the same pronunciation but have different meanings, whether spelled the same or not.

Try saying what you're attempting to remember out loud or very quickly, and see if anything leaps out. If you know other languages, using similar-sounding words from those can be effective.

You could also browse this list of homonyms
at http://www.cooper.com/alan/homonym_list.html.

## 4. Onomatopoeia

An Onomatopeia is a word that phonetically imitates, resembles or suggests the source of the sound that it describes. Are there any noises made by the thing you're trying to memorize? Is it often associated with some other sound? Failing that, just make up a noise that seems to fit.

Achoo, ahem, baa, bam, bark, beep, beep beep, belch, bleat, boo, boo hoo, boom, burp, buzz, chirp, click clack, crash, croak, crunch, cuckoo, dash, drip, ding dong, eek, fizz, flit, flutter, gasp, grrr, ha ha, hee hee, hiccup, hiss, hissing, honk, icky, itchy, jiggly, jangle, knock knock, lush, la la la, mash, meow, moan, murmur, neigh, oink, ouch, plop, pow, quack, quick, rapping, rattle, ribbit, roar, rumble, rustle, scratch, sizzle, skittering, snap crackle pop, splash, splish splash, spurt, swish, swoosh, tap, tapping, tick tock, tinkle, tweet, ugh, vroom, wham, whinny, whip, whooping, woof.

## 5. Acronyms

An acronym is a word or name formed as an abbreviation from the initial components of a word, such as NATO, which stands for North Atlantic Treaty Organization. If you're trying to memorize something involving letters, this is often a good bet. A lot of famous mnemonics are acronyms, such as ROYGBIV which stands for the order of colors in the light spectrum (Red, Orange, Yellow, Green, Blue, Indigo, and Violet).

A great acronym generator to try is: www.all-acronyms.com.

A different spin on an acronym is a backronym. A **backronym** is a specially constructed phrase that is supposed to be the source of a word that is an acronym. A backronym is constructed by creating a new phrase to fit an already existing word, name, or acronym.

The word is a combination of *backward* and *acronym*, and has been defined as a "reverse acronym." For example, the United States Department of Justice assigns to their Amber Alert program the meaning "**A**merica's **M**issing: **B**roadcast **E**mergency **R**esponse." The process can go either way to make good mnemonics.

Visit: https://arthurdick.com/projects/backronym/ to try out a simple backronym generator.

## 6. Anagrams

An anagram is a direct word switch or word play, the result of rearranging the letters of a word or phrase to produce a new word or phrase, using all the original letters exactly once; for example, the word anagram can be rearranged into nag-a-ram.

Try re-arranging letters or components and see if anything memorable emerges. Visit http://www.nameacronym.net/ to use a simple anagram generator.

One particularly memorable form of anagram is the spoonerism, where you swap the initial syllables or letters of words to make new phrases. These are usually humorous, and this makes them easier to remember. Here are some examples:

"Is it kisstomary to cuss the bride?" (as opposed to "customary to kiss")
"The Lord is a shoving leopard." (instead of "a loving shepherd")
"A blushing crow." ("crushing blow")
"A well-boiled icicle" ("well-oiled bicycle")
"You were fighting a liar in the quadrangle." ("lighting a fire")
"Is the bean dizzy?" (as opposed to "is the dean busy?")

## 7. Stories

Make up quick stories or incidents involving the material you want to memorize. For larger chunks of information, the stories can get more elaborate. Structured stories are particularly good for remembering lists or other sequenced information. Have a look at https://en.wikipedia.org/wiki/Method_of_loci for a more advanced memory sequencing technique.

# Visual Metaphors

"LIMITS, LIKE FEAR, IS OFTEN AN ILLUSION." –MICHAEL JORDAN

What is a Metaphor?

A metaphor is a figure of speech that refers to one thing by mentioning another thing. Metaphors provide clarity and identify hidden similarities between two seemingly unrelated ideas. A visual metaphor is an image that creates a link between different ideas.

Visual metaphors help us use our understanding of the world to learn new concepts, skills, and ideas. Visual metaphors help us relate new material to what we already know. Visual metaphors must be clear and simple enough to spark a connection and understanding. Visual metaphors should use familiar things to help you be less fearful of new, complex, or challenging topics. Metaphors trigger a sense of familiarity so that you are more accepting of the new idea. Metaphors work best when you associate a familiar, easy to understand idea with a challenging, obscure, or abstract concept.

**How to make a visual metaphor**

1. Brainstorm using the words of the concept. Use different fonts, colors, or shapes to represent parts of the concept.

2. Merge these images together

3. Show the process using arrows, accents, etc.

4. Think about the story line your metaphor projects.

**Examples of visual metaphors:**

A skeleton used to show a framework of something.

A cloud showing an outline.

A bodybuilder whose muscles represent supporting ideas and details.

A sandwich where the meat, tomato, and lettuce represent supporting ideas.

A recipe card to show a process.

Your metaphor should be accurate. It should be complex enough to convey meaning, but simple and clear enough to be easily understood.

# Morphology
## "SCIENCE IS THE CAPTAIN, AND PRACTICE THE SOLDIERS." LEONARDO DA VINCI

Morphology is the study of the origin, roots, suffixes, and prefixes of the words. Understanding the meaning of prefixes, suffixes, and roots make it easier to decode the meaning of new vocabulary. Having the ability to decode using morphology increases text comprehension when initially reading as well.

The capability of identifying meaningful parts of words (morphemes), including prefixes, suffixes, and roots can be helpful. Identifying morphemes improves decoding accuracy and fluency. Reading speed improves when you can decode larger chunks of text quickly. When you can recognize morphemes in words, you will be better able to make sense of new words in context. Below are charts containing the most common prefixes, suffixes, and root words. Use them to help you decode your vocabulary terms.

**Prefixes**

| Prefix | Meaning | Example words and meanings | |
|---|---|---|---|
| a, ab, abs | away from | absent | not to be present, to give up an office or throne. |
| | | abdicate | |
| ad, a, ac, af, ag, an, ar, at, as | to, toward | Advance | To move forward |
| | | advantage | To have the upper hand |
| anti | against | Antidote | To repair poisoning |
| | | antisocial | refers to someone who's not social |
| | | antibiotic | |
| bi, bis | two | bicycle | two-wheeled cycle |
| | | binary | two number system |
| | | biweekly | every two weeks |
| circum, cir | around | circumnavigate | Travel around the world |
| | | circle | a figure that goes all around |
| com, con, co, col | with, together | Complete | To finish |
| | | Complement | To go along with |
| de | away from, down, the opposite of | depart | to go away from |
| | | detour | to go out of your way |
| dis, dif, di | apart | dislike | not to like |
| | | dishonest | not honest |
| | | distant | away |
| En-, em- | Cause to | Entrance | the way in. |
| epi | upon, on top of | epitaph | writing upon a tombstone |
| | | epilogue | speech at the end, on top of the rest |
| | | epidemic | |
| equ, equi | equal | equalize | to make equal |
| | | equitable | fair, equal |
| ex, e, ef | out, from | exit | to go out |
| | | eject | to throw out |
| | | exhale | to breathe out |
| Fore- | Before | Forewarned | To have prior warning |

| Prefix | Meaning | Example Words and Meanings | |
|---|---|---|---|
| in, il, ir, im, en | in, into | Infield<br>Imbibe | The inner playing field<br>to take part in |
| in, il, ig, ir, im | not | inactive<br>ignorant<br>irreversible<br>irritate | not active<br>not knowing<br>not reversible<br>to put into discomfort |
| inter | between, among | international<br>interact | among nations<br>to mix with |
| mal, male | bad, ill, wrong | malpractice<br>malfunction | bad practice<br>fail to function, bad function |
| Mid | Middle | Amidships | In the middle of a ship |
| mis | wrong, badly | misnomer | The wrong name |
| mono | one, alone, single | monocle | one lensed glasses |
| non | not, the reverse of | nonprofit | not making a profit |
| ob | in front, against, in front of, in the way of | Obsolete | No longer needed |
| omni | everywhere, all | omnipresent<br>omnipotent | always present, everywhere<br>all powerful |
| Over | On top | Overdose | Take too much medication |
| Pre | Before | Preview | Happens before a show. |
| per | through | Permeable<br>pervasive | to pass through,<br>all encompassing |
| poly | many | Polygamy<br>polygon | many spouses<br>figure with many sides |
| post | after | postpone<br>postmortem | to do after<br>after death |
| pre | before, earlier than | Predict<br>Preview | To know before<br>To view before release |
| pro | forward, going ahead of, supporting | proceed<br>pro-war<br>promote | to go forward<br>supporting the war<br>to raise or move forward |
| re | again, back | retell<br>recall<br>reverse | to tell again<br>to call back<br>to go back |
| se | apart | secede<br>seclude | to withdraw, become apart<br>to stay apart from others |
| Semi | Half | Semipermeable | Half-permeable |

| Prefix | Meaning | Example Words and Meanings | |
|---|---|---|---|
| Sub | under, less than | Submarine | under water |
| super | over, above, greater | superstar<br>superimpose | a start greater than her stars<br>to put over something else |
| trans | across | transcontinental<br>transverse | across the continent<br>to lie or go across |
| un, uni | one | unidirectional<br>unanimous<br>unilateral | having one direction<br>sharing one view<br>having one side |
| un | not | uninterested<br>unhelpful<br>unethical | not interested<br>not helpful<br>not ethical |

## Roots

| Root | Meaning | Example words & meanings | |
|---|---|---|---|
| act, ag | to do, to act | Agent<br>Activity | One who acts as a representative<br>Action |
| Aqua | Water | Aquamarine | The color of water |
| Aud | To hear | Auditorium | A place to hear music |
| apert | open | Aperture | An opening |
| bas | low | Basement<br>Basement | Something that is low, at the bottom<br>A room that is low |
| Bio | Living thing | Biological | Living matter |
| cap, capt, cip, cept, ceive | to take, to hold, to seize | Captive<br>Receive<br>Capable<br>Recipient | One who is held<br>To take<br>Able to take hold of things<br>One who takes hold or receives |
| ced, cede, ceed, cess | to go, to give in | Precede<br>Access<br>Proceed | To go before<br>Means of going to<br>To go forward |
| Cogn | Know | Cognitive | Ability to think |
| cred, credit | to believe | Credible<br>Incredible<br>Credit | Believable<br>Not believable<br>Belief, trust |
| curr, curs, cours | to run | Current<br>Precursory<br>Recourse | Now in progress, running<br>Running (going) before<br>To run for aid |
| Cycle | Circle | Lifecycle | The circle of life |
| dic, dict | to say | Dictionary<br>Indict | A book explaining words (sayings) |

| Root | Meaning | Examples and meanings | |
|---|---|---|---|
| duc, duct | to lead | Induce<br>Conduct<br>Aqueduct | To lead to action<br>To lead or guide<br>Pipe that leads water somewhere |
| equ | equal, even | Equality<br>Equanimity | Equal in social, political rights<br>Evenness of mind, tranquility |
| fac, fact, fic, fect, fy | to make, to do | Facile<br>Fiction<br>Factory<br>Affect | Easy to do<br>Something that is made up<br>Place that makes things<br>To make a change in |
| fer, ferr | to carry, bring | Defer<br>Referral | To carry away<br>Bring a source for help/information |
| Gen | Birth | Generate | To create something |
| graph | write | Monograph<br>Graphite | A writing on a particular subject<br>A form of carbon used for writing |
| Loc | Place | Location | A place |
| Mater | Mother | Maternity | Expecting birth |
| Mem | Recall | Memory | The recall experiences |
| mit, mis | to send | Admit<br>Missile | To send in<br>Something sent through the air |
| Nat | Born | Native | Born in a place |
| par | equal | Parity<br>Disparate | Equality<br>No equal, not alike |
| Ped | Foot | Podiatrist | Foot doctor |
| Photo | Light | Photograph | A picture |
| plic | to fold, to bend, to turn | Complicate<br>Implicate | To fold (mix) together<br>To fold in, to involve |
| pon, pos, posit, pose | to place | Component<br>Transpose<br>Compose<br>Deposit | A part placed together with others<br>A place across<br>To put many parts into place<br>To place for safekeeping |
| scrib, script | to write | Describe<br>Transcript<br>Subscription | To write about or tell about<br>A written copy<br>A written signature or document |
| sequ, secu | to follow | Sequence | In following order |

| Root | Meaning | Examples and Meanings | |
|---|---|---|---|
| Sign | Mark | Signal | to alert somebody |
| spec, spect, spic | to appear, to look, to see | Specimen<br>Aspect | An example to look at<br>One way to see something |
| sta, stat, sist,<br>stit, sisto | to stand, or make stand<br>Stable, steady | Constant<br>Status<br>Stable<br>Desist | Standing with<br>Social standing<br>Steady (standing)<br>To stand away from |
| Struct | To build | Construction | To build a thing |
| tact | to touch | Contact<br>Tactile | To touch together<br>To be able to be touched |
| ten, tent, tain | to hold | Tenable<br>Retentive<br>Maintain | Able to be held, holding<br>Holding<br>To keep or hold up |
| tend, tens, tent | to stretch | Extend<br>Tension | To stretch or draw out<br>Stretched |
| Therm | Temperature | Thermometer | Detects temperature |
| tract | to draw | Attract<br>Contract | To draw together<br>An agreement drawn up |
| ven, vent | to come | Convene<br>Advent | To come together<br>A coming |
| Vis | See | Invisible | Cannot be seen |
| ver, vert, vers | to turn | Avert<br>Revert<br>Reverse | To turn away<br>To turn back<br>To turn around |

# Crossword Puzzles

1. Using the Across and Down clues, write the correct words in the numbered grid below.

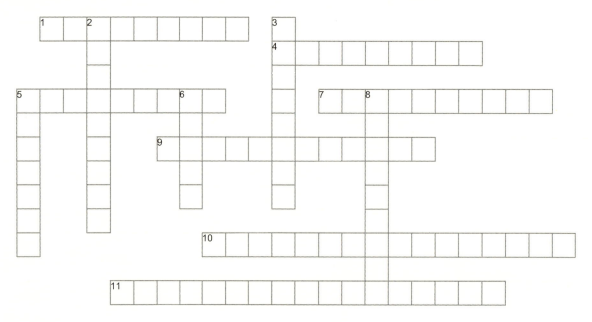

## ACROSS

1. The process whereby molecules and ions flow through the cell membrane from an area of higher concentration to an area of lower concentration; mixing of particles in a gas or liquid.
4. The process whereby cells build molecules and store energy.
5. Breakdown of ingested particles into molecules that can be absorbed by the body.
7. When both alleles for a given gene are the same in an individual.
9. A particle at rest will stay at rest and a particle in motion will stay in motion until acted upon by an outside force.
10. Momentary force of attraction that exist between molecules and are much weaker than the forces of chemical bonding.
11. The number of individuals of a species living in an area.

## DOWN

1. The process whereby molecules and ions flow through the cell membrane from an area of higher concentration to an area of lower concentration; mixing of particles in a gas or liquid.
4. The process whereby cells build molecules and store energy.
5. Breakdown of ingested particles into molecules that can be absorbed by the body.
7. When both alleles for a given gene are the same in an individual.
9. A particle at rest will stay at rest and a particle in motion will stay in motion until acted upon by an outside force.
10. Momentary force of attraction that exist between molecules and are much weaker than the forces of chemical bonding.
11. The number of individuals of a species living in an area.

A. Van der Waals Force
B. Law of Inertia
C. Metaphase
D. Half Life
E. Population Density
F. Forebrain
G. Homozygous
H. Diffusion
I. Density
J. Digestion
K. Ovary
L. Anabolism

© 2017 Network4Learning, Inc.

2. *Using the Across and Down clues, write the correct words in the numbered grid below.*

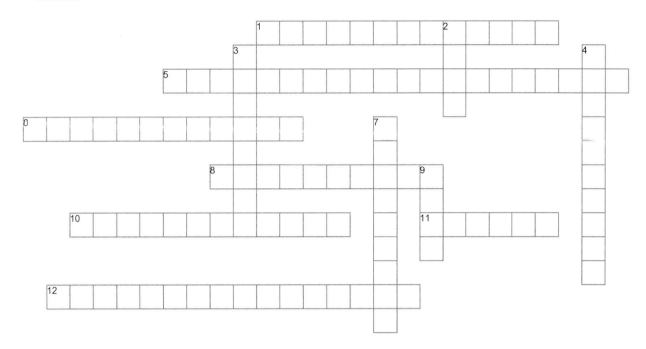

## ACROSS

1. The introduction of new genes from an immigrant, which results in a change of the gene pool.
5. Allows for the transfer of substances across the cell membrane with the help of specialized proteins.
6. The number of protons found in the nucleus of an atom of that element.
8. The distance from one crest (or top) of a wave to the next crest on the same side.
10. Occurs when a hydrogen atom is involved with a polar intermolecular attraction to a more electronegative atom.
11. Larger vessels that carry blood away from the heart.
12. traits are expressed from a pair of genes in the individual (on homologous chromosomes).

## DOWN

1. The introduction of new genes from an immigrant, which results in a change of the gene pool.
5. Allows for the transfer of substances across the cell membrane with the help of specialized proteins.
6. The number of protons found in the nucleus of an atom of that element.
8. The distance from one crest (or top) of a wave to the next crest on the same side.
10. Occurs when a hydrogen atom is involved with a polar intermolecular attraction to a more electronegative atom.
11. Larger vessels that carry blood away from the heart.
12. traits are expressed from a pair of genes in the individual (on homologous chromosomes).

A. Wavelength
E. Heat
I. Acid
B. Gene Migration
F. Hydrogen Bond
J. Midbrain
C. Atomic Number
G. Facilitated Diffusion
K. Law of Segregation
D. Homozygous
H. Migration
L. Artery

3. Using the Across and Down clues, write the correct words in the numbered grid below.

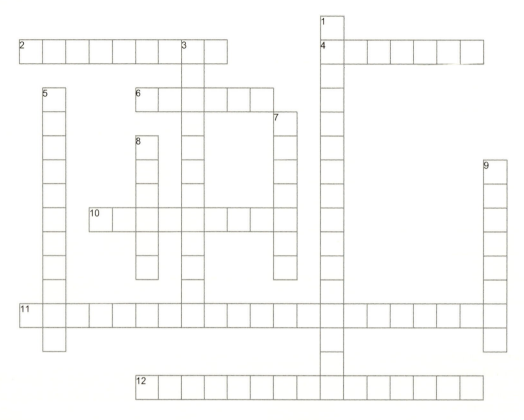

## ACROSS

2. Visual center connected to the eyes by the optic nerves.
4. A substance that cannot be broken down into any other substances.
6. The force of gravity acting upon that object.
10. Step four in mitosis; occurs as nuclear membranes form around the chromosomes and disperse through the new nucleoplasm; spindle fibers also disappear.
11. Scientific model that proposes that adaptations of species arise suddenly and rapidly.
12. The boundary between the nucleus and the cytoplasm.

## DOWN

2. Visual center connected to the eyes by the optic nerves.
4. A substance that cannot be broken down into any other substances.
6. The force of gravity acting upon that object.
10. Step four in mitosis; occurs as nuclear membranes form around the chromosomes and disperse through the new nucleoplasm; spindle fibers also disappear.
11. Scientific model that proposes that adaptations of species arise suddenly and rapidly.
12. The boundary between the nucleus and the cytoplasm.

A. Punctuated Equilibrium  B. Nuclear Membrane  C. Telophase
D. Ovules  E. Element  F. Optic Lobe
G. Weight  H. Secretory Vesicle  I. Ribosome
J. Nerve Tissue  K. Boiling Point  L. Nucleus

© 2017 Network4Learning, Inc.

4. Using the Across and Down clues, write the correct words in the numbered grid below.

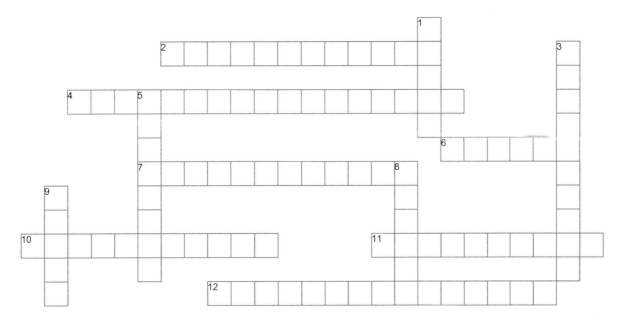

## ACROSS

2. The process of cell reproduction that centers on the replication and separation of strands of DNA.
4. A single species can develop into several diverse species over time; over time a species will specially adapt to live more effectively in a new environment.
6. What a zygote eventually grown into.
7. Makes up the walls of internal organs and functions in involuntary movement. (breathing, etc.)
10. The measure of the average kinetic energy of a substance.
11. Plants that produce seeds without flowers.
12. Reduces friction between bones and supports and connects them.

## DOWN

1. Negative ion.
3. Plants that produce flowers as reproductive organs.
5. A measure of the amount of force applied per unit of area.
8. Protein molecules that act as catalysts for organic reactions.
9. Class of lymphocyte cell that emerge from the bone marrow mature and produce antibodies, which enter the bloodstream.

A. Smooth Muscle
B. B Cell
C. Embryo
D. Cartilage Tissue
E. Adaptive Radiation
F. Angiosperm
G. Anion
H. Cell Division
I. Pressure
J. Enzyme
K. Gymnosperm
L. Temperature

5. Using the Across and Down clues, write the correct words in the numbered grid below.

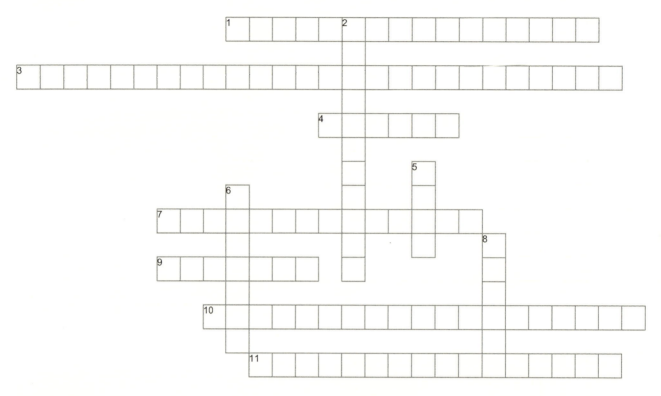

## ACROSS

1. Holds tissues and organs together, stabilizing the body structure.
3. Network of membranous channels; does not have attached ribosomes.
4. The force of gravity acting upon that object.
7. One gene is usually dominant over the other.
9. The physical place where a species lives.
10. Pressure that results from the total weight of the atmosphere exerting force on the Earth; can be measured with a barometer.
11. Part of the brain that controls involuntary responses such as breathing and heartbeat.

## DOWN

2. Results when two or more species living within the same area and that overlap niches both require a resource that is in limited supply.
5. A chain of about 80 nucleotides that provide the link between the "language" of nucleotides (codon and anticodon) and the "language" of amino acids; also known as transfer RNA.
6. An organization of individuals in a population in which tasks are divided for the group to work together.
8. What a zygote eventually grown into.

A. Medulla Oblongata
C. Atmospheric Pressure
E. Embryo
G. tRNA
I. Habitat
K. Competition

B. Smooth Endoplasmic Reticulum
D. Society
F. Connective Tissue
H. Weight
J. Law of Dominance

6. *Using the Across and Down clues, write the correct words in the numbered grid below.*

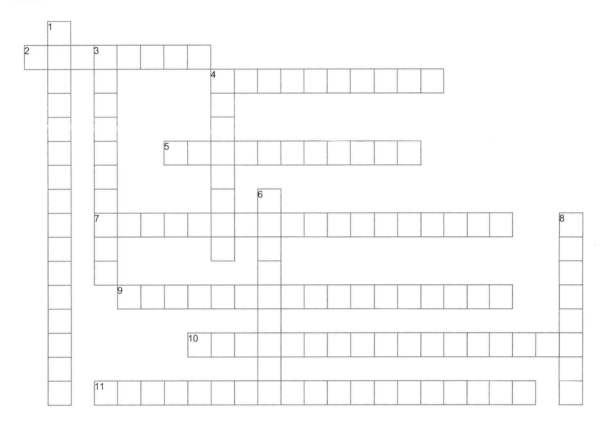

## ACROSS

2. Part of the brain that controls sensory and motor responses, memory, speech, and most factors of intelligence.
4. Structures that exist in two different species because they share a common ancestry.
5. The bending of a light wave around an obstacle.
7. Requires only one recessive gene to be expressed if there is no counteracting dominant gene.
9. The number of individuals of a species living in an area.
10. Carry impulses to skeletal muscle from the CNS.
11. Pressure that results from the total weight of the atmosphere exerting force on the Earth; can be measured with a barometer.

## DOWN

1. Carry substances produced within the cell to the cell membrane; packets of material packaged by the Golgi apparatus or endoplasmic reticulum.
3. The export of substances from the cell.
4. The time it takes for 50 percent of an isotope to decay.
6. Particular substance of an enzyme that fits within the active site.
8. The precursor of the gut lining and various accessory structures.

A. Half Life  
B. Endoderm  
C. Substrate  
D. Homologous  
E. Diffraction  
F. Atmospheric Pressure  
G. Exocytosis  
H. Cerebrum  
I. Population Density  
J. Secretory Vesicle  
K. Somatic Motor Nerve  
L. Sex Influenced Trait

7. Using the Across and Down clues, write the correct words in the numbered grid below.

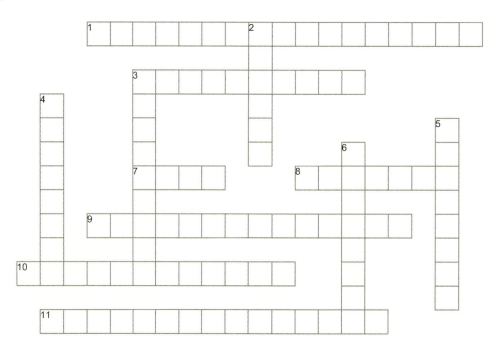

## ACROSS

1. The conduit for delivering nutrients and gases to all cells and for removing waste products from them.
3. When both alleles for a given gene are the same in an individual.
7. A chemical that accepts protons (H+ ions) when dissolved in water.
8. The process of producing four daughter cells, each with single unduplicated chromosomes.
9. A process in which bacteria absorb and incorporate pieces of DNA from their environment (usually from dead bacterial cells).
10. Temperature at which a substance changes from solid to liquid form.
11. The boundary between the nucleus and the cytoplasm.

## DOWN

2. A mass of lymph tissue that is active only through the teen years, fighting infection and producing T cells.
3. Consists of the cerebellum and medulla oblongata.
4. The first phase in mitosis.
5. Membrane-bound organelles containing digestive enzymes; digest unused material within the cell, damaged organelles, or materials absorbed by the cell for use.
6. Distributes the remaining set of chromosomes in a mitosis-like process.

A. Transformation  B. Hindbrain  C. Lysosome  D. Meiosis
E. Thymus  F. Division  G. Nuclear Membrane  H. Circulatory System
I. Melting Point  J. Prophase  K. Base  L. Homozygous

© 2017 Network4Learning, Inc.

8. *Using the Across and Down clues, write the correct words in the numbered grid below.*

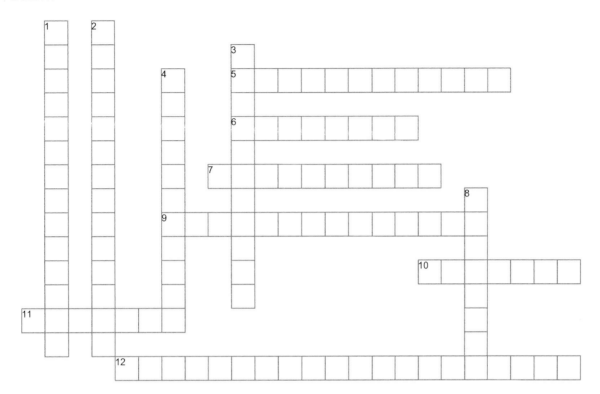

## ACROSS

5. Involved in hunger, thirst, blood pressure, body temperature, hostility, pain, pleasure, etc.
6. An individual of a species.
7. Structures that exist in two different species because they share a common ancestry.
9. Attaches bones of the skeleton to each other and surrounding tissues, which enables voluntary movement.
10. Present in every living cell, large un-branched chains of amino acids; may also be called polypeptides.
11. An organelle surrounded by two lipid bilayer membranes that is located near the center of the cell and contains chromosomes, nuclear pores, nucleoplasm, and nucleoli.
12. Two main components, the brain and the spinal cord; which control all other organs and systems of the body.

## DOWN

1. Instrumental in the storing, packaging, and shipping of proteins; also known as Golgi bodies or the Golgi complex.
2. Cells that contain membrane-bound intracellular organelles, including a nucleus.
3. The site of photosynthesis within plant cells.
4. Three laws that form the basis of most of our understanding of things in motion.
8. The rate of change of displacement; includes both speed and direction.

A. Protein
D. Newtons Laws
G. Central Nervous System
J. Organism

B. Hypothalamus
E. Skeletal Muscle
H. Chloroplast
K. Eukaryotic Cell

C. Golgi Apparatus
F. Homologous
I. Nucleus
L. Velocity

9. Using the Across and Down clues, write the correct words in the numbered grid below.

## ACROSS

3. The introduction of new genes from an immigrant, which results in a change of the gene pool.
6. Carries electrical and chemical impulses to and from organs and limbs to the brain.
8. Scientific model that proposes that adaptations of species arise suddenly and rapidly.
9. Large organization of folded membranes; responsible for the delivery of lipids and proteins to certain areas within the cytoplasm.
10. traits are expressed from a pair of genes in the individual (on homologous chromosomes).
11. A ring inside the epidermis that is made up of large parenchyma cells.

## DOWN

1. A chemical that donates proton (H+ ions) when dissolved in water.
2. The primary reproductive organ for a plant.
4. Produced by the male gametophyte; also known as a male gamete.
5. the period when the cell is active in carrying on its functions.
7. Negative ion.
8. Present in every living cell, large un-branched chains of amino acids; may also be called polypeptides.

A. Nerve Tissue
D. Law of Segregation
G. Protein
J. Anion

B. Sperm
E. Flower
H. Gene Migration
K. Cortex

C. Endoplasmic Reticulum
F. Interphase
I. Punctuated Equilibrium
L. Acid

10. *Using the Across and Down clues, write the correct words in the numbered grid below.*

## ACROSS

3. Membrane-bound organelles containing digestive enzymes; digest unused material within the cell, damaged organelles, or materials absorbed by the cell for use.
5. Steps in the cellular respiration process that do not require oxygen.
7. Small round cases within the ovary that contain one or more egg cells.
9. Individuals within a population that are most adapted to the environment and are also the most likely individuals to reproduce successfully.
10. Bond of attraction between positive and negative ions.
11. The outermost occupied energy level of an element.
12. Step four in mitosis; occurs as nuclear membranes form around the chromosomes and disperse through the new nucleoplasm; spindle fibers also disappear.

## DOWN

1. The process of cell reproduction that centers on the replication and separation of strands of DNA.
2. One gene is usually dominant over the other.
4. Located most anterior, it contains the olfactory lobes and cerebrum as well as the thalamus, hypothalamus, and pituitary gland.
6. Class of lymphocyte cell that emerge from the bone marrow mature and produce antibodies, which enter the bloodstream.
8. Carry impulses via electrochemical responses.

A. Anaerobic
D. Law of Dominance
G. Lysosome
J. Forebrain

B. Ovules
E. Neuron
H. Telophase
K. Valence Shell

C. Differential Reproduction
F. Cell Division
I. Ionic Bond
L. B Cell

11. *Using the Across and Down clues, write the correct words in the numbered grid below.*

## ACROSS

1. Requires only one recessive gene to be expressed if there is no counteracting dominant gene.
6. Some traits have no genes that are dominant and instead produce offspring that are a mix of the two parents.
7. Occurs when the nucleus emits a beta particle that degrades into an electron as it passes out of the atom.
8. Scientific model that proposes that adaptations of species arise suddenly and rapidly.
9. The two identical strands of duplicated chromatin in a cell that is getting ready to divide.
10. A ring inside the epidermis that is made up of large parenchyma cells.

## DOWN

1. Attaches bones of the skeleton to each other and surrounding tissues, which enables voluntary movement.
2. The principal infection-fighting component of the immune system.
3. Theoretical temperature at which particle motion stops; also known as 0 Kelvin.
4. The primary reproductive organ for a plant.
5. Energy that flows from an object that is warm to an object that is cooler.

A. Punctuated Equilibrium
D. Flower
G. Skeletal Muscle
J. Lymphatic System

B. Beta Decay
E. Chromatid
H. Cortex
K. Absolute Zero

C. Sex Influenced Trait
F. Incomplete Dominance
I. Heat

© 2017 Network4Learning, Inc.

12. *Using the Across and Down clues, write the correct words in the numbered grid below.*

## ACROSS

7. Located most anterior, it contains the olfactory lobes and cerebrum as well as the thalamus, hypothalamus, and pituitary gland.
8. The measure of the average kinetic energy of a substance.
9. Carry impulses via electrochemical responses.
10. Flows through the blood vessels and heart and is essential for carrying oxygen to cells, fighting infection, and carrying nutrients and wastes to and from cells.
11. Occurs when a hydrogen atom is involved with a polar intermolecular attraction to a more electronegative atom.
12. Three laws that form the basis of most of our understanding of things in motion.

## DOWN

1. The change in direction of a wave as it passes from one medium to another.
2. Movement of energy by transfer from particle to particle; can only occur when objects are touching.
3. A special process of diffusion that occurs when the water concentration inside the cell differs from the concentration outside the cell.
4. The parent cell that has a normal set of paired chromosomes.
5. Formed when two or more different atoms bond together chemically to form a unique substance.
6. Larger vessels that carry blood away from the heart.

A. Conduction
B. Compound
C. Diploid
D. Neuron
E. Artery
F. Osmosis
G. Refraction
H. Temperature
I. Blood Tissue
J. Newtons Laws
K. Forebrain
L. Hydrogen Bond

13. *Using the Across and Down clues, write the correct words in the numbered grid below.*

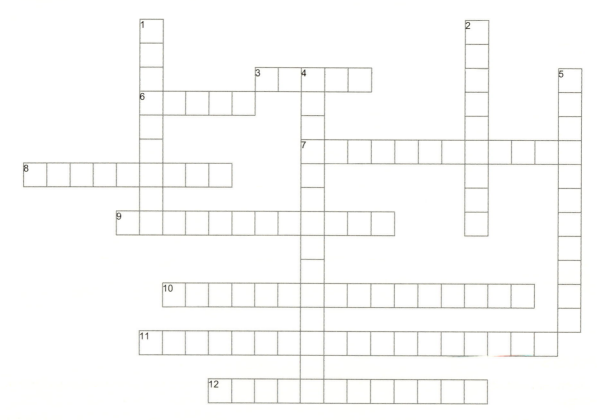

## ACROSS

3. the rate of change of an object's distance traveled.
6. Negative ion.
7. The average mass number.
8. Poor conductors of electrical currents.
9. Temperature at which a substance changes from solid to liquid form.
10. Named after scientists who discovered and modeled the structure of DNA.
11. The intentional alteration of genetic material of a living organism.
12. Bond formed between the atoms when atoms share electrons.

## DOWN

1. Step two of mitosis; occurs when the spindle fibers pull the chromosomes into alignment along the equatorial plane of the cell, creating the metaphase plate.
2. The number of wavelengths that pass a point in a second.
4. Cells that contain membrane-bound intracellular organelles, including a nucleus.
5. Three laws that form the basis of most of our understanding of things in motion.

A. Speed  
E. Eukaryotic Cell  
I. Newtons Laws  
B. Anion  
F. Watson Crick Model  
J. Melting Point  
C. Frequency  
G. Genetic Engineering  
K. Covalent Bond  
D. Insulator  
H. Atomic Weight  
L. Metaphase  

© 2017 Network4Learning, Inc.

14. *Using the Across and Down clues, write the correct words in the numbered grid below.*

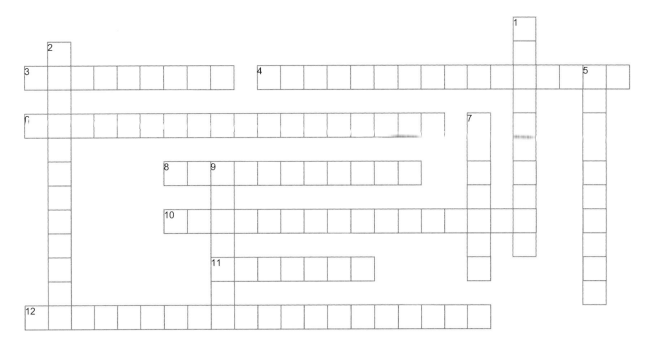

## ACROSS

3. The process whereby cells build molecules and store energy.
4. Named after scientists who discovered and modeled the structure of DNA.
6. The intentional alteration of genetic material of a living organism.
8. The process by which characteristics pass from one generation to another.
10. Substances freely pass across the membrane without the cell expending any energy.
11. A special process of diffusion that occurs when the water concentration inside the cell differs from the concentration outside the cell.
12. Two main components, the brain and the spinal cord; which control all other organs and systems of the body.

## DOWN

1. Begin in bone marrow as stem cells and are collected and distributed via the lymph nodes.
2. Those species having no internal backbone structure.
5. When the entire population of a particular species is eliminated.
7. The parent cell that has a normal set of paired chromosomes.
9. Short length of DNA wrapped around a core of small proteins.

A. Invertebrate
B. Inheritance
C. Histone
D. Diploid
E. Genetic Engineering
F. Lymphocyte
G. Watson Crick Model
H. Passive Transport
I. Extinction
J. Anabolism
K. Central Nervous System
L. Osmosis

15. *Using the Across and Down clues, write the correct words in the numbered grid below.*

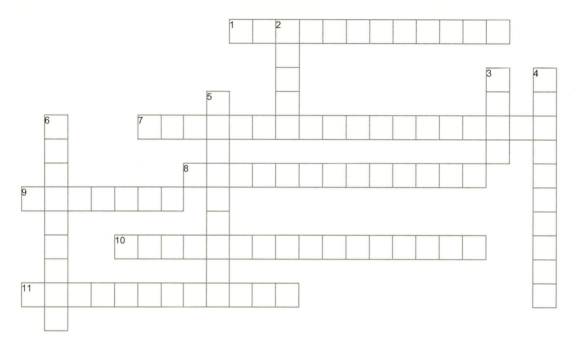

## ACROSS

1. Center of cellular respiration
7. Requires only one recessive gene to be expressed if there is no counteracting dominant gene.
8. A process in which some water that has traveled up through the plant to the leaves is evaporated.
9. The path that an electrical current follows.
10. Substances freely pass across the membrane without the cell expending any energy.
11. Studied the relationships between traits expressed in parents and offspring and the hereditary factors that caused expression of traits.

## DOWN

2. Mature cells in the thymus gland that patrol the blood for antigens but are also equipped to destroy antigens themselves.
3. Energy that flows from an object that is warm to an object that is cooler.
4. Process of breaking down molecules and releasing stored energy.
5. Temporary movement out of one range into another and back.
6. Tiny vessels that surround all tissues of the body and exchange carbon dioxide for oxygen.

A. Mitochondria
E. Sex Influenced Trait
I. Catabolism
B. Heat
F. Capillary
J. Passive Transport
C. Gregor Mendel
G. Circuit
K. Migration
D. T Cell
H. Transpiration

© 2017 Network4Learning, Inc.

16. *Using the Across and Down clues, write the correct words in the numbered grid below.*

## ACROSS

1. Molecule that has regions of partial change.
3. Study that organizes living things into groups based on morphology or, more recently, genetics.
4. Potential of hydrogen scale, which is a measurement of H+ ions in solutions.
6. Homologous chromosomes separate and independently sort in gamete formation.
7. An organization of individuals in a population in which tasks are divided for the group to work together.
8. Permanent one-way movement out of the original range.
9. Located most anterior, it contains the olfactory lobes and cerebrum as well as the thalamus, hypothalamus, and pituitary gland.
10. Responsible for the intake and processing of gases required by an organism and for expelling gases produced as waste products.

## DOWN

1. Notation that allow us to easily predict the results of a genetic cross.
2. The transfer or genetic material (portions of a bacterial chromosome) from one bacteria cell to another.
4. The first phase in mitosis.
5. The study of things in motion.

A. Taxonomy
D. Society
G. Mechanics
J. Independent Assortment

B. Transduction
E. Prophase
H. Punnett Square
K. Emigration

C. Polar Molecule
F. pH
I. Forebrain
L. Respiratory System

17. *Using the Across and Down clues, write the correct words in the numbered grid below.*

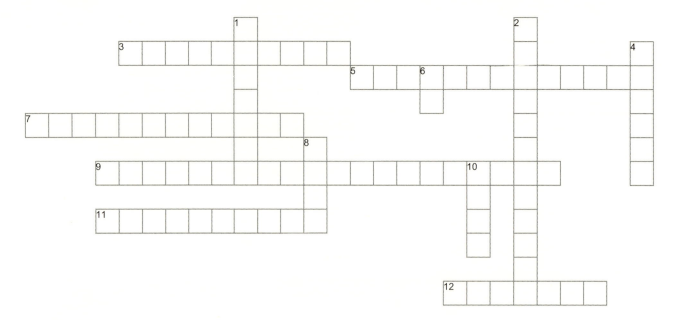

## ACROSS

3. The total number of a single species of organism found in an ecosystem.
5. Found beneath the skin and around organs, providing cushioning, insulation, and fat storage.
7. Functions to defend the body from infection by bacteria and viruses.
9. Allows for the transfer of substances across the cell membrane with the help of specialized proteins.
11. Enzyme control that may occur when the product of the reaction is also an inhibitor to the reaction.
12. Point at which homologous chromosomes pair up during meiosis.

## DOWN

1. The physical place where a species lives.
2. Center of cellular respiration
4. Mathematical quantities that recognize both the size and direction of the dimension being considered.
6. Potential of hydrogen scale, which is a measurement of H+ ions in solutions.
8. Vessels that carry blood toward the heart.
10. An accessory excretory organ that secretes wastes with water from sweat glands.

A. Regulation  B. Adipose Tissue  C. Population  D. Vector
E. Immune System  F. Habitat  G. Synapse  H. pH
I. Facilitated Diffusion  J. Skin  K. Vein  L. Mitochondria

© 2017 Network4Learning, Inc.

18. *Using the Across and Down clues, write the correct words in the numbered grid below.*

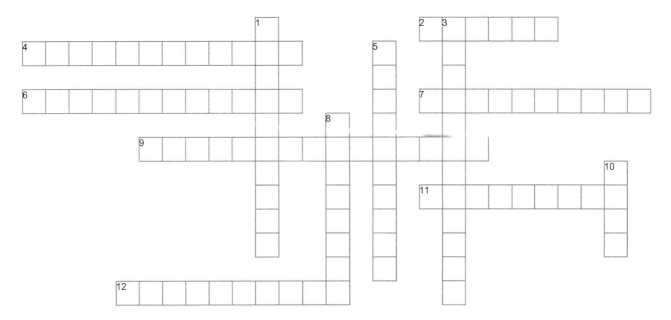

## ACROSS

2. Positive ion.
4. Functions to defend the body from infection by bacteria and viruses.
6. The transfer or genetic material (portions of a bacterial chromosome) from one bacteria cell to another.
7. The total number of a single species of organism found in an ecosystem.
9. Reduces friction between bones and supports and connects them.
11. A sequence of events ending in cell division, which produces two daughter cells.
12. Process of breaking down molecules and releasing stored energy.

## DOWN

1. Component of blood responsible for carrying oxygen.
3. Theoretical temperature at which particle motion stops; also known as 0 Kelvin.
5. A learned behavior that develops in a critical or sensitive period of the animal's lifespan.
8. Part of the brain that controls sensory and motor responses, memory, speech, and most factors of intelligence.
10. Length of DNA that encodes a particular protein.

A. Transduction
B. Immune System
C. Cerebrum
D. Imprinting
E. Hemoglobin
F. Cartilage Tissue
G. Cation
H. Population
I. Absolute Zero
J. Cell Cycle
K. Catabolism
L. Gene

19. *Using the Across and Down clues, write the correct words in the numbered grid below.*

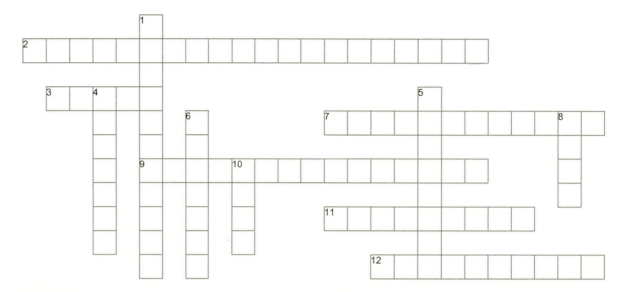

## ACROSS

2. Two main components, the brain and the spinal cord; which control all other organs and systems of the body.
3. An ecosystem that is generally defined by its climate characteristics.
7. The study of how photosynthetic organisms and animals are distributed in a location plus the history of their distribution in the past.
9. Cells with no nucleus or any other membrane-bound organelles.
11. Steps in the cellular respiration process that do not require oxygen.
12. Plants that produce seeds without flowers.

## DOWN

1. Generated by the reproductive organs of the sporophyte through the process of meiosis.
4. A special process of diffusion that occurs when the water concentration inside the cell differs from the concentration outside the cell.
5. Part of the brain that controls sensory and motor responses, memory, speech, and most factors of intelligence.
6. Present in every living cell, large un-branched chains of amino acids; may also be called polypeptides.
8. Energy that flows from an object that is warm to an object that is cooler.
10. The simplest unit of an element that retains the element's characteristics.

A. Gametophyte
D. Biome
G. Atom
J. Protein

B. Heat
E. Biogeography
H. Cerebrum
K. Osmosis

C. Central Nervous System
F. Gymnosperm
I. Prokaryotic Cell
L. Anaerobic

© 2017 Network4Learning, Inc.

20. *Using the Across and Down clues, write the correct words in the numbered grid below.*

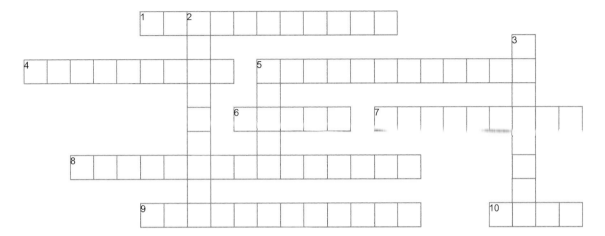

## ACROSS

1. The bending of a light wave around an obstacle.
4. The process whereby molecules and ions flow through the cell membrane from an area of higher concentration to an area of lower concentration; mixing of particles in a gas or liquid.
5. The study of how photosynthetic organisms and animals are distributed in a location plus the history of their distribution in the past.
6. The push or pull exerted on an object.
7. An area of land that lies within the home range that the individual will defend as his own.
8. The boundary between the nucleus and the cytoplasm.
9. Over time, a gene pool (particularly in a small population) may experience a change in frequency of particular genes simply due to change fluctuations.
10. The smallest and most basic unit of most living things.

## DOWN

2. Energy generally flows through the entire ecosystem in one direction from producers to consumers and on to decomposers.
3. Membrane-bound organelles containing digestive enzymes; digest unused material within the cell, damaged organelles, or materials absorbed by the cell for use.
5. An ecosystem that is generally defined by its climate characteristics.

A. Food Chain
B. Territory
C. Biogeography
D. Force
E. Lysosome
F. Diffraction
G. Genetic Drift
H. Diffusion
I. Biome
J. Nuclear Membrane
K. Cell

21. *Using the Across and Down clues, write the correct words in the numbered grid below.*

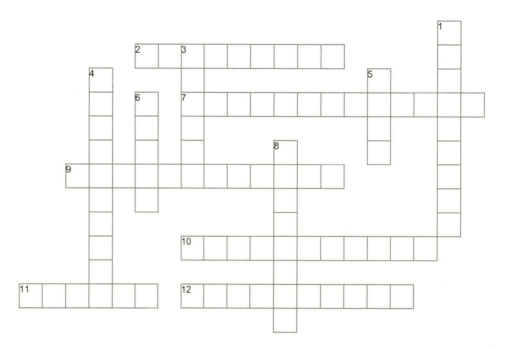

## ACROSS

2. The study of things in motion.
7. A process in which some water that has traveled up through the plant to the leaves is evaporated.
9. Another name for anaerobic respiration, which breaks down the two pyruvic acid molecules (three carbons each) into end products (such as ethyl alcohol, or lactic acid), plus carbon dioxide.
10. Pigment molecules that give the chloroplast their green color.
11. Filter metabolic waste from the blood and excrete them as urine
12. Calculated by adding up the masses of the protons and neutrons.

## DOWN

1. Step four in mitosis; occurs as nuclear membranes form around the chromosomes and disperse through the new nucleoplasm; spindle fibers also disappear.
3. Positive ion.
4. When one community completely replaces another over time in an area.
5. The amount of matter that is contained by the object.
6. The body of the chloroplast.
8. Located between the forebrain and hindbrain; contains the optic lobes.

A. Succession   B. Mass          C. Chlorophyll   D. Midbrain   E. Telophase
F. Stoma        G. Atomic Mass   H. Mechanics     I. Cation     J. Transpiration
K. Fermentation L. Kidney

© 2017 Network4Learning, Inc.

22. *Using the Across and Down clues, write the correct words in the numbered grid below.*

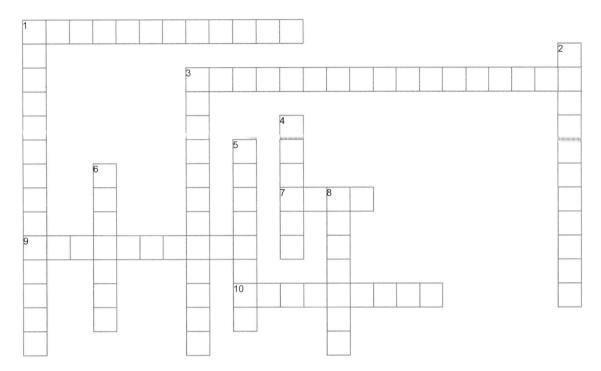

## ACROSS

1. Over time, a gene pool (particularly in a small population) may experience a change in frequency of particular genes simply due to change fluctuations.
3. The conduit for delivering nutrients and gases to all cells and for removing waste products from them.
7. Length of DNA that encodes a particular protein.
9. The bouncing of a wave of light off an object.
10. the ability of a substance to produce a magnetic field.

## DOWN

1. Instrumental in the storing, packaging, and shipping of proteins; also known as Golgi bodies or the Golgi complex.
2. Permanent one-way movement into a new range.
3. The process of cell reproduction that centers on the replication and separation of strands of DNA.
4. The force of gravity acting upon that object.
5. Study that organizes living things into groups based on morphology or, more recently, genetics.
6. Single unduplicated chromosomes.
8. An organelle surrounded by two lipid bilayer membranes that is located near the center of the cell and contains chromosomes, nuclear pores, nucleoplasm, and nucleoli.

A. Genetic Drift
B. Circulatory System
C. Haploid
D. Reflection
E. Immigration
F. Gene
G. Magnetism
H. Cell Division
I. Nucleus
J. Weight
K. Taxonomy
L. Golgi Apparatus

23. Using the Across and Down clues, write the correct words in the numbered grid below.

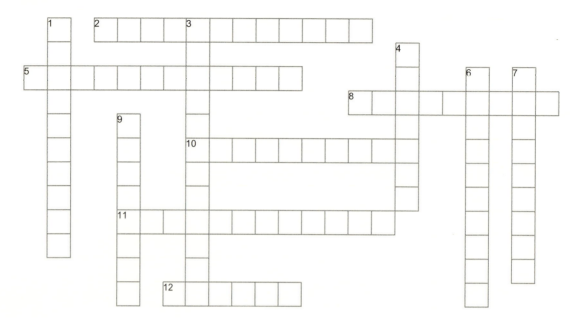

## ACROSS

2. Center of cellular respiration
5. Involved in hunger, thirst, blood pressure, body temperature, hostility, pain, pleasure, etc.
8. Occurs when the nucleus emits a beta particle that degrades into an electron as it passes out of the atom.
10. The export of substances from the cell.
11. Occurs when a hydrogen atom is involved with a polar intermolecular attraction to a more electronegative atom.
12. The force of gravity acting upon that object.

## DOWN

1. The breaking down of the six-carbon sugar (glucose) into smaller carbon-containing molecules yielding ATP.
3. Structure that encloses the cell and separates it from the environment; also known as the plasma membrane.
4. the process by which a cell distributes its duplicated chromosomes so that each daughter cell has a full set of chromosomes.
6. The bouncing of a wave of light off an object.
7. the ability of a substance to produce a magnetic field.
9. The first phase in mitosis.

A. Cell Membrane   B. Hypothalamus   C. Magnetism   D. Mitochondria
E. Reflection      F. Exocytosis     G. Beta Decay  H. Hydrogen Bond
I. Mitosis         J. Glycolysis     K. Prophase    L. Weight

© 2017 Network4Learning, Inc.

24. *Using the Across and Down clues, write the correct words in the numbered grid below.*

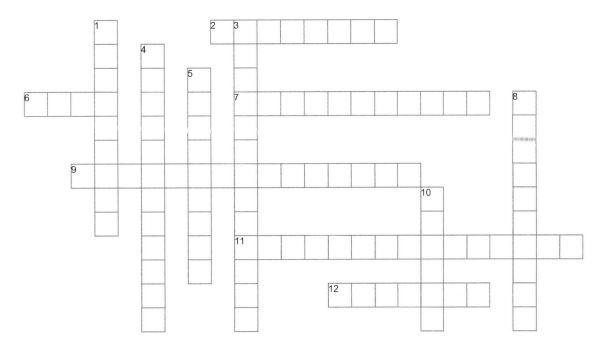

## ACROSS

2. The entire collection of genes within a given population.
6. The amount of matter that is contained by the object.
7. The site of photosynthesis within plant cells.
9. Code proteins that determine fictional or physiological events.
11. The principal infection-fighting component of the immune system.
12. Single unduplicated chromosomes.

## DOWN

1. Part of the Earth that includes all living things.
3. Three-dimensional space where electrons travel freely; also known as an electron shell or orbital.
4. Theoretical temperature at which particle motion stops; also known as 0 Kelvin.
5. The transfer of energy via waves.
8. When the entire population of a particular species is eliminated.
10. Mathematical quantities that recognize both the size and direction of the dimension being considered.

A. Lymphatic System
E. Regulatory Genes
I. Vector
B. Electron Cloud
F. Haploid
J. Chloroplast
C. Extinction
G. Absolute Zero
K. Biosphere
D. Mass
H. Gene Pool
L. Radiation

© 2017 Network4Learning, Inc.

25. *Using the Across and Down clues, write the correct words in the numbered grid below.*

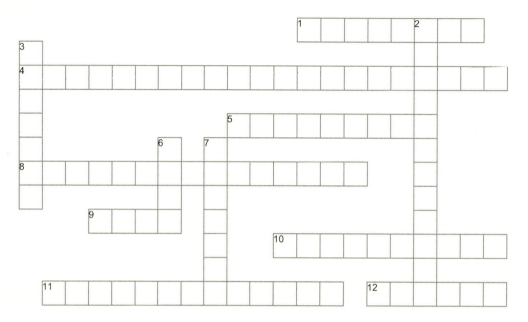

## ACROSS

1. The rate of change of displacement; includes both speed and direction.
4. Homologous chromosomes separate and independently sort in gamete formation.
5. The combination of DNA with histones.
8. The boundary between the nucleus and the cytoplasm.
9. RNA strand that migrates form the nucleus to the cytoplasm; also known as messenger RNA.
10. Enzyme control that may occur when the product of the reaction is also an inhibitor to the reaction.
11. Notation that allow us to easily predict the results of a genetic cross.
12. Classification category even more general than kingdoms.

## DOWN

2. Functions to defend the body from infection by bacteria and viruses.
3. Short length of DNA wrapped around a core of small proteins.
6. A chain of about 80 nucleotides that provide the link between the "language" of nucleotides (codon and anticodon) and the "language" of amino acids; also known as transfer RNA.
7. The process of producing four daughter cells, each with single unduplicated chromosomes.

A. tRNA
D. Nuclear Membrane
G. Punnett Square
J. Immune System

B. Velocity
E. Chromatin
H. Domain
K. mRNA

C. Histone
F. Regulation
I. Meiosis
L. Independent Assortment

1. Using the Across and Down clues, write the correct words in the numbered grid below.

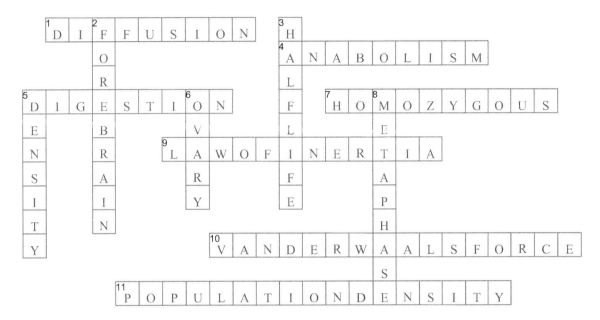

## ACROSS

1. The process whereby molecules and ions flow through the cell membrane from an area of higher concentration to an area of lower concentration; mixing of particles in a gas or liquid.
4. The process whereby cells build molecules and store energy.
5. Breakdown of ingested particles into molecules that can be absorbed by the body.
7. When both alleles for a given gene are the same in an individual.
9. A particle at rest will stay at rest and a particle in motion will stay in motion until acted upon by an outside force.
10. Momentary force of attraction that exist between molecules and are much weaker than the forces of chemical bonding.
11. The number of individuals of a species living in an area.

## DOWN

1. The process whereby molecules and ions flow through the cell membrane from an area of higher concentration to an area of lower concentration; mixing of particles in a gas or liquid.
4. The process whereby cells build molecules and store energy.
5. Breakdown of ingested particles into molecules that can be absorbed by the body.
7. When both alleles for a given gene are the same in an individual.
9. A particle at rest will stay at rest and a particle in motion will stay in motion until acted upon by an outside force.
10. Momentary force of attraction that exist between molecules and are much weaker than the forces of chemical bonding.
11. The number of individuals of a species living in an area.

A. Van der Waals Force  B. Law of Inertia  C. Metaphase  D. Half Life
E. Population Density  F. Forebrain  G. Homozygous  H. Diffusion
I. Density  J. Digestion  K. Ovary  L. Anabolism

© 2017 Network4Learning, Inc.

2. Using the Across and Down clues, write the correct words in the numbered grid below.

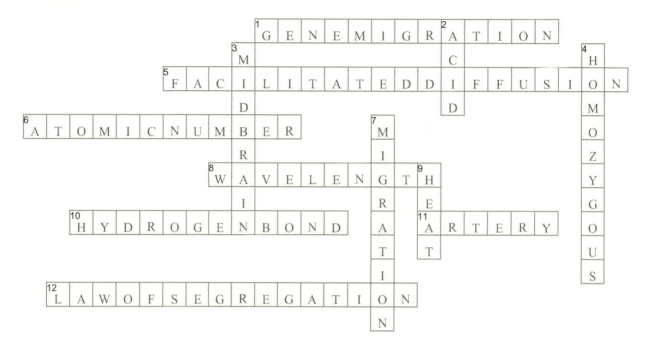

## ACROSS

1. The introduction of new genes from an immigrant, which results in a change of the gene pool.
5. Allows for the transfer of substances across the cell membrane with the help of specialized proteins.
6. The number of protons found in the nucleus of an atom of that element.
8. The distance from one crest (or top) of a wave to the next crest on the same side.
10. Occurs when a hydrogen atom is involved with a polar intermolecular attraction to a more electronegative atom.
11. Larger vessels that carry blood away from the heart.
12. traits are expressed from a pair of genes in the individual (on homologous chromosomes).

## DOWN

1. The introduction of new genes from an immigrant, which results in a change of the gene pool.
5. Allows for the transfer of substances across the cell membrane with the help of specialized proteins.
6. The number of protons found in the nucleus of an atom of that element.
8. The distance from one crest (or top) of a wave to the next crest on the same side.
10. Occurs when a hydrogen atom is involved with a polar intermolecular attraction to a more electronegative atom.
11. Larger vessels that carry blood away from the heart.
12. traits are expressed from a pair of genes in the individual (on homologous chromosomes).

A. Wavelength
E. Heat
I. Acid
B. Gene Migration
F. Hydrogen Bond
J. Midbrain
C. Atomic Number
G. Facilitated Diffusion
K. Law of Segregation
D. Homozygous
H. Migration
L. Artery

© 2017 Network4Learning, Inc.

3. Using the Across and Down clues, write the correct words in the numbered grid below.

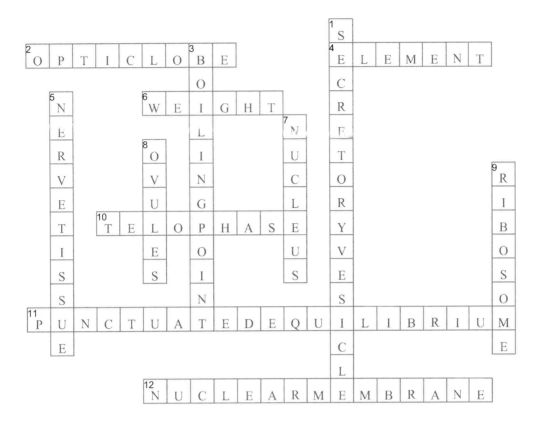

## ACROSS

2. Visual center connected to the eyes by the optic nerves.
4. A substance that cannot be broken down into any other substances.
6. The force of gravity acting upon that object.
10. Step four in mitosis; occurs as nuclear membranes form around the chromosomes and disperse through the new nucleoplasm; spindle fibers also disappear.
11. Scientific model that proposes that adaptations of species arise suddenly and rapidly.
12. The boundary between the nucleus and the cytoplasm.

## DOWN

2. Visual center connected to the eyes by the optic nerves.
4. A substance that cannot be broken down into any other substances.
6. The force of gravity acting upon that object.
10. Step four in mitosis; occurs as nuclear membranes form around the chromosomes and disperse through the new nucleoplasm; spindle fibers also disappear.
11. Scientific model that proposes that adaptations of species arise suddenly and rapidly.
12. The boundary between the nucleus and the cytoplasm.

A. Punctuated Equilibrium
B. Nuclear Membrane
C. Telophase
D. Ovules
E. Element
F. Optic Lobe
G. Weight
H. Secretory Vesicle
I. Ribosome
J. Nerve Tissue
K. Boiling Point
L. Nucleus

4. Using the Across and Down clues, write the correct words in the numbered grid below.

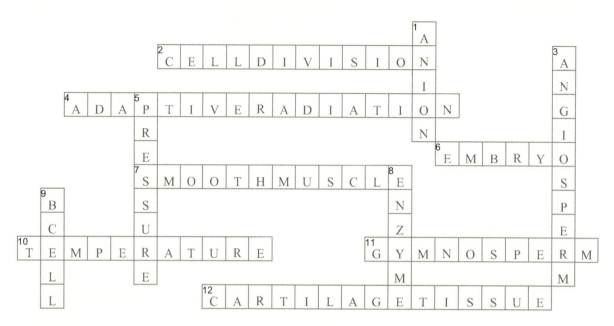

## ACROSS

2. The process of cell reproduction that centers on the replication and separation of strands of DNA.
4. A single species can develop into several diverse species over time; over time a species will specially adapt to live more effectively in a new environment.
6. What a zygote eventually grown into.
7. Makes up the walls of internal organs and functions in involuntary movement. (breathing, etc.)
10. The measure of the average kinetic energy of a substance.
11. Plants that produce seeds without flowers.
12. Reduces friction between bones and supports and connects them.

## DOWN

1. Negative ion.
3. Plants that produce flowers as reproductive organs.
5. A measure of the amount of force applied per unit of area.
8. Protein molecules that act as catalysts for organic reactions.
9. Class of lymphocyte cell that emerge from the bone marrow mature and produce antibodies, which enter the bloodstream.

A. Smooth Muscle
B. B Cell
C. Embryo
D. Cartilage Tissue
E. Adaptive Radiation
F. Angiosperm
G. Anion
H. Cell Division
I. Pressure
J. Enzyme
K. Gymnosperm
L. Temperature

5. Using the Across and Down clues, write the correct words in the numbered grid below.

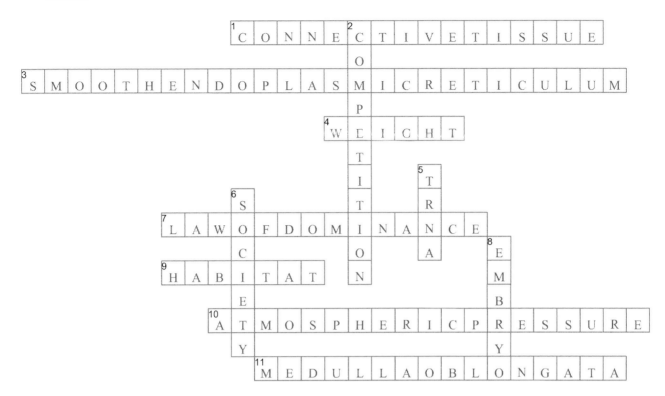

## ACROSS

1. Holds tissues and organs together, stabilizing the body structure.
3. Network of membranous channels; does not have attached ribosomes.
4. The force of gravity acting upon that object.
7. One gene is usually dominant over the other.
9. The physical place where a species lives.
10. Pressure that results from the total weight of the atmosphere exerting force on the Earth; can be measured with a barometer.
11. Part of the brain that controls involuntary responses such as breathing and heartbeat.

## DOWN

2. Results when two or more species living within the same area and that overlap niches both require a resource that is in limited supply.
5. A chain of about 80 nucleotides that provide the link between the "language" of nucleotides (codon and anticodon) and the "language" of amino acids; also known as transfer RNA.
6. An organization of individuals in a population in which tasks are divided for the group to work together.
8. What a zygote eventually grown into.

A. Medulla Oblongata
C. Atmospheric Pressure
E. Embryo
G. tRNA
I. Habitat
K. Competition

B. Smooth Endoplasmic Reticulum
D. Society
F. Connective Tissue
H. Weight
J. Law of Dominance

© 2017 Network4Learning, Inc.

6. Using the Across and Down clues, write the correct words in the numbered grid below.

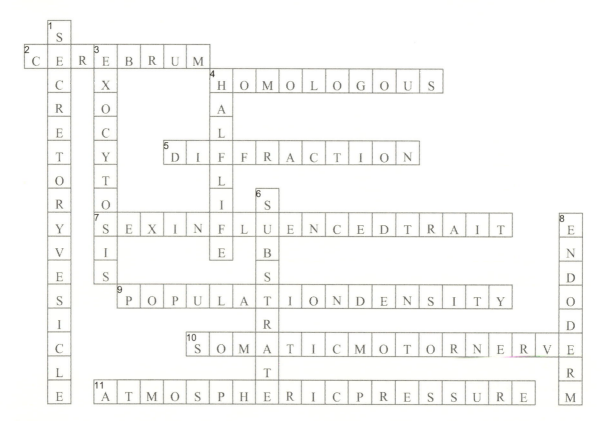

## ACROSS

2. Part of the brain that controls sensory and motor responses, memory, speech, and most factors of intelligence.
4. Structures that exist in two different species because they share a common ancestry.
5. The bending of a light wave around an obstacle.
7. Requires only one recessive gene to be expressed if there is no counteracting dominant gene.
9. The number of individuals of a species living in an area.
10. Carry impulses to skeletal muscle from the CNS.
11. Pressure that results from the total weight of the atmosphere exerting force on the Earth; can be measured with a barometer.

## DOWN

1. Carry substances produced within the cell to the cell membrane; packets of material packaged by the Golgi apparatus or endoplasmic reticulum.
3. The export of substances from the cell.
4. The time it takes for 50 percent of an isotope to decay.
6. Particular substance of an enzyme that fits within the active site.
8. The precursor of the gut lining and various accessory structures.

A. Half Life
D. Homologous
G. Exocytosis
J. Secretory Vesicle
B. Endoderm
E. Diffraction
H. Cerebrum
K. Somatic Motor Nerve
C. Substrate
F. Atmospheric Pressure
I. Population Density
L. Sex Influenced Trait

© 2017 Network4Learning, Inc.

7. Using the Across and Down clues, write the correct words in the numbered grid below.

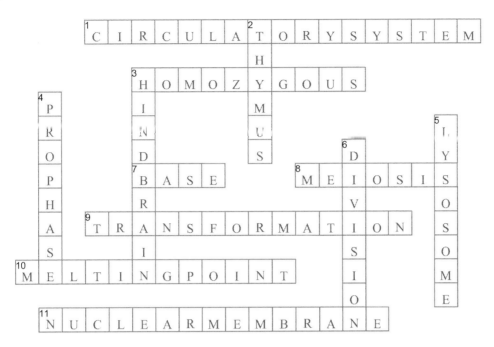

## ACROSS

1. The conduit for delivering nutrients and gases to all cells and for removing waste products from them.
3. When both alleles for a given gene are the same in an individual.
7. A chemical that accepts protons (H+ ions) when dissolved in water.
8. The process of producing four daughter cells, each with single unduplicated chromosomes.
9. A process in which bacteria absorb and incorporate pieces of DNA from their environment (usually from dead bacterial cells).
10. Temperature at which a substance changes from solid to liquid form.
11. The boundary between the nucleus and the cytoplasm.

## DOWN

2. A mass of lymph tissue that is active only through the teen years, fighting infection and producing T cells.
3. Consists of the cerebellum and medulla oblongata.
4. The first phase in mitosis.
5. Membrane-bound organelles containing digestive enzymes; digest unused material within the cell, damaged organelles, or materials absorbed by the cell for use.
6. Distributes the remaining set of chromosomes in a mitosis-like process.

A. Transformation  B. Hindbrain  C. Lysosome  D. Meiosis
E. Thymus  F. Division  G. Nuclear Membrane  H. Circulatory System
I. Melting Point  J. Prophase  K. Base  L. Homozygous

© 2017 Network4Learning, Inc.

8. Using the Across and Down clues, write the correct words in the numbered grid below.

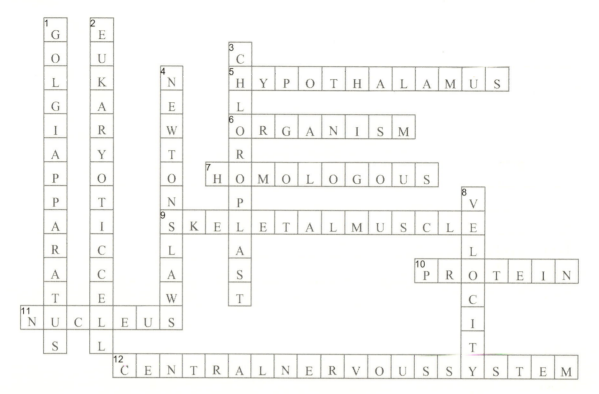

## ACROSS

5. Involved in hunger, thirst, blood pressure, body temperature, hostility, pain, pleasure, etc.
6. An individual of a species.
7. Structures that exist in two different species because they share a common ancestry.
9. Attaches bones of the skeleton to each other and surrounding tissues, which enables voluntary movement.
10. Present in every living cell, large un-branched chains of amino acids; may also be called polypeptides.
11. An organelle surrounded by two lipid bilayer membranes that is located near the center of the cell and contains chromosomes, nuclear pores, nucleoplasm, and nucleoli.
12. Two main components, the brain and the spinal cord; which control all other organs and systems of the body.

## DOWN

1. Instrumental in the storing, packaging, and shipping of proteins; also known as Golgi bodies or the Golgi complex.
2. Cells that contain membrane-bound intracellular organelles, including a nucleus.
3. The site of photosynthesis within plant cells.
4. Three laws that form the basis of most of our understanding of things in motion.
8. The rate of change of displacement; includes both speed and direction.

A. Protein
D. Newtons Laws
G. Central Nervous System
J. Organism
B. Hypothalamus
E. Skeletal Muscle
H. Chloroplast
K. Eukaryotic Cell
C. Golgi Apparatus
F. Homologous
I. Nucleus
L. Velocity

© 2017 Network4Learning, Inc.

9. Using the Across and Down clues, write the correct words in the numbered grid below.

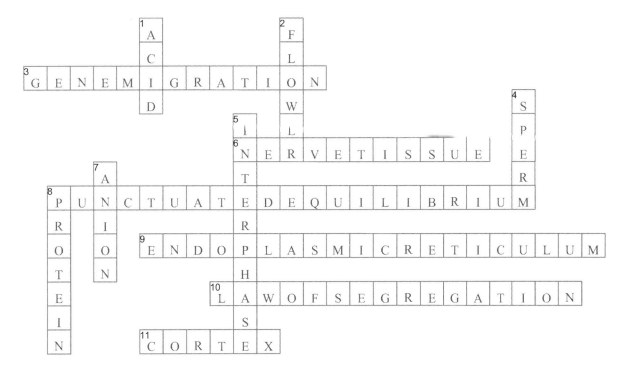

## ACROSS

3. The introduction of new genes from an immigrant, which results in a change of the gene pool.
6. Carries electrical and chemical impulses to and from organs and limbs to the brain.
8. Scientific model that proposes that adaptations of species arise suddenly and rapidly.
9. Large organization of folded membranes; responsible for the delivery of lipids and proteins to certain areas within the cytoplasm.
10. traits are expressed from a pair of genes in the individual (on homologous chromosomes).
11. A ring inside the epidermis that is made up of large parenchyma cells.

## DOWN

1. A chemical that donates proton (H+ ions) when dissolved in water.
2. The primary reproductive organ for a plant.
4. Produced by the male gametophyte; also known as a male gamete.
5. the period when the cell is active in carrying on its functions.
7. Negative ion.
8. Present in every living cell, large un-branched chains of amino acids; may also be called polypeptides.

A. Nerve Tissue
D. Law of Segregation
G. Protein
J. Anion

B. Sperm
E. Flower
H. Gene Migration
K. Cortex

C. Endoplasmic Reticulum
F. Interphase
I. Punctuated Equilibrium
L. Acid

10. Using the Across and Down clues, write the correct words in the numbered grid below.

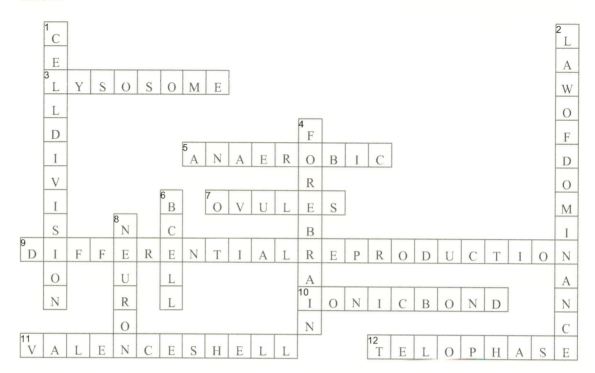

## ACROSS

3. Membrane-bound organelles containing digestive enzymes; digest unused material within the cell, damaged organelles, or materials absorbed by the cell for use.
5. Steps in the cellular respiration process that do not require oxygen.
7. Small round cases within the ovary that contain one or more egg cells.
9. Individuals within a population that are most adapted to the environment and are also the most likely individuals to reproduce successfully.
10. Bond of attraction between positive and negative ions.
11. The outermost occupied energy level of an element.
12. Step four in mitosis; occurs as nuclear membranes form around the chromosomes and disperse through the new nucleoplasm; spindle fibers also disappear.

## DOWN

1. The process of cell reproduction that centers on the replication and separation of strands of DNA.
2. One gene is usually dominant over the other.
4. Located most anterior, it contains the olfactory lobes and cerebrum as well as the thalamus, hypothalamus, and pituitary gland.
6. Class of lymphocyte cell that emerge from the bone marrow mature and produce antibodies, which enter the bloodstream.
8. Carry impulses via electrochemical responses.

A. Anaerobic
D. Law of Dominance
G. Lysosome
J. Forebrain

B. Ovules
E. Neuron
H. Telophase
K. Valence Shell

C. Differential Reproduction
F. Cell Division
I. Ionic Bond
L. B Cell

© 2017 Network4Learning, Inc.

11. *Using the Across and Down clues, write the correct words in the numbered grid below.*

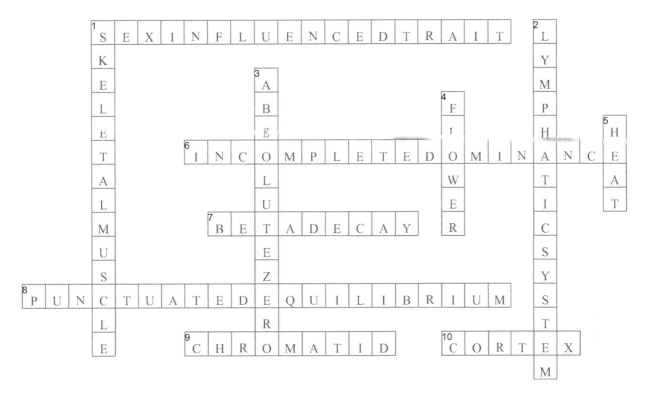

## ACROSS

1. Requires only one recessive gene to be expressed if there is no counteracting dominant gene.
6. Some traits have no genes that are dominant and instead produce offspring that are a mix of the two parents.
7. Occurs when the nucleus emits a beta particle that degrades into an electron as it passes out of the atom.
8. Scientific model that proposes that adaptations of species arise suddenly and rapidly.
9. The two identical strands of duplicated chromatin in a cell that is getting ready to divide.
10. A ring inside the epidermis that is made up of large parenchyma cells.

## DOWN

1. Attaches bones of the skeleton to each other and surrounding tissues, which enables voluntary movement.
2. The principal infection-fighting component of the immune system.
3. Theoretical temperature at which particle motion stops; also known as 0 Kelvin.
4. The primary reproductive organ for a plant.
5. Energy that flows from an object that is warm to an object that is cooler.

A. Punctuated Equilibrium   B. Beta Decay          C. Sex Influenced Trait
D. Flower                   E. Chromatid           F. Incomplete Dominance
G. Skeletal Muscle          H. Cortex              I. Heat
J. Lymphatic System         K. Absolute Zero

© 2017 Network4Learning, Inc.

12. *Using the Across and Down clues, write the correct words in the numbered grid below.*

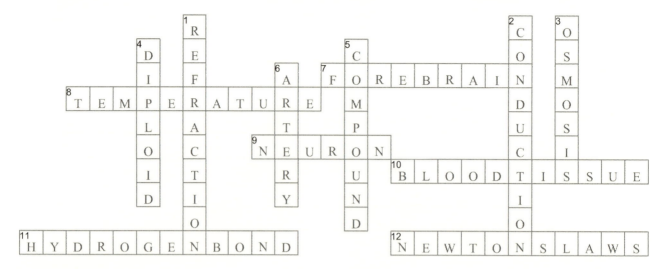

## ACROSS

7. Located most anterior, it contains the olfactory lobes and cerebrum as well as the thalamus, hypothalamus, and pituitary gland.
8. The measure of the average kinetic energy of a substance.
9. Carry impulses via electrochemical responses.
10. Flows through the blood vessels and heart and is essential for carrying oxygen to cells, fighting infection, and carrying nutrients and wastes to and from cells.
11. Occurs when a hydrogen atom is involved with a polar intermolecular attraction to a more electronegative atom.
12. Three laws that form the basis of most of our understanding of things in motion.

## DOWN

1. The change in direction of a wave as it passes from one medium to another.
2. Movement of energy by transfer from particle to particle; can only occur when objects are touching.
3. A special process of diffusion that occurs when the water concentration inside the cell differs from the concentration outside the cell.
4. The parent cell that has a normal set of paired chromosomes.
5. Formed when two or more different atoms bond together chemically to form a unique substance.
6. Larger vessels that carry blood away from the heart.

A. Conduction  B. Compound  C. Diploid  D. Neuron
E. Artery  F. Osmosis  G. Refraction  H. Temperature
I. Blood Tissue  J. Newtons Laws  K. Forebrain  L. Hydrogen Bond

© 2017 Network4Learning, Inc.

13. *Using the Across and Down clues, write the correct words in the numbered grid below.*

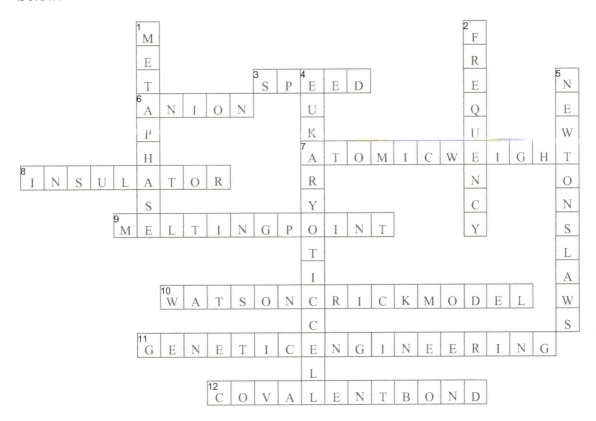

## ACROSS

3. the rate of change of an object's distance traveled.
6. Negative ion.
7. The average mass number.
8. Poor conductors of electrical currents.
9. Temperature at which a substance changes from solid to liquid form.
10. Named after scientists who discovered and modeled the structure of DNA.
11. The intentional alteration of genetic material of a living organism.
12. Bond formed between the atoms when atoms share electrons.

## DOWN

1. Step two of mitosis; occurs when the spindle fibers pull the chromosomes into alignment along the equatorial plane of the cell, creating the metaphase plate.
2. The number of wavelengths that pass a point in a second.
4. Cells that contain membrane-bound intracellular organelles, including a nucleus.
5. Three laws that form the basis of most of our understanding of things in motion.

A. Speed  
B. Anion  
C. Frequency  
D. Insulator  
E. Eukaryotic Cell  
F. Watson Crick Model  
G. Genetic Engineering  
H. Atomic Weight  
I. Newtons Laws  
J. Melting Point  
K. Covalent Bond  
L. Metaphase  

© 2017 Network4Learning, Inc.

14. Using the Across and Down clues, write the correct words in the numbered grid below.

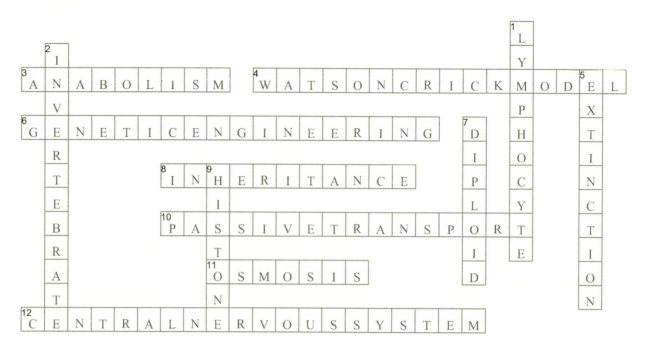

## ACROSS

3. The process whereby cells build molecules and store energy.
4. Named after scientists who discovered and modeled the structure of DNA.
6. The intentional alteration of genetic material of a living organism.
8. The process by which characteristics pass from one generation to another.
10. Substances freely pass across the membrane without the cell expending any energy.
11. A special process of diffusion that occurs when the water concentration inside the cell differs from the concentration outside the cell.
12. Two main components, the brain and the spinal cord; which control all other organs and systems of the body.

## DOWN

1. Begin in bone marrow as stem cells and are collected and distributed via the lymph nodes.
2. Those species having no internal backbone structure.
5. When the entire population of a particular species is eliminated.
7. The parent cell that has a normal set of paired chromosomes.
9. Short length of DNA wrapped around a core of small proteins.

A. Invertebrate  
B. Inheritance  
C. Histone  
D. Diploid  
E. Genetic Engineering  
F. Lymphocyte  
G. Watson Crick Model  
H. Passive Transport  
I. Extinction  
J. Anabolism  
K. Central Nervous System  
L. Osmosis

15. *Using the Across and Down clues, write the correct words in the numbered grid below.*

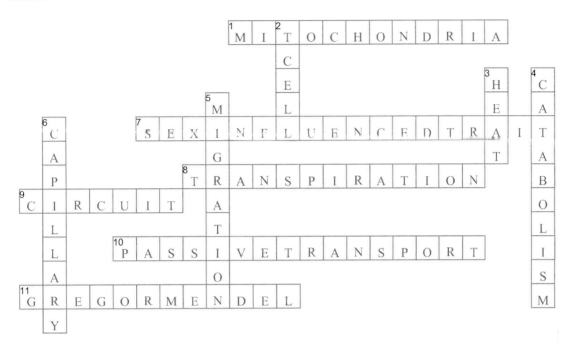

## ACROSS

1. Center of cellular respiration
7. Requires only one recessive gene to be expressed if there is no counteracting dominant gene.
8. A process in which some water that has traveled up through the plant to the leaves is evaporated.
9. The path that an electrical current follows.
10. Substances freely pass across the membrane without the cell expending any energy.
11. Studied the relationships between traits expressed in parents and offspring and the hereditary factors that caused expression of traits.

## DOWN

2. Mature cells in the thymus gland that patrol the blood for antigens but are also equipped to destroy antigens themselves.
3. Energy that flows from an object that is warm to an object that is cooler.
4. Process of breaking down molecules and releasing stored energy.
5. Temporary movement out of one range into another and back.
6. Tiny vessels that surround all tissues of the body and exchange carbon dioxide for oxygen.

A. Mitochondria
B. Heat
C. Gregor Mendel
D. T Cell
E. Sex Influenced Trait
F. Capillary
G. Circuit
H. Transpiration
I. Catabolism
J. Passive Transport
K. Migration

16. *Using the Across and Down clues, write the correct words in the numbered grid below.*

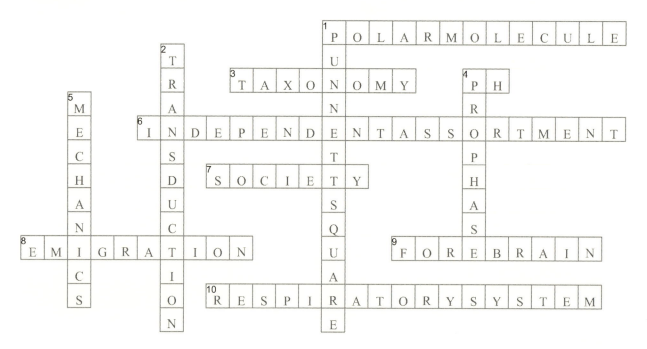

## ACROSS

1. Molecule that has regions of partial change.
3. Study that organizes living things into groups based on morphology or, more recently, genetics.
4. Potential of hydrogen scale, which is a measurement of H+ ions in solutions.
6. Homologous chromosomes separate and independently sort in gamete formation.
7. An organization of individuals in a population in which tasks are divided for the group to work together.
8. Permanent one-way movement out of the original range.
9. Located most anterior, it contains the olfactory lobes and cerebrum as well as the thalamus, hypothalamus, and pituitary gland.
10. Responsible for the intake and processing of gases required by an organism and for expelling gases produced as waste products.

## DOWN

1. Notation that allow us to easily predict the results of a genetic cross.
2. The transfer or genetic material (portions of a bacterial chromosome) from one bacteria cell to another.
4. The first phase in mitosis.
5. The study of things in motion.

A. Taxonomy
D. Society
G. Mechanics
J. Independent Assortment

B. Transduction
E. Prophase
H. Punnett Square
K. Emigration

C. Polar Molecule
F. pH
I. Forebrain
L. Respiratory System

© 2017 Network4Learning, Inc.

17. *Using the Across and Down clues, write the correct words in the numbered grid below.*

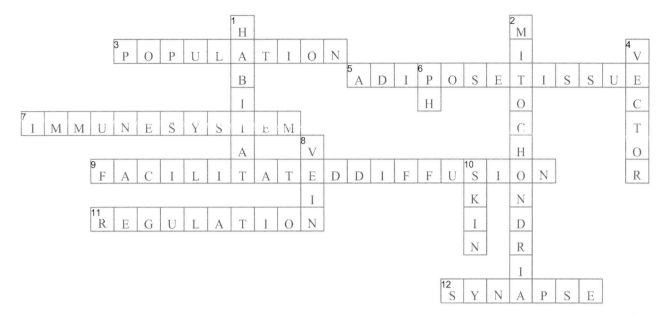

## ACROSS

3. The total number of a single species of organism found in an ecosystem.
5. Found beneath the skin and around organs, providing cushioning, insulation, and fat storage.
7. Functions to defend the body from infection by bacteria and viruses.
9. Allows for the transfer of substances across the cell membrane with the help of specialized proteins.
11. Enzyme control that may occur when the product of the reaction is also an inhibitor to the reaction.
12. Point at which homologous chromosomes pair up during meiosis.

## DOWN

1. The physical place where a species lives.
2. Center of cellular respiration
4. Mathematical quantities that recognize both the size and direction of the dimension being considered.
6. Potential of hydrogen scale, which is a measurement of H+ ions in solutions.
8. Vessels that carry blood toward the heart.
10. An accessory excretory organ that secretes wastes with water from sweat glands.

A. Regulation  B. Adipose Tissue  C. Population  D. Vector
E. Immune System  F. Habitat  G. Synapse  H. pH
I. Facilitated Diffusion  J. Skin  K. Vein  L. Mitochondria

18. *Using the Across and Down clues, write the correct words in the numbered grid below.*

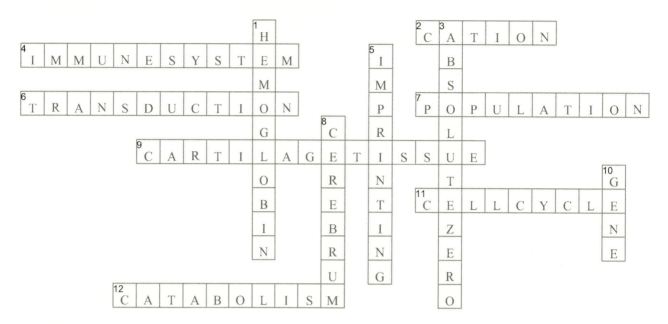

## ACROSS

2. Positive ion.
4. Functions to defend the body from infection by bacteria and viruses.
6. The transfer or genetic material (portions of a bacterial chromosome) from one bacteria cell to another.
7. The total number of a single species of organism found in an ecosystem.
9. Reduces friction between bones and supports and connects them.
11. A sequence of events ending in cell division, which produces two daughter cells.
12. Process of breaking down molecules and releasing stored energy.

## DOWN

1. Component of blood responsible for carrying oxygen.
3. Theoretical temperature at which particle motion stops; also known as 0 Kelvin.
5. A learned behavior that develops in a critical or sensitive period of the animal's lifespan.
8. Part of the brain that controls sensory and motor responses, memory, speech, and most factors of intelligence.
10. Length of DNA that encodes a particular protein.

A. Transduction  B. Immune System  C. Cerebrum  D. Imprinting
E. Hemoglobin   F. Cartilage Tissue  G. Cation    H. Population
I. Absolute Zero  J. Cell Cycle     K. Catabolism  L. Gene

© 2017 Network4Learning, Inc.

19. Using the Across and Down clues, write the correct words in the numbered grid below.

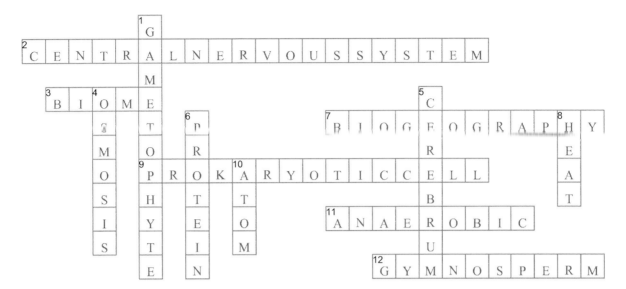

## ACROSS

2. Two main components, the brain and the spinal cord; which control all other organs and systems of the body.
3. An ecosystem that is generally defined by its climate characteristics.
7. The study of how photosynthetic organisms and animals are distributed in a location plus the history of their distribution in the past.
9. Cells with no nucleus or any other membrane-bound organelles.
11. Steps in the cellular respiration process that do not require oxygen.
12. Plants that produce seeds without flowers.

## DOWN

1. Generated by the reproductive organs of the sporophyte through the process of meiosis.
4. A special process of diffusion that occurs when the water concentration inside the cell differs from the concentration outside the cell.
5. Part of the brain that controls sensory and motor responses, memory, speech, and most factors of intelligence.
6. Present in every living cell, large un-branched chains of amino acids; may also be called polypeptides.
8. Energy that flows from an object that is warm to an object that is cooler.
10. The simplest unit of an element that retains the element's characteristics.

A. Gametophyte
D. Biome
G. Atom
J. Protein

B. Heat
E. Biogeography
H. Cerebrum
K. Osmosis

C. Central Nervous System
F. Gymnosperm
I. Prokaryotic Cell
L. Anaerobic

© 2017 Network4Learning, Inc.

20. Using the Across and Down clues, write the correct words in the numbered grid below.

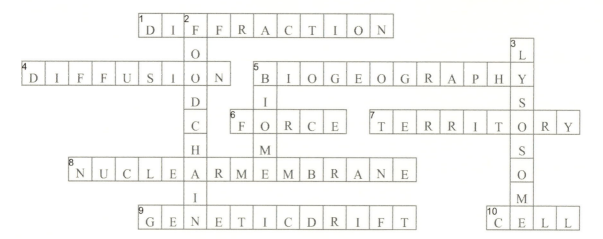

## ACROSS

1. The bending of a light wave around an obstacle.
4. The process whereby molecules and ions flow through the cell membrane from an area of higher concentration to an area of lower concentration; mixing of particles in a gas or liquid.
5. The study of how photosynthetic organisms and animals are distributed in a location plus the history of their distribution in the past.
6. The push or pull exerted on an object.
7. An area of land that lies within the home range that the individual will defend as his own.
8. The boundary between the nucleus and the cytoplasm.
9. Over time, a gene pool (particularly in a small population) may experience a change in frequency of particular genes simply due to change fluctuations.
10. The smallest and most basic unit of most living things.

## DOWN

2. Energy generally flows through the entire ecosystem in one direction from producers to consumers and on to decomposers.
3. Membrane-bound organelles containing digestive enzymes; digest unused material within the cell, damaged organelles, or materials absorbed by the cell for use.
5. An ecosystem that is generally defined by its climate characteristics.

A. Food Chain
B. Territory
C. Biogeography
D. Force
E. Lysosome
F. Diffraction
G. Genetic Drift
H. Diffusion
I. Biome
J. Nuclear Membrane
K. Cell

21. *Using the Across and Down clues, write the correct words in the numbered grid below.*

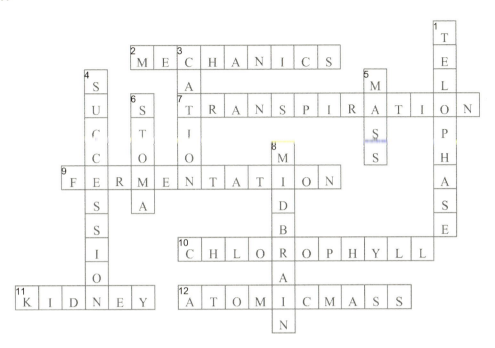

## ACROSS

2. The study of things in motion.
7. A process in which some water that has traveled up through the plant to the leaves is evaporated.
9. Another name for anaerobic respiration, which breaks down the two pyruvic acid molecules (three carbons each) into end products (such as ethyl alcohol, or lactic acid), plus carbon dioxide.
10. Pigment molecules that give the chloroplast their green color.
11. Filter metabolic waste from the blood and excrete them as urine
12. Calculated by adding up the masses of the protons and neutrons.

## DOWN

1. Step four in mitosis; occurs as nuclear membranes form around the chromosomes and disperse through the new nucleoplasm; spindle fibers also disappear.
3. Positive ion.
4. When one community completely replaces another over time in an area.
5. The amount of matter that is contained by the object.
6. The body of the chloroplast.
8. Located between the forebrain and hindbrain; contains the optic lobes.

A. Succession  B. Mass  C. Chlorophyll  D. Midbrain  E. Telophase
F. Stoma  G. Atomic Mass  H. Mechanics  I. Cation  J. Transpiration
K. Fermentation  L. Kidney

© 2017 Network4Learning, Inc.

22. Using the Across and Down clues, write the correct words in the numbered grid below.

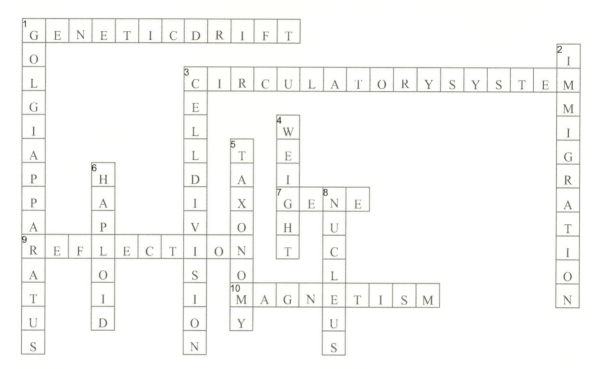

## ACROSS

1. Over time, a gene pool (particularly in a small population) may experience a change in frequency of particular genes simply due to change fluctuations.
3. The conduit for delivering nutrients and gases to all cells and for removing waste products from them.
7. Length of DNA that encodes a particular protein.
9. The bouncing of a wave of light off an object.
10. the ability of a substance to produce a magnetic field.

## DOWN

1. Instrumental in the storing, packaging, and shipping of proteins; also known as Golgi bodies or the Golgi complex.
2. Permanent one-way movement into a new range.
3. The process of cell reproduction that centers on the replication and separation of strands of DNA.
4. The force of gravity acting upon that object.
5. Study that organizes living things into groups based on morphology or, more recently, genetics.
6. Single unduplicated chromosomes.
8. An organelle surrounded by two lipid bilayer membranes that is located near the center of the cell and contains chromosomes, nuclear pores, nucleoplasm, and nucleoli.

A. Genetic Drift
B. Circulatory System
C. Haploid
D. Reflection
E. Immigration
F. Gene
G. Magnetism
H. Cell Division
I. Nucleus
J. Weight
K. Taxonomy
L. Golgi Apparatus

© 2017 Network4Learning, Inc.

23. *Using the Across and Down clues, write the correct words in the numbered grid below.*

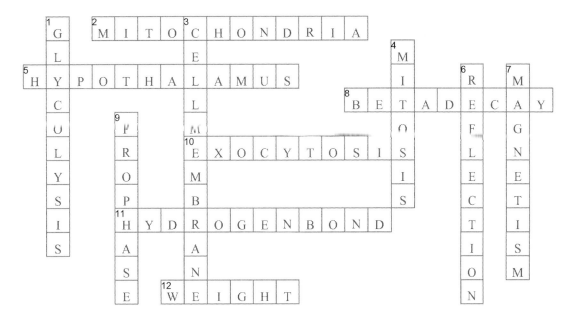

## ACROSS

2. Center of cellular respiration
5. Involved in hunger, thirst, blood pressure, body temperature, hostility, pain, pleasure, etc.
8. Occurs when the nucleus emits a beta particle that degrades into an electron as it passes out of the atom.
10. The export of substances from the cell.
11. Occurs when a hydrogen atom is involved with a polar intermolecular attraction to a more electronegative atom.
12. The force of gravity acting upon that object.

## DOWN

1. The breaking down of the six-carbon sugar (glucose) into smaller carbon-containing molecules yielding ATP.
3. Structure that encloses the cell and separates it from the environment; also known as the plasma membrane.
4. the process by which a cell distributes its duplicated chromosomes so that each daughter cell has a full set of chromosomes.
6. The bouncing of a wave of light off an object.
7. the ability of a substance to produce a magnetic field.
9. The first phase in mitosis.

A. Cell Membrane  B. Hypothalamus  C. Magnetism  D. Mitochondria
E. Reflection  F. Exocytosis  G. Beta Decay  H. Hydrogen Bond
I. Mitosis  J. Glycolysis  K. Prophase  L. Weight

© 2017 Network4Learning, Inc.

24. *Using the Across and Down clues, write the correct words in the numbered grid below.*

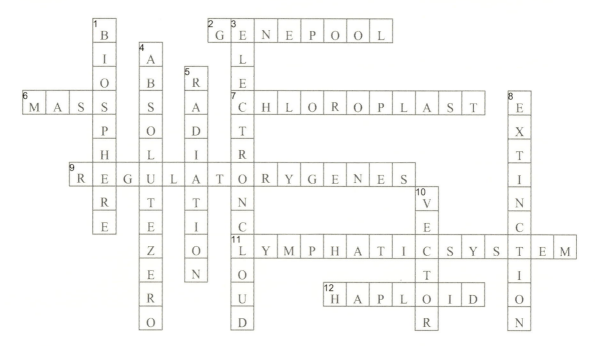

## ACROSS

2. The entire collection of genes within a given population.
6. The amount of matter that is contained by the object.
7. The site of photosynthesis within plant cells.
9. Code proteins that determine fictional or physiological events.
11. The principal infection-fighting component of the immune system.
12. Single unduplicated chromosomes.

## DOWN

1. Part of the Earth that includes all living things.
3. Three-dimensional space where electrons travel freely; also known as an electron shell or orbital.
4. Theoretical temperature at which particle motion stops; also known as 0 Kelvin.
5. The transfer of energy via waves.
8. When the entire population of a particular species is eliminated.
10. Mathematical quantities that recognize both the size and direction of the dimension being considered.

A. Lymphatic System
E. Regulatory Genes
I. Vector
B. Electron Cloud
F. Haploid
J. Chloroplast
C. Extinction
G. Absolute Zero
K. Biosphere
D. Mass
H. Gene Pool
L. Radiation

25. Using the Across and Down clues, write the correct words in the numbered grid below.

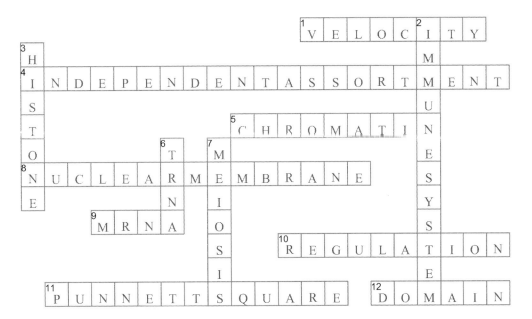

## ACROSS

1. The rate of change of displacement; includes both speed and direction.
4. Homologous chromosomes separate and independently sort in gamete formation.
5. The combination of DNA with histones.
8. The boundary between the nucleus and the cytoplasm.
9. RNA strand that migrates form the nucleus to the cytoplasm; also known as messenger RNA.
10. Enzyme control that may occur when the product of the reaction is also an inhibitor to the reaction.
11. Notation that allow us to easily predict the results of a genetic cross.
12. Classification category even more general than kingdoms.

## DOWN

2. Functions to defend the body from infection by bacteria and viruses.
3. Short length of DNA wrapped around a core of small proteins.
6. A chain of about 80 nucleotides that provide the link between the "language" of nucleotides (codon and anticodon) and the "language" of amino acids; also known as transfer RNA.
7. The process of producing four daughter cells, each with single unduplicated chromosomes.

A. tRNA
D. Nuclear Membrane
G. Punnett Square
J. Immune System

B. Velocity
E. Chromatin
H. Domain
K. mRNA

C. Histone
F. Regulation
I. Meiosis
L. Independent Assortment

© 2017 Network4Learning, Inc.

## Multiple Choice

*From the words provided for each clue, provide the letter of the word which best matches the clue.*

1. ___ The push or pull exerted on an object.
   A. Positron Decay   B. Evolution   C. Organelle   D. Force

2. ___ Carry impulses from body organs to the CNS.
   A. Visceral Sensory Nerve   B. Gamma Radiation   C. Ovules   D. Chromatin

3. ___ Membrane-bound organelles containing digestive enzymes; digest unused material within the cell, damaged organelles, or materials absorbed by the cell for use.
   A. Diffraction   B. Lysosome   C. Punnett Square   D. Incomplete Dominance

4. ___ A learned behavior that develops in a critical or sensitive period of the animal's lifespan.
   A. Optic Lobe   B. Visceral Sensory Nerve   C. Endocytosis   D. Imprinting

5. ___ Reactions that release energy.
   A. Organelle   B. Exothermic   C. Base   D. Diffraction

6. ___ Center of cellular respiration
   A. Biosphere   B. Passive Transport   C. Exothermic   D. Mitochondria

7. ___ Network of membranous channels; does not have attached ribosomes.
   A. Electron Cloud   B. Smooth Endoplasmic Reticulum   C. Diffraction   D. Molecule

8. ___ The boundary between the nucleus and the cytoplasm.
   A. Evaporation   B. Covalent Bond   C. Biosphere   D. Nuclear Membrane

9. ___ Short length of DNA wrapped around a core of small proteins.
   A. Ovary   B. Histone   C. Law of Segregation   D. Kidney

10. ___ Step three in mitosis.
    A. Anaphase   B. Chloroplast   C. Golgi Apparatus   D. Biogeography

11. ___ Mature cells in the thymus gland that patrol the blood for antigens but are also equipped to destroy antigens themselves.
    A. Sympathetic Nervous System   B. Gamete   C. T Cell   D. mRNA

12. ___ The gradual change of characteristics within a population, producing a change in a species over time.
    A. Passive Transport   B. Evolution   C. Chromatin   D. Velocity

13. ___ Pressure that results from the total weight of the atmosphere exerting force on the Earth; can be measured with a barometer.
    A. Base   B. Pituitary Gland   C. Atmospheric Pressure   D. Photosynthesis

14. ___ The combination of alleles that make a particular trait.
    A. Insulator   B. Genotype   C. Chemistry   D. Evaporation

15. ___ RNA strand that migrates form the nucleus to the cytoplasm; also known as messenger RNA.
    A. Regulatory Genes   B. mRNA   C. Incomplete Dominance   D. Oogenesis

16. __ A communication network that connects the entire body of an organism and provides control over bodily functions.
    A.Pressure  B.Velocity  C.Exocytosis  D.Nervous System

17. __ The simplest unit of an element that retains the element's characteristics.
    A.Vein  B.Molecule  C.Cellular Metabolism  D.Atom

18. __ The study of matter.
    A.Beta Decay  B.Chemistry  C.Temperature  D.Immigration

19. __ Calculated by adding up the masses of the protons and neutrons.
    A.Positron Decay  B.Photosynthesis  C.Vertebrate  D.Atomic Mass

20. __ Notation that allow us to easily predict the results of a genetic cross.
    A.Heat  B.Angiosperm  C.T Cell  D.Punnett Square

21. __ The site of photosynthesis within plant cells.
    A.Substrate  B.Melting Point  C.Covalent Bond  D.Chloroplast

22. __ Code proteins that form organs and structural characteristics.
    A.Transformation  B.Structural Gene  C.Acid  D.Kidney

23. __ Formation of egg cells.
    A.Oogenesis  B.Nervous System  C.Atomic Mass  D.Immigration

24. __ Cell that results when a sperm cell fertilizes an egg cell.
    A.Endoderm  B.Chloroplast  C.Sex Limited Trait  D.Zygote

25. __ Visual center connected to the eyes by the optic nerves.
    A.Histone  B.Optic Lobe  C.Biogeography  D.Allopatric Speciation

26. __ Substances freely pass across the membrane without the cell expending any energy.
    A.Regulatory Genes  B.Passive Transport  C.Force  D.Photosynthesis

27. __ The rate of change of displacement; includes both speed and direction.
    A.Velocity  B.Population  C.Molecule  D.Histone

28. __ Plants that have tissue organized in such a way as to conduct food and water throughout their structure.
    A.Vascular  B.Molecule  C.Law of Dominance  D.Ribosome

29. __ Particular substance of an enzyme that fits within the active site.
    A.Imprinting  B.Regulatory Genes  C.Kidney  D.Substrate

30. __ Genes located on a gender chromosome.
    A.Velocity  B.Genotype  C.Sex Limited Trait  D.Adipose Tissue

31. __ The process whereby large molecules are taken up into a pocket of membrane; the pocket pinches off, delivering the molecules, still inside a membrane sack into the cytoplasm.
    A.Beta Decay  B.Angiosperm  C.Endocytosis  D.Exocytosis

32. __ The first phase in mitosis.
    A.Prophase  B.Homozygous  C.Succession  D.Zygote

33. __ Forms the barrier between the environment and the interior of the body.
    A.Punnett Square   B.Zygote   C.Epithelial Tissue   D.Heat

34. __ Consists of gamma rays, which are high-frequency, high-energy, electromagnetic radiation that are usually given off in combination with alpha and beta decay.
    A.T Cell   B.Beta Decay   C.Gamete   D.Gamma Radiation

35. __ When both alleles for a given gene are the same in an individual.
    A.Homozygous   B.T Cell   C.Allopatric Speciation   D.Pressure

36. __ Serves as a processing plant for ingested food.
    A.Innate Behaviors   B.Digestive System   C.Chemistry   D.Microvilli

37. __ Occurs when the nucleus emits a beta particle that degrades into an electron as it passes out of the atom.
    A.Heat   B.Ovules   C.Beta Decay   D.Angiosperm

38. __ When one community completely replaces another over time in an area.
    A.Lymphocyte   B.Succession   C.Positron Decay   D.Genome

39. __ The process by which characteristics pass from one generation to another.
    A.Diffraction   B.Inheritance   C.Atmospheric Pressure   D.Chloroplast

40. __ The four haploid cells (egg and sperm) that are found in reproductive organs as a result of meiosis.
    A.Ovules   B.Pituitary Gland   C.Gamete   D.Parasympathetic Nervous System

41. __ Temperature at which a substance changes from solid to liquid form.
    A.Molecule   B.Melting Point   C.Ribosome   D.Exothermic

42. __ A crucial set of reactions that convert the light energy of the sun into chemical energy usable by living things.
    A.Temperature   B.Heat   C.Photosynthesis   D.Biogeography

43. __ Temporary movement out of one range into another and back.
    A.Migration   B.Diffraction   C.Anaphase   D.Atomic Mass

44. __ The study of how photosynthetic organisms and animals are distributed in a location plus the history of their distribution in the past.
    A.Oogenesis   B.Chemistry   C.Biogeography   D.Genetic Drift

45. __ Found beneath the skin and around organs, providing cushioning, insulation, and fat storage.
    A.Exocytosis   B.Adipose Tissue   C.Heat   D.Diffraction

46. __ Instrumental in the storing, packaging, and shipping of proteins; also known as Golgi bodies or the Golgi complex.
    A.Golgi Apparatus   B.Lymphocyte   C.Evolution   D.Heat

47. __ Cells components that perform functions.
    A.Gamma Radiation   B.Newtons Laws   C.Organelle   D.Zygote

48. __ traits are expressed from a pair of genes in the individual (on homologous chromosomes).
    A.Chromatin   B.Prophase   C.Diffusion   D.Law of Segregation

49. __ Releases various hormones.
    A.Pituitary Gland  B.Genetic Drift  C.Ribosome  D.Newtons Laws

50. __ Projections of the cell extending from the cell membrane; increase the surface area of the cell membrane, increasing the area available to absorb nutrients.
    A.Structural Gene  B.Atom  C.Microvilli  D.Mass

51. __ Filter metabolic waste from the blood and excrete them as urine
    A.Incomplete Dominance  B.Kidney  C.Lymphocyte  D.Gene

52. __ Begin in bone marrow as stem cells and are collected and distributed via the lymph nodes.
    A.Catabolism  B.Melting Point  C.Lymphocyte  D.Electron Cloud

53. __ The precursor of the gut lining and various accessory structures.
    A.Endoderm  B.Homozygous  C.Ovary  D.Catabolism

54. __ Scientific model that proposes that adaptations of species arise suddenly and rapidly.
    A.Punctuated Equilibrium  B.Evaporation  C.Angiosperm  D.Adipose Tissue

55. __ The combination of DNA with histones.
    A.Chromatin  B.Hydrogen Bond  C.Beta Decay  D.Melting Point

56. __ One gene is usually dominant over the other.
    A.Covalent Bond  B.Van der Waals Force  C.Law of Dominance  D.Melting Point

57. __ Occurs when two populations are geographically isolated from each other.
    A.Immigration  B.Allopatric Speciation  C.Epithelial Tissue  D.Punctuated Equilibrium

58. __ A measure of the amount of force applied per unit of area.
    A.Gene  B.Electron Cloud  C.mRNA  D.Pressure

59. __ Small round cases within the ovary that contain one or more egg cells.
    A.Ovules  B.Vein  C.Beta Decay  D.Digestive System

60. __ Energy that flows from an object that is warm to an object that is cooler.
    A.Heat  B.Angiosperm  C.Kidney  D.Gene

61. __ Three-dimensional space where electrons travel freely; also known as an electron shell or orbital.
    A.Electron Cloud  B.Histone  C.Diffusion  D.Visceral Sensory Nerve

62. __ Plants that produce flowers as reproductive organs.
    A.Beta Decay  B.Angiosperm  C.Vein  D.Gamma Radiation

63. __ A process in which bacteria absorb and incorporate pieces of DNA from their environment (usually from dead bacterial cells).
    A.Transformation  B.Exothermic  C.Migration  D.Punnett Square

64. __ Occurs when the nucleus emits a particle that degrades into a positron as it passes out of the atom.
    A.Genome  B.Punnett Square  C.Positron Decay  D.Atom

65. __ Escape of individual particles of a substance into gaseous form.
    A.Evaporation  B.Gamma Radiation  C.Insulator  D.mRNA

66. __ Theoretical temperature at which particle motion stops; also known as 0 Kelvin.
    A.Absolute Zero   B.Genome   C.Smooth Endoplasmic Reticulum   D.Transformation

67. __ Carries electrical and chemical impulses to and from organs and limbs to the brain.
    A.Chemistry   B.Nerve Tissue   C.Vascular   D.Nervous System

68. __ Process of breaking down molecules and releasing stored energy.
    A.Smooth Endoplasmic Reticulum   B.Law of Segregation   C.Catabolism   D.Pressure

69. __ The site of protein synthesis within cells.
    A.Population   B.Angiosperm   C.Ribosome   D.Evolution

70. __ Permanent one-way movement into a new range.
    A.Endocytosis   B.Immigration   C.Endoderm   D.Passive Transport

71. __ Two or more atoms held together by shared electrons (covalent bonds).
    A.Digestive System   B.Diffusion   C.Population Density   D.Molecule

72. __ Chemicals produced in the endocrine glands of an organism which modify metabolic activities.
    A.Hormones   B.Angiosperm   C.Heat   D.Allopatric Speciation

73. __ The bending of a light wave around an obstacle.
    A.Biogeography   B.Force   C.Punctuated Equilibrium   D.Diffraction

74. __ Carries impulses back from organs.
    A.Atmospheric Pressure   B.Transformation   C.Newtons Laws   D.Parasympathetic Nervous System

75. __ Carries impulses that stimulate organs.
    A.Angiosperm   B.Organelle   C.Endoderm   D.Sympathetic Nervous System

76. __ Length of DNA that encodes a particular protein.
    A.Passive Transport   B.Gene   C.Photosynthesis   D.Parasympathetic Nervous System

77. __ Occurs when a hydrogen atom is involved with a polar intermolecular attraction to a more electronegative atom.
    A.Golgi Apparatus   B.Gamma Radiation   C.Exocytosis   D.Hydrogen Bond

78. __ A general term that includes all types of energy transformation processes, including photosynthesis, respiration, growth, movement, etc.
    A.Cellular Metabolism   B.Organelle   C.Law of Segregation   D.Lysosome

79. __ Momentary force of attraction that exist between molecules and are much weaker than the forces of chemical bonding.
    A.Punnett Square   B.Van der Waals Force   C.Velocity   D.Chromatin

80. __ The actions in animals we call instincts; highly stereotyped.
    A.Passive Transport   B.Regulatory Genes   C.Innate Behaviors   D.Biogeography

81. __ The export of substances from the cell.
    A.Sympathetic Nervous System   B.Nerve Tissue   C.Exocytosis   D.Biosphere

82. __ Code proteins that determine fictional or physiological events.
    A.Regulatory Genes   B.Innate Behaviors   C.Acid   D.Epithelial Tissue

83. __ Bond formed between the atoms when atoms share electrons.
    A.Cellular Metabolism  B.Lysosome  C.Covalent Bond  D.Vascular

84. __ The process whereby molecules and ions flow through the cell membrane from an area of higher concentration to an area of lower concentration; mixing of particles in a gas or liquid.
    A.Positron Decay  B.Atom  C.Succession  D.Diffusion

85. __ Over time, a gene pool (particularly in a small population) may experience a change in frequency of particular genes simply due to change fluctuations.
    A.Genetic Drift  B.Epithelial Tissue  C.Sex Limited Trait  D.Endoderm

86. __ The conduit for delivering nutrients and gases to all cells and for removing waste products from them.
    A.Biosphere  B.Adipose Tissue  C.Smooth Endoplasmic Reticulum  D.Circulatory System

87. __ Some traits have no genes that are dominant and instead produce offspring that are a mix of the two parents.
    A.Digestive System  B.Immigration  C.Adipose Tissue  D.Incomplete Dominance

88. __ Vessels that carry blood toward the heart.
    A.Circulatory System  B.Vein  C.Lymphocyte  D.Hormones

89. __ Poor conductors of electrical currents.
    A.Kidney  B.Mass  C.Insulator  D.Golgi Apparatus

90. __ The amount of matter that is contained by the object.
    A.Digestive System  B.Mitochondria  C.Chromatin  D.Mass

91. __ The total number of a single species of organism found in an ecosystem.
    A.Homozygous  B.Force  C.Gene  D.Population

92. __ Sum total of genetic information.
    A.Genome  B.Ribosome  C.Atom  D.Vertebrate

93. __ The number of individuals of a species living in an area.
    A.Organelle  B.Chloroplast  C.Positron Decay  D.Population Density

94. __ The measure of the average kinetic energy of a substance.
    A.Catabolism  B.Newtons Laws  C.Evaporation  D.Temperature

95. __ Part of the Earth that includes all living things.
    A.Biosphere  B.Molecule  C.Chemistry  D.Nuclear Membrane

96. __ A chemical that accepts protons (H+ ions) when dissolved in water.
    A.Atom  B.Biosphere  C.Chemistry  D.Base

97. __ The hollow, bulb-shaped structure in the lower interior of the pistil.
    A.Heat  B.Immigration  C.Ovary  D.Covalent Bond

98. __ Three laws that form the basis of most of our understanding of things in motion.
    A.Vertebrate  B.Newtons Laws  C.Atmospheric Pressure  D.Law of Dominance

99. __ A chemical that donates proton (H+ ions) when dissolved in water.
    A.Insulator  B.Migration  C.Acid  D.Golgi Apparatus

© 2017 Network4Learning, Inc.

100. __ Species that have internal backbones.
   A.Vertebrate   B.Regulatory Genes   C.Biosphere   D.Punctuated Equilibrium

*From the words provided for each clue, provide the letter of the word which best matches the clue.*

101. __ Tiny vessels that surround all tissues of the body and exchange carbon dioxide for oxygen.
   A.Central Nervous System   B.Capillary   C.Chemistry   D.Cerebellum

102. __ Plants that have tissue organized in such a way as to conduct food and water throughout their structure.
   A.Community   B.Vertebrate   C.Vascular   D.Prokaryotic Cell

103. __ Filter metabolic waste from the blood and excrete them as urine
   A.Kidney   B.Newtons Laws   C.Competition   D.Nucleolus

104. __ Escape of individual particles of a substance into gaseous form.
   A.Law of Segregation   B.Evaporation   C.Circulatory System   D.Vascular

105. __ Responsible for the sense of smell.
   A.Law of Dominance   B.Somatic Sensory Nerve   C.Cytoplasm   D.Olfactory Lobe

106. __ Genes located on a gender chromosome.
   A.Cerebellum   B.Blood Tissue   C.Population   D.Sex Limited Trait

107. __ Cells with no nucleus or any other membrane-bound organelles.
   A.Prokaryotic Cell   B.Organism   C.Refraction   D.Electron Cloud

108. __ An allele that masks the effect of its partner allele.
   A.Biogeography   B.Territory   C.Dominant Allele   D.Wavelength

109. __ Occurs when a hydrogen atom is involved with a polar intermolecular attraction to a more electronegative atom.
   A.Weight   B.Respiratory System   C.Hydrogen Bond   D.Organic Compound

110. __ Uses energy to move molecules across a cell membrane against a concentration gradient.
   A.Law of Segregation   B.Refraction   C.Active Transport   D.Olfactory Lobe

111. __ The bouncing of a wave of light off an object.
   A.Independent Assortment   B.Hydrogen Bond   C.Flower   D.Reflection

112. __ Smaller than even the smallest cells; survive and replicate by invading a living cell.
   A.Heat   B.Nucleolus   C.Adaptive Radiation   D.Viruses

113. __ Reacting molecules.
   A.Enzyme   B.Reactants   C.Photosynthesis   D.Refraction

114. __ A process in which bacteria absorb and incorporate pieces of DNA from their environment (usually from dead bacterial cells).
   A.Transformation   B.Epithelial Tissue   C.Meiosis   D.Electron Cloud

115. __ Carry impulses from body organs to the CNS.
   A.Somatic Sensory Nerve   B.Visceral Sensory Nerve   C.Endoplasmic Reticulum   D.Blood Tissue

116. __ Part of the brain that controls balance, equilibrium, and muscle coordination.
   A.Mitosis   B.Biogeography   C.Cerebellum   D.Ecology

117. __ Species that have internal backbones.
   A.Vertebrate   B.Sex Influenced Trait   C.Newtons Laws   D.Organic Compound

118. __ Carry impulses from body surface to the CNS.
   A.Immigration   B.Osmosis   C.Chlorophyll   D.Somatic Sensory Nerve

119. __ Instrumental in the storing, packaging, and shipping of proteins; also known as Golgi bodies or the Golgi complex.
   A.Society   B.Weight   C.Golgi Apparatus   D.Osmosis

120. __ Bond of attraction between positive and negative ions.
   A.Population   B.Ionic Bond   C.Osmosis   D.Differential Reproduction

121. __ Process of breaking down molecules and releasing stored energy.
   A.Ecology   B.Watson Crick Model   C.Heterozygous   D.Catabolism

122. __ Scientific model that proposes that adaptations of species arise suddenly and rapidly.
   A.Chlorophyll   B.Punctuated Equilibrium   C.Law of Dominance   D.Visceral Sensory Nerve

123. __ Occurs when two populations are geographically isolated from each other.
   A.Allopatric Speciation   B.Laws of Thermodynamics   C.Olfactory Lobe   D.Prophase

124. __ The force of gravity acting upon that object.
   A.Transduction   B.Weight   C.Immigration   D.Connective Tissue

125. __ Provides structural support to a cell.
   A.Atmospheric Pressure   B.Cytoskeleton   C.Active Transport   D.Sympatric Speciation

126. __ Forms the barrier between the environment and the interior of the body.
   A.Competition   B.Momentum   C.Epithelial Tissue   D.Reflection

127. __ Calculated by adding up the masses of the protons and neutrons.
   A.Cytoskeleton   B.Atomic Mass   C.Active Transport   D.Evaporation

128. __ Holds tissues and organs together, stabilizing the body structure.
   A.Independent Assortment   B.Circuit   C.Momentum   D.Connective Tissue

129. __ One gene is usually dominant over the other.
   A.Law of Dominance   B.Flower   C.Circulatory System   D.Evolution

130. __ The path that an electrical current follows.
   A.Atmospheric Pressure   B.Prokaryotic Cell   C.Somatic Sensory Nerve   D.Circuit

131. __ The actions in animals we call instincts; highly stereotyped.
   A.Olfactory Lobe   B.Innate Behaviors   C.Sperm   D.Habitat

132. __ A special process of diffusion that occurs when the water concentration inside the cell differs from the concentration outside the cell.
   A.Atmospheric Pressure   B.Osmosis   C.Allopatric Speciation   D.Population

133. __ The total number of a single species of organism found in an ecosystem.
   A.Sex Influenced Trait   B.Medulla Oblongata   C.Population   D.Circulatory System

134. ___ Membrane-bound organelles containing digestive enzymes; digest unused material within the cell, damaged organelles, or materials absorbed by the cell for use.
A.Atomic Weight   B.Society   C.Lysosome   D.Wavelength

135. ___ Small round cases within the ovary that contain one or more egg cells.
A.Ovules   B.Epithelial Tissue   C.Food Chain   D.Transduction

136. ___ Poor conductors of electrical currents.
A.Insulator   B.Evaporation   C.Digestive System   D.Organic Compound

137. ___ Energy that flows from an object that is warm to an object that is cooler.
A.Refraction   B.Sympatric Speciation   C.Heat   D.Krebs Cycle

138. ___ The transfer or genetic material (portions of a bacterial chromosome) from one bacteria cell to another.
A.Allopatric Speciation   B.Transduction   C.Genetic Drift   D.Habitat

139. ___ Protein molecules that act as catalysts for organic reactions.
A.Enzyme   B.Osmosis   C.Cerebellum   D.Olfactory Lobe

140. ___ The average mass number.
A.Absolute Zero   B.Adaptive Radiation   C.Atomic Weight   D.Golgi Apparatus

141. ___ Explain the interaction between heat and work (energy) in the universe.
A.Laws of Thermodynamics   B.Territory   C.Cell   D.Lysosome

142. ___ The movement of mass over a distance.
A.Ovules   B.Work   C.Territory   D.Biogeography

143. ___ Populations that interact with each other in a ecosystem.
A.Golgi Apparatus   B.Reactants   C.Cytoskeleton   D.Community

144. ___ The study of how photosynthetic organisms and animals are distributed in a location plus the history of their distribution in the past.
A.Biogeography   B.Society   C.Positron Decay   D.Heterozygous

145. ___ Over time, a gene pool (particularly in a small population) may experience a change in frequency of particular genes simply due to change fluctuations.
A.Genetic Drift   B.Translation   C.Evaporation   D.Territory

146. ___ The precursor of the gut lining and various accessory structures.
A.Endoderm   B.Law of Dominance   C.Watson Crick Model   D.Biogeography

147. ___ An organization of individuals in a population in which tasks are divided for the group to work together.
A.Punctuated Equilibrium   B.Society   C.Refraction   D.Chemistry

148. ___ Genetically different members reproduce with each other, producing a population, which is separate from the original species.
A.Sex Influenced Trait   B.Olfactory Lobe   C.Sympatric Speciation   D.Respiratory System

149. ___ Individuals within a population that are most adapted to the environment and are also the most likely individuals to reproduce successfully.
A.Differential Reproduction   B.Territory   C.Translation   D.Polar Molecule

150. __ The first phase in mitosis.
    A.Law of Dominance   B.Prophase   C.Momentum   D.Ovules

151. __ Three-dimensional space where electrons travel freely; also known as an electron shell or orbital.
    A.Electron Cloud   B.Atmospheric Pressure   C.Endoderm   D.Prokaryotic Cell

152. __ Pressure that results from the total weight of the atmosphere exerting force on the Earth; can be measured with a barometer.
    A.Independent Assortment   B.Connective Tissue   C.Reactants   D.Atmospheric Pressure

153. __ Serves as a processing plant for ingested food.
    A.Habitat   B.Viruses   C.Digestive System   D.Cytoplasm

154. __ The change in direction of a wave as it passes from one medium to another.
    A.Refraction   B.Polar Molecule   C.Electron Cloud   D.Laws of Thermodynamics

155. __ Occurs when the nucleus emits a particle that degrades into a positron as it passes out of the atom.
    A.Laws of Thermodynamics   B.Adaptive Radiation   C.Law of Segregation   D.Positron Decay

156. __ Energy generally flows through the entire ecosystem in one direction from producers to consumers and on to decomposers.
    A.Transduction   B.Work   C.Digestive System   D.Food Chain

157. __ the process by which a cell distributes its duplicated chromosomes so that each daughter cell has a full set of chromosomes.
    A.Kidney   B.Mitosis   C.Community   D.Density

158. __ An area of land that lies within the home range that the individual will defend as his own.
    A.Territory   B.Meiosis   C.Evolution   D.Central Nervous System

159. __ The site of photosynthesis within plant cells.
    A.Independent Assortment   B.Sperm   C.Chemistry   D.Chloroplast

160. __ An individual of a species.
    A.Organism   B.Genetic Drift   C.Medulla Oblongata   D.Capillary

161. __ The measure of how much matter exists in a volume.
    A.Sympatric Speciation   B.Competition   C.Chemistry   D.Density

162. __ A learned behavior that develops in a critical or sensitive period of the animal's lifespan.
    A.Capillary   B.Vascular   C.Imprinting   D.Differential Reproduction

163. __ Permanent one-way movement into a new range.
    A.Golgi Apparatus   B.Genetic Drift   C.Organic Compound   D.Immigration

164. __ A single species can develop into several diverse species over time; over time a species will specially adapt to live more effectively in a new environment.
    A.Vertebrate   B.Immigration   C.Olfactory Lobe   D.Adaptive Radiation

165. __ Part of the brain that controls involuntary responses such as breathing and heartbeat.
    A.Connective Tissue   B.Medulla Oblongata   C.Enzyme   D.Biogeography

166. ___ The conduit for delivering nutrients and gases to all cells and for removing waste products from them.
   A. Flower   B. Circulatory System   C. Laws of Thermodynamics   D. Reactants

167. ___ Two main components, the brain and the spinal cord; which control all other organs and systems of the body.
   A. Golgi Apparatus   B. Central Nervous System   C. Chloroplast   D. Catabolism

168. ___ Responsible for the intake and processing of gases required by an organism and for expelling gases produced as waste products.
   A. Osmosis   B. Respiratory System   C. Cytoplasm   D. Heat

169. ___ Region between the nucleus and cell membrane.
   A. Cytoplasm   B. Laws of Thermodynamics   C. Population   D. Differential Reproduction

170. ___ The distance from one crest (or top) of a wave to the next crest on the same side.
   A. Ovules   B. Pressure   C. Population   D. Wavelength

171. ___ Phase of photosynthesis that requires a second type of RNA.
   A. Law of Segregation   B. Translation   C. Respiratory System   D. Olfactory Lobe

172. ___ Short length of DNA wrapped around a core of small proteins.
   A. Evaporation   B. Sperm   C. Histone   D. Nucleolus

173. ___ A learned behavior where the organism produces less and less response as a stimulus is repeated, without a subsequent negative or positive action.
   A. Chemistry   B. Immigration   C. Chlorophyll   D. Habituation

174. ___ Named after scientists who discovered and modeled the structure of DNA.
   A. Circulatory System   B. Watson Crick Model   C. Chlorophyll   D. Lysosome

175. ___ The gradual change of characteristics within a population, producing a change in a species over time.
   A. Evolution   B. Cell   C. Enzyme   D. Newtons Laws

176. ___ The building blocks of all living things.
   A. Insulator   B. Organic Compound   C. Allopatric Speciation   D. Wavelength

177. ___ The primary reproductive organ for a plant.
   A. Transformation   B. Digestive System   C. Cytoplasm   D. Flower

178. ___ Molecule that has regions of partial change.
   A. Endoderm   B. Polar Molecule   C. Pressure   D. Independent Assortment

179. ___ Results when two or more species living within the same area and that overlap niches both require a resource that is in limited supply.
   A. Reflection   B. Competition   C. Catabolism   D. Sympatric Speciation

180. ___ Flows through the blood vessels and heart and is essential for carrying oxygen to cells, fighting infection, and carrying nutrients and wastes to and from cells.
   A. Vertebrate   B. Blood Tissue   C. Organism   D. Digestive System

181. ___ Homologous chromosomes separate and independently sort in gamete formation.
   A. Independent Assortment   B. Lysosome   C. Reactants   D. Work

182. __ Behavior patterns that take into account other individuals.
   A.Habituation  B.Prophase  C.Sex Influenced Trait  D.Social Behavior

183. __ A crucial set of reactions that convert the light energy of the sun into chemical energy usable by living things.
   A.Ovules  B.Food Chain  C.Lysosome  D.Photosynthesis

184. __ The product of mass and velocity.
   A.Absolute Zero  B.Competition  C.Prophase  D.Momentum

185. __ When the two alleles for a given gene are different in an individual.
   A.Connective Tissue  B.Heterozygous  C.Pressure  D.Central Nervous System

186. __ A measure of the amount of force applied per unit of area.
   A.Kidney  B.Translation  C.Pressure  D.Endoderm

187. __ Three laws that form the basis of most of our understanding of things in motion.
   A.Newtons Laws  B.Adaptive Radiation  C.Meiosis  D.Blood Tissue

188. __ Theoretical temperature at which particle motion stops; also known as 0 Kelvin.
   A.Polar Molecule  B.Social Behavior  C.Medulla Oblongata  D.Absolute Zero

189. __ A rounded area within the nucleus of the cell where ribosomal RNA is synthesized.
   A.Nucleolus  B.Chloroplast  C.Transformation  D.Photosynthesis

190. __ The study of matter.
   A.Chemistry  B.Cerebellum  C.Respiratory System  D.Chlorophyll

191. __ traits are expressed from a pair of genes in the individual (on homologous chromosomes).
   A.Law of Segregation  B.Heat  C.Flower  D.Kidney

192. __ Large organization of folded membranes; responsible for the delivery of lipids and proteins to certain areas within the cytoplasm.
   A.Independent Assortment  B.Capillary  C.Endoplasmic Reticulum  D.Cytoskeleton

193. __ Pigment molecules that give the chloroplast their green color.
   A.Heat  B.Chlorophyll  C.Atomic Weight  D.Epithelial Tissue

194. __ Produced by the male gametophyte; also known as a male gamete.
   A.Insulator  B.Vascular  C.Sperm  D.Respiratory System

195. __ The physical place where a species lives.
   A.Evolution  B.Golgi Apparatus  C.Habitat  D.Epithelial Tissue

196. __ The first step in aerobic respiration that occurs in the matrix of a cell's mitochondria.
   A.Density  B.Krebs Cycle  C.Golgi Apparatus  D.Digestive System

197. __ The process of producing four daughter cells, each with single unduplicated chromosomes.
   A.Meiosis  B.Electron Cloud  C.Vascular  D.Laws of Thermodynamics

198. __ The smallest and most basic unit of most living things.
   A.Ionic Bond  B.Cell  C.Watson Crick Model  D.Territory

199. __ The study of how organisms interact with other organisms and how they influence or are influenced by their physical environment.
   A.Ecology   B.Wavelength   C.Organism   D.Differential Reproduction

200. __ Requires only one recessive gene to be expressed if there is no counteracting dominant gene.
   A.Respiratory System   B.Habitat   C.Sex Influenced Trait   D.Laws of Thermodynamics

*From the words provided for each clue, provide the letter of the word which best matches the clue.*

201. __ When one community completely replaces another over time in an area.
   A.Community   B.Transpiration   C.Succession   D.Osmosis

202. __ The number of individuals of a species living in an area.
   A.Embryo   B.Wavelength   C.Electron Transport   D.Population Density

203. __ Temporary movement out of one range into another and back.
   A.Refraction   B.Prokaryotic Cell   C.Allopatric Speciation   D.Migration

204. __ The path that an electrical current follows.
   A.Organelle   B.Circuit   C.Refraction   D.Adaptive Radiation

205. __ The first phase in mitosis.
   A.Krebs Cycle   B.Force   C.Prophase   D.Reactants

206. __ Pressure that results from the total weight of the atmosphere exerting force on the Earth; can be measured with a barometer.
   A.Atmospheric Pressure   B.Lysosome   C.Photosynthesis   D.Digestion

207. __ Two or more atoms held together by shared electrons (covalent bonds).
   A.Diffraction   B.Habitat   C.Protein   D.Molecule

208. __ The simplest unit of an element that retains the element's characteristics.
   A.Atom   B.Natural Selection   C.Immune System   D.Smooth Endoplasmic Reticulum

209. __ Tiny vessels that surround all tissues of the body and exchange carbon dioxide for oxygen.
   A.Cardiac Muscle   B.Diffraction   C.Connective Tissue   D.Capillary

210. __ One gene is usually dominant over the other.
   A.Law of Dominance   B.Electron Cloud   C.Olfactory Lobe   D.Neuron

211. __ The two identical strands of duplicated chromatin in a cell that is getting ready to divide.
   A.Molecule   B.Community   C.Dominant Allele   D.Chromatid

212. __ The study of how photosynthetic organisms and animals are distributed in a location plus the history of their distribution in the past.
   A.Hindbrain   B.Pressure   C.Natural Selection   D.Biogeography

213. __ The site of protein synthesis within cells.
   A.Capillary   B.Visceral Sensory Nerve   C.Weight   D.Ribosome

214. ___ The introduction of new genes from an immigrant, which results in a change of the gene pool.
A.Histone  B.Sympatric Speciation  C.Gene Migration  D.Diploid

215. ___ Begin in bone marrow as stem cells and are collected and distributed via the lymph nodes.
A.Lymphocyte  B.Protein  C.Habituation  D.Innate Behaviors

216. ___ Occurs when the nucleus emits a beta particle that degrades into an electron as it passes out of the atom.
A.Beta Decay  B.Friction  C.Atom  D.Cerebellum

217. ___ A feature of population genetics that is the driving force behind evolution.
A.Natural Selection  B.Cell Membrane  C.Chromatid  D.Lymphocyte

218. ___ Tissue forming the walls of the heart with strength and electrical properties that are vital to the heart's ability to pump blood.
A.Krebs Cycle  B.Eukaryotic Cell  C.Cardiac Muscle  D.Histone

219. ___ A flow of electrons through a conductor.
A.Electrical Current  B.Atom  C.Cerebellum  D.Eukaryotic Cell

220. ___ The distance from one crest (or top) of a wave to the next crest on the same side.
A.Histone  B.Photosynthesis  C.Lymphocyte  D.Wavelength

221. ___ The parent cell that has a normal set of paired chromosomes.
A.Diploid  B.Weight  C.Organelle  D.Biogeography

222. ___ Occurs when two populations are geographically isolated from each other.
A.Mitosis  B.Allopatric Speciation  C.Dominant Allele  D.Adaptive Radiation

223. ___ Part of the brain that controls involuntary responses such as breathing and heartbeat.
A.Competition  B.Genotype  C.Nuclear Membrane  D.Medulla Oblongata

224. ___ The second step of aerobic respiration that captures the energy created by the release of electrons from the Krebs cycle.
A.Electron Transport  B.Circuit  C.Cell Cycle  D.Histone

225. ___ Cells that contain membrane-bound intracellular organelles, including a nucleus.
A.Organelle  B.Exothermic  C.Prophase  D.Eukaryotic Cell

226. ___ The physical place where a species lives.
A.Weight  B.Atmospheric Pressure  C.Community  D.Habitat

227. ___ Protein molecules that act as catalysts for organic reactions.
A.Sympatric Speciation  B.Vein  C.Visceral Sensory Nerve  D.Enzyme

228. ___ The rubbing force that acts against motion between two touching surfaces.
A.Element  B.Catabolism  C.Taxonomy  D.Friction

229. ___ An organization of individuals in a population in which tasks are divided for the group to work together.
A.Succession  B.Element  C.Alpha Decay  D.Society

230. ___ The formation of an RNA molecule, which corresponds to a gene.
A.Protein  B.Mutation  C.Transcription  D.Wavelength

231. __ Thin-walled air sacs, which are the site of gas exchange.
    A. Alpha Decay   B. Alveoli   C. Reactants   D. Law of Dominance

232. __ What a zygote eventually grown into.
    A. Capillary   B. Cell Cycle   C. Embryo   D. Medulla Oblongata

233. __ Center of cellular respiration
    A. Circuit   B. Wavelength   C. Immune System   D. Mitochondria

234. __ The precursor of the gut lining and various accessory structures.
    A. Golgi Apparatus   B. Photosynthesis   C. Endoderm   D. Friction

235. __ Short length of DNA wrapped around a core of small proteins.
    A. Biogeography   B. Migration   C. Histone   D. Innate Behaviors

236. __ An allele that masks the effect of its partner allele.
    A. Transcription   B. Diffraction   C. Dominant Allele   D. Society

237. __ Membrane-bound organelles containing digestive enzymes; digest unused material within the cell, damaged organelles, or materials absorbed by the cell for use.
    A. Vein   B. Lysosome   C. Midbrain   D. Mutation

238. __ A process in which some water that has traveled up through the plant to the leaves is evaporated.
    A. Transpiration   B. Diploid   C. Natural Selection   D. Eukaryotic Cell

239. __ Present in every living cell, large un-branched chains of amino acids; may also be called polypeptides.
    A. Mitosis   B. Electron Transport   C. Enzyme   D. Protein

240. __ Vessels that carry blood toward the heart.
    A. Histone   B. Vertebrate   C. Vein   D. Golgi Apparatus

241. __ Requires only one recessive gene to be expressed if there is no counteracting dominant gene.
    A. Wavelength   B. Law of Dominance   C. Sex Influenced Trait   D. Beta Decay

242. __ Populations that interact with each other in a ecosystem.
    A. Community   B. Olfactory Lobe   C. Lysosome   D. Electron Cloud

243. __ A substance that cannot be broken down into any other substances.
    A. Pressure   B. Element   C. Energy Cycle   D. Visceral Sensory Nerve

244. __ Network of membranous channels; does not have attached ribosomes.
    A. Smooth Endoplasmic Reticulum   B. Allopatric Speciation   C. Cell Membrane   D. Dominant Allele

245. __ A measure of the amount of force applied per unit of area.
    A. Cell Cycle   B. Sympatric Speciation   C. Pressure   D. Biogeography

246. __ Explain the interaction between heat and work (energy) in the universe.
    A. Laws of Thermodynamics   B. Embryo   C. Endoderm   D. Frequency

247. __ Consists of the cerebellum and medulla oblongata.
    A. Nuclear Membrane   B. Electron Transport   C. Hindbrain   D. Refraction

248. __ The boundary between the nucleus and the cytoplasm.
    A.Nuclear Membrane   B.Dominant Allele   C.Taxonomy   D.Digestion

249. __ Results when two or more species living within the same area and that overlap niches both require a resource that is in limited supply.
    A.Eukaryotic Cell   B.Competition   C.Exothermic   D.Refraction

250. __ Process of breaking down molecules and releasing stored energy.
    A.Allopatric Speciation   B.Reflex   C.Digestive System   D.Catabolism

251. __ A special process of diffusion that occurs when the water concentration inside the cell differs from the concentration outside the cell.
    A.Habitat   B.Cell Membrane   C.Osmosis   D.Catabolism

252. __ Reactions that release energy.
    A.Photosynthesis   B.Smooth Endoplasmic Reticulum   C.Osmosis   D.Exothermic

253. __ Carry impulses via electrochemical responses.
    A.Neuron   B.pH   C.Reflection   D.Cell Membrane

254. __ Provides the body with structure, stability, and the ability to move.
    A.Musculoskeletal System   B.Connective Tissue   C.Gene Migration   D.Nuclear Membrane

255. __ Cells with no nucleus or any other membrane-bound organelles.
    A.Cytoplasm   B.Connective Tissue   C.Weight   D.Prokaryotic Cell

256. __ the process by which a cell distributes its duplicated chromosomes so that each daughter cell has a full set of chromosomes.
    A.Mitosis   B.Electron Cloud   C.Ribosome   D.Enzyme

257. __ Responsible for the sense of smell.
    A.Eukaryotic Cell   B.Lysosome   C.Olfactory Lobe   D.Genotype

258. __ The bending of a light wave around an obstacle.
    A.Gene Pool   B.Prokaryotic Cell   C.Reflection   D.Diffraction

259. __ Three-dimensional space where electrons travel freely; also known as an electron shell or orbital.
    A.Electron Cloud   B.Law of Dominance   C.Cell Membrane   D.Krebs Cycle

260. __ A crucial set of reactions that convert the light energy of the sun into chemical energy usable by living things.
    A.Cardiac Muscle   B.Photosynthesis   C.Frequency   D.Digestive System

261. __ The combination of alleles that make a particular trait.
    A.Competition   B.Cell Membrane   C.Biogeography   D.Genotype

262. __ Occurs when the nucleus of an atom emits a package of two protons and two neutrons, called an alpha particle, which is equivalent to the nucleus of a helium atom.
    A.Diploid   B.Organelle   C.Alpha Decay   D.Reflex

263. __ Region between the nucleus and cell membrane.
    A.Atom   B.Vein   C.Neuron   D.Cytoplasm

**264.** ___ The entire collection of genes within a given population.
A. Element   B. Immune System   C. Gene Pool   D. Alpha Decay

**265.** ___ The push or pull exerted on an object.
A. Chromatid   B. Cytoplasm   C. Force   D. Neuron

**266.** ___ Structures that are similar because of their common function, although they do not share a common ancestry.
A. Prophase   B. Mitosis   C. Analogous   D. Homozygous

**267.** ___ Cells components that perform functions.
A. Organelle   B. Diffraction   C. Lysosome   D. Eukaryotic Cell

**268.** ___ A sequence of events ending in cell division, which produces two daughter cells.
A. Analogous   B. Competition   C. Adaptive Radiation   D. Cell Cycle

**269.** ___ The force of gravity acting upon that object.
A. Weight   B. Cerebellum   C. Reactants   D. Atmospheric Pressure

**270.** ___ Structure that encloses the cell and separates it from the environment; also known as the plasma membrane.
A. Cell Membrane   B. Homozygous   C. Newtons Laws   D. Community

**271.** ___ The change in direction of a wave as it passes from one medium to another.
A. Exothermic   B. Digestive System   C. Refraction   D. Molecule

**272.** ___ The bouncing of a wave of light off an object.
A. Immune System   B. Force   C. Reflection   D. Homozygous

**273.** ___ Arteries, veins, and capillaries.
A. Competition   B. Vessel   C. Organelle   D. Electrical Current

**274.** ___ When both alleles for a given gene are the same in an individual.
A. Cerebellum   B. Genotype   C. Exothermic   D. Homozygous

**275.** ___ A learned behavior where the organism produces less and less response as a stimulus is repeated, without a subsequent negative or positive action.
A. Reactants   B. Habituation   C. Cytoplasm   D. Diffusion

**276.** ___ The actions in animals we call instincts; highly stereotyped.
A. Innate Behaviors   B. Digestive System   C. Law of Dominance   D. Smooth Endoplasmic Reticulum

**277.** ___ Class of lymphocyte cell that emerge from the bone marrow mature and produce antibodies, which enter the bloodstream.
A. Olfactory Lobe   B. B Cell   C. Atmospheric Pressure   D. Analogous

**278.** ___ Functions to defend the body from infection by bacteria and viruses.
A. Alpha Decay   B. Society   C. Immune System   D. Cytoplasm

**279.** ___ Instrumental in the storing, packaging, and shipping of proteins; also known as Golgi bodies or the Golgi complex.
A. Biogeography   B. Reflection   C. Gene Pool   D. Golgi Apparatus

**280.** ___ The first step in aerobic respiration that occurs in the matrix of a cell's mitochondria.
A. Alpha Decay   B. Alveoli   C. Habitat   D. Krebs Cycle

281. __ Three laws that form the basis of most of our understanding of things in motion.
A.Force   B.Diffusion   C.Newtons Laws   D.Enzyme

282. __ A change of the DNA sequence of a gene, resulting in a change of the trait.
A.Weight   B.Chromatid   C.B Cell   D.Mutation

283. __ Positive ion.
A.Refraction   B.Cation   C.Atomic Weight   D.Hindbrain

284. __ Located between the forebrain and hindbrain; contains the optic lobes.
A.Atom   B.Habituation   C.Midbrain   D.Digestive System

285. __ Holds tissues and organs together, stabilizing the body structure.
A.Adaptive Radiation   B.Transpiration   C.Connective Tissue   D.Atom

286. __ Serves as a processing plant for ingested food.
A.Digestive System   B.Dominant Allele   C.Musculoskeletal System   D.Organelle

287. __ The number of wavelengths that pass a point in a second.
A.Immune System   B.Diploid   C.Frequency   D.Exothermic

288. __ Part of the brain that controls balance, equilibrium, and muscle coordination.
A.Cerebellum   B.Innate Behaviors   C.Capillary   D.Connective Tissue

289. __ Study that organizes living things into groups based on morphology or, more recently, genetics.
A.Taxonomy   B.Olfactory Lobe   C.Atomic Weight   D.Laws of Thermodynamics

290. __ The average mass number.
A.Law of Dominance   B.Atomic Weight   C.Molecule   D.Neuron

291. __ Genetically different members reproduce with each other, producing a population, which is separate from the original species.
A.Dominant Allele   B.Electron Transport   C.Sympatric Speciation   D.Olfactory Lobe

292. __ Supports life throughout the environment.
A.Habitat   B.Energy Cycle   C.Reflex   D.Atomic Weight

293. __ Potential of hydrogen scale, which is a measurement of H+ ions in solutions.
A.Exothermic   B.pH   C.Habitat   D.Medulla Oblongata

294. __ Species that have internal backbones.
A.Lymphocyte   B.Adaptive Radiation   C.Vertebrate   D.Diploid

295. __ Reacting molecules.
A.Krebs Cycle   B.Cation   C.Reactants   D.Diffusion

296. __ An automatic movement of a body part in response to a stimulus.
A.Reflex   B.Prokaryotic Cell   C.Embryo   D.Eukaryotic Cell

297. __ Carry impulses from body organs to the CNS.
A.Visceral Sensory Nerve   B.Enzyme   C.Lysosome   D.Law of Dominance

298. \_\_ A single species can develop into several diverse species over time; over time a species will specially adapt to live more effectively in a new environment.
A. Force   B. Sex Influenced Trait   C. Homozygous   D. Adaptive Radiation

299. \_\_ The process whereby molecules and ions flow through the cell membrane from an area of higher concentration to an area of lower concentration; mixing of particles in a gas or liquid.
A. Diffusion   B. Gene Migration   C. Frequency   D. Exothermic

300. \_\_ Breakdown of ingested particles into molecules that can be absorbed by the body.
A. Genotype   B. Diploid   C. Allopatric Speciation   D. Digestion

© 2017 Network4Learning, Inc.

*From the words provided for each clue, provide the letter of the word which best matches the clue.*

1. __D__  The push or pull exerted on an object.
   A.Positron Decay   B.Evolution   C.Organelle   D.Force

2. __A__  Carry impulses from body organs to the CNS.
   A.Visceral Sensory Nerve   B.Gamma Radiation   C.Ovules   D.Chromatin

3. __B__  Membrane-bound organelles containing digestive enzymes; digest unused material within the cell, damaged organelles, or materials absorbed by the cell for use.
   A.Diffraction   B.Lysosome   C.Punnett Square   D.Incomplete Dominance

4. __D__  A learned behavior that develops in a critical or sensitive period of the animal's lifespan.
   A.Optic Lobe   B.Visceral Sensory Nerve   C.Endocytosis   D.Imprinting

5. __B__  Reactions that release energy.
   A.Organelle   B.Exothermic   C.Base   D.Diffraction

6. __D__  Center of cellular respiration
   A.Biosphere   B.Passive Transport   C.Exothermic   D.Mitochondria

7. __B__  Network of membranous channels; does not have attached ribosomes.
   A.Electron Cloud   B.Smooth Endoplasmic Reticulum   C.Diffraction   D.Molecule

8. __D__  The boundary between the nucleus and the cytoplasm.
   A.Evaporation   B.Covalent Bond   C.Biosphere   D.Nuclear Membrane

9. __B__  Short length of DNA wrapped around a core of small proteins.
   A.Ovary   B.Histone   C.Law of Segregation   D.Kidney

10. __A__  Step three in mitosis.
    A.Anaphase   B.Chloroplast   C.Golgi Apparatus   D.Biogeography

11. __C__  Mature cells in the thymus gland that patrol the blood for antigens but are also equipped to destroy antigens themselves.
    A.Sympathetic Nervous System   B.Gamete   C.T Cell   D.mRNA

12. __B__  The gradual change of characteristics within a population, producing a change in a species over time.
    A.Passive Transport   B.Evolution   C.Chromatin   D.Velocity

13. __C__  Pressure that results from the total weight of the atmosphere exerting force on the Earth; can be measured with a barometer.
    A.Base   B.Pituitary Gland   C.Atmospheric Pressure   D.Photosynthesis

14. __B__  The combination of alleles that make a particular trait.
    A.Insulator   B.Genotype   C.Chemistry   D.Evaporation

15. __B__  RNA strand that migrates form the nucleus to the cytoplasm; also known as messenger RNA.
    A.Regulatory Genes   B.mRNA   C.Incomplete Dominance   D.Oogenesis

16. __D__ A communication network that connects the entire body of an organism and provides control over bodily functions.
    A.Pressure   B.Velocity   C.Exocytosis   D.Nervous System

17. __D__ The simplest unit of an element that retains the element's characteristics.
    A.Vein   B.Molecule   C.Cellular Metabolism   D.Atom

18. __B__ The study of matter.
    A.Beta Decay   B.Chemistry   C.Temperature   D.Immigration

19. __D__ Calculated by adding up the masses of the protons and neutrons.
    A.Positron Decay   B.Photosynthesis   C.Vertebrate   D.Atomic Mass

20. __D__ Notation that allow us to easily predict the results of a genetic cross.
    A.Heat   B.Angiosperm   C.T Cell   D.Punnett Square

21. __D__ The site of photosynthesis within plant cells.
    A.Substrate   B.Melting Point   C.Covalent Bond   D.Chloroplast

22. __B__ Code proteins that form organs and structural characteristics.
    A.Transformation   B.Structural Gene   C.Acid   D.Kidney

23. __A__ Formation of egg cells.
    A.Oogenesis   B.Nervous System   C.Atomic Mass   D.Immigration

24. __D__ Cell that results when a sperm cell fertilizes an egg cell.
    A.Endoderm   B.Chloroplast   C.Sex Limited Trait   D.Zygote

25. __B__ Visual center connected to the eyes by the optic nerves.
    A.Histone   B.Optic Lobe   C.Biogeography   D.Allopatric Speciation

26. __B__ Substances freely pass across the membrane without the cell expending any energy.
    A.Regulatory Genes   B.Passive Transport   C.Force   D.Photosynthesis

27. __A__ The rate of change of displacement; includes both speed and direction.
    A.Velocity   B.Population   C.Molecule   D.Histone

28. __A__ Plants that have tissue organized in such a way as to conduct food and water throughout their structure.
    A.Vascular   B.Molecule   C.Law of Dominance   D.Ribosome

29. __D__ Particular substance of an enzyme that fits within the active site.
    A.Imprinting   B.Regulatory Genes   C.Kidney   D.Substrate

30. __C__ Genes located on a gender chromosome.
    A.Velocity   B.Genotype   C.Sex Limited Trait   D.Adipose Tissue

31. __C__ The process whereby large molecules are taken up into a pocket of membrane; the pocket pinches off, delivering the molecules, still inside a membrane sack into the cytoplasm.
    A.Beta Decay   B.Angiosperm   C.Endocytosis   D.Exocytosis

32. __A__ The first phase in mitosis.
    A.Prophase   B.Homozygous   C.Succession   D.Zygote

© 2017 Network4Learning, Inc.

33. C   Forms the barrier between the environment and the interior of the body.
    A.Punnett Square   B.Zygote   C.Epithelial Tissue   D.Heat

34. D   Consists of gamma rays, which are high-frequency, high-energy, electromagnetic radiation that are usually given off in combination with alpha and beta decay.
    A.T Cell   B.Beta Decay   C.Gamete   D.Gamma Radiation

35. A   When both alleles for a given gene are the same in an individual.
    A.Homozygous   B.T Cell   C.Allopatric Speciation   D.Pressure

36. B   Serves as a processing plant for ingested food.
    A.Innate Behaviors   B.Digestive System   C.Chemistry   D.Microvilli

37. C   Occurs when the nucleus emits a beta particle that degrades into an electron as it passes out of the atom.
    A.Heat   B.Ovules   C.Beta Decay   D.Angiosperm

38. B   When one community completely replaces another over time in an area.
    A.Lymphocyte   B.Succession   C.Positron Decay   D.Genome

39. B   The process by which characteristics pass from one generation to another.
    A.Diffraction   B.Inheritance   C.Atmospheric Pressure   D.Chloroplast

40. C   The four haploid cells (egg and sperm) that are found in reproductive organs as a result of meiosis.
    A.Ovules   B.Pituitary Gland   C.Gamete   D.Parasympathetic Nervous System

41. B   Temperature at which a substance changes from solid to liquid form.
    A.Molecule   B.Melting Point   C.Ribosome   D.Exothermic

42. C   A crucial set of reactions that convert the light energy of the sun into chemical energy usable by living things.
    A.Temperature   B.Heat   C.Photosynthesis   D.Biogeography

43. A   Temporary movement out of one range into another and back.
    A.Migration   B.Diffraction   C.Anaphase   D.Atomic Mass

44. C   The study of how photosynthetic organisms and animals are distributed in a location plus the history of their distribution in the past.
    A.Oogenesis   B.Chemistry   C.Biogeography   D.Genetic Drift

45. B   Found beneath the skin and around organs, providing cushioning, insulation, and fat storage.
    A.Exocytosis   B.Adipose Tissue   C.Heat   D.Diffraction

46. A   Instrumental in the storing, packaging, and shipping of proteins; also known as Golgi bodies or the Golgi complex.
    A.Golgi Apparatus   B.Lymphocyte   C.Evolution   D.Heat

47. C   Cells components that perform functions.
    A.Gamma Radiation   B.Newtons Laws   C.Organelle   D.Zygote

48. D   traits are expressed from a pair of genes in the individual (on homologous chromosomes).
    A.Chromatin   B.Prophase   C.Diffusion   D.Law of Segregation

49. _A_  Releases various hormones.
    A.Pituitary Gland  B.Genetic Drift  C.Ribosome  D.Newtons Laws

50. _C_  Projections of the cell extending from the cell membrane; increase the surface area of the cell membrane, increasing the area available to absorb nutrients.
    A.Structural Gene  B.Atom  C.Microvilli  D.Mass

51. _B_  Filter metabolic waste from the blood and excrete them as urine
    A.Incomplete Dominance  B.Kidney  C.Lymphocyte  D.Gene

52. _C_  Begin in bone marrow as stem cells and are collected and distributed via the lymph nodes.
    A.Catabolism  B.Melting Point  C.Lymphocyte  D.Electron Cloud

53. _A_  The precursor of the gut lining and various accessory structures.
    A.Endoderm  B.Homozygous  C.Ovary  D.Catabolism

54. _A_  Scientific model that proposes that adaptations of species arise suddenly and rapidly.
    A.Punctuated Equilibrium  B.Evaporation  C.Angiosperm  D.Adipose Tissue

55. _A_  The combination of DNA with histones.
    A.Chromatin  B.Hydrogen Bond  C.Beta Decay  D.Melting Point

56. _C_  One gene is usually dominant over the other.
    A.Covalent Bond  B.Van der Waals Force  C.Law of Dominance  D.Melting Point

57. _B_  Occurs when two populations are geographically isolated from each other.
    A.Immigration  B.Allopatric Speciation  C.Epithelial Tissue  D.Punctuated Equilibrium

58. _D_  A measure of the amount of force applied per unit of area.
    A.Gene  B.Electron Cloud  C.mRNA  D.Pressure

59. _A_  Small round cases within the ovary that contain one or more egg cells.
    A.Ovules  B.Vein  C.Beta Decay  D.Digestive System

60. _A_  Energy that flows from an object that is warm to an object that is cooler.
    A.Heat  B.Angiosperm  C.Kidney  D.Gene

61. _A_  Three-dimensional space where electrons travel freely; also known as an electron shell or orbital.
    A.Electron Cloud  B.Histone  C.Diffusion  D.Visceral Sensory Nerve

62. _B_  Plants that produce flowers as reproductive organs.
    A.Beta Decay  B.Angiosperm  C.Vein  D.Gamma Radiation

63. _A_  A process in which bacteria absorb and incorporate pieces of DNA from their environment (usually from dead bacterial cells).
    A.Transformation  B.Exothermic  C.Migration  D.Punnett Square

64. _C_  Occurs when the nucleus emits a particle that degrades into a positron as it passes out of the atom.
    A.Genome  B.Punnett Square  C.Positron Decay  D.Atom

65. _A_  Escape of individual particles of a substance into gaseous form.
    A.Evaporation  B.Gamma Radiation  C.Insulator  D.mRNA

66. __A__ Theoretical temperature at which particle motion stops; also known as 0 Kelvin.
    A.Absolute Zero   B.Genome   C.Smooth Endoplasmic Reticulum   D.Transformation

67. __B__ Carries electrical and chemical impulses to and from organs and limbs to the brain.
    A.Chemistry   B.Nerve Tissue   C.Vascular   D.Nervous System

68. __C__ Process of breaking down molecules and releasing stored energy.
    A.Smooth Endoplasmic Reticulum   B.Law of Segregation   C.Catabolism   D.Pressure

69. __C__ The site of protein synthesis within cells.
    A.Population   B.Angiosperm   C.Ribosome   D.Evolution

70. __B__ Permanent one-way movement into a new range.
    A.Endocytosis   B.Immigration   C.Endoderm   D.Passive Transport

71. __D__ Two or more atoms held together by shared electrons (covalent bonds).
    A.Digestive System   B.Diffusion   C.Population Density   D.Molecule

72. __A__ Chemicals produced in the endocrine glands of an organism which modify metabolic activities.
    A.Hormones   B.Angiosperm   C.Heat   D.Allopatric Speciation

73. __D__ The bending of a light wave around an obstacle.
    A.Biogeography   B.Force   C.Punctuated Equilibrium   D.Diffraction

74. __D__ Carries impulses back from organs.
    A.Atmospheric Pressure   B.Transformation   C.Newtons Laws   D.Parasympathetic Nervous System

75. __D__ Carries impulses that stimulate organs.
    A.Angiosperm   B.Organelle   C.Endoderm   D.Sympathetic Nervous System

76. __B__ Length of DNA that encodes a particular protein.
    A.Passive Transport   B.Gene   C.Photosynthesis   D.Parasympathetic Nervous System

77. __D__ Occurs when a hydrogen atom is involved with a polar intermolecular attraction to a more electronegative atom.
    A.Golgi Apparatus   B.Gamma Radiation   C.Exocytosis   D.Hydrogen Bond

78. __A__ A general term that includes all types of energy transformation processes, including photosynthesis, respiration, growth, movement, etc.
    A.Cellular Metabolism   B.Organelle   C.Law of Segregation   D.Lysosome

79. __B__ Momentary force of attraction that exist between molecules and are much weaker than the forces of chemical bonding.
    A.Punnett Square   B.Van der Waals Force   C.Velocity   D.Chromatin

80. __C__ The actions in animals we call instincts; highly stereotyped.
    A.Passive Transport   B.Regulatory Genes   C.Innate Behaviors   D.Biogeography

81. __C__ The export of substances from the cell.
    A.Sympathetic Nervous System   B.Nerve Tissue   C.Exocytosis   D.Biosphere

82. __A__ Code proteins that determine fictional or physiological events.
    A.Regulatory Genes   B.Innate Behaviors   C.Acid   D.Epithelial Tissue

83. __C__  Bond formed between the atoms when atoms share electrons.
    A.Cellular Metabolism   B.Lysosome   C.Covalent Bond   D.Vascular

84. __D__  The process whereby molecules and ions flow through the cell membrane from an area of higher concentration to an area of lower concentration; mixing of particles in a gas or liquid.
    A.Positron Decay   B.Atom   C.Succession   D.Diffusion

85. __A__  Over time, a gene pool (particularly in a small population) may experience a change in frequency of particular genes simply due to change fluctuations.
    A.Genetic Drift   B.Epithelial Tissue   C.Sex Limited Trait   D.Endoderm

86. __D__  The conduit for delivering nutrients and gases to all cells and for removing waste products from them.
    A.Biosphere   B.Adipose Tissue   C.Smooth Endoplasmic Reticulum   D.Circulatory System

87. __D__  Some traits have no genes that are dominant and instead produce offspring that are a mix of the two parents.
    A.Digestive System   B.Immigration   C.Adipose Tissue   D.Incomplete Dominance

88. __B__  Vessels that carry blood toward the heart.
    A.Circulatory System   B.Vein   C.Lymphocyte   D.Hormones

89. __C__  Poor conductors of electrical currents.
    A.Kidney   B.Mass   C.Insulator   D.Golgi Apparatus

90. __D__  The amount of matter that is contained by the object.
    A.Digestive System   B.Mitochondria   C.Chromatin   D.Mass

91. __D__  The total number of a single species of organism found in an ecosystem.
    A.Homozygous   B.Force   C.Gene   D.Population

92. __A__  Sum total of genetic information.
    A.Genome   B.Ribosome   C.Atom   D.Vertebrate

93. __D__  The number of individuals of a species living in an area.
    A.Organelle   B.Chloroplast   C.Positron Decay   D.Population Density

94. __D__  The measure of the average kinetic energy of a substance.
    A.Catabolism   B.Newtons Laws   C.Evaporation   D.Temperature

95. __A__  Part of the Earth that includes all living things.
    A.Biosphere   B.Molecule   C.Chemistry   D.Nuclear Membrane

96. __D__  A chemical that accepts protons (H+ ions) when dissolved in water.
    A.Atom   B.Biosphere   C.Chemistry   D.Base

97. __C__  The hollow, bulb-shaped structure in the lower interior of the pistil.
    A.Heat   B.Immigration   C.Ovary   D.Covalent Bond

98. __B__  Three laws that form the basis of most of our understanding of things in motion.
    A.Vertebrate   B.Newtons Laws   C.Atmospheric Pressure   D.Law of Dominance

99. __C__  A chemical that donates proton (H+ ions) when dissolved in water.
    A.Insulator   B.Migration   C.Acid   D.Golgi Apparatus

© 2017 Network4Learning, Inc.

100. A  Species that have internal backbones.
   A.Vertebrate  B.Regulatory Genes  C.Biosphere  D.Punctuated Equilibrium

*From the words provided for each clue, provide the letter of the word which best matches the clue.*

101. B  Tiny vessels that surround all tissues of the body and exchange carbon dioxide for oxygen.
   A.Central Nervous System  B.Capillary  C.Chemistry  D.Cerebellum

102. C  Plants that have tissue organized in such a way as to conduct food and water throughout their structure.
   A.Community  B.Vertebrate  C.Vascular  D.Prokaryotic Cell

103. A  Filter metabolic waste from the blood and excrete them as urine
   A.Kidney  B.Newtons Laws  C.Competition  D.Nucleolus

104. B  Escape of individual particles of a substance into gaseous form.
   A.Law of Segregation  B.Evaporation  C.Circulatory System  D.Vascular

105. D  Responsible for the sense of smell.
   A.Law of Dominance  B.Somatic Sensory Nerve  C.Cytoplasm  D.Olfactory Lobe

106. D  Genes located on a gender chromosome.
   A.Cerebellum  B.Blood Tissue  C.Population  D.Sex Limited Trait

107. A  Cells with no nucleus or any other membrane-bound organelles.
   A.Prokaryotic Cell  B.Organism  C.Refraction  D.Electron Cloud

108. C  An allele that masks the effect of its partner allele.
   A.Biogeography  B.Territory  C.Dominant Allele  D.Wavelength

109. C  Occurs when a hydrogen atom is involved with a polar intermolecular attraction to a more electronegative atom.
   A.Weight  B.Respiratory System  C.Hydrogen Bond  D.Organic Compound

110. C  Uses energy to move molecules across a cell membrane against a concentration gradient.
   A.Law of Segregation  B.Refraction  C.Active Transport  D.Olfactory Lobe

111. D  The bouncing of a wave of light off an object.
   A.Independent Assortment  B.Hydrogen Bond  C.Flower  D.Reflection

112. D  Smaller than even the smallest cells; survive and replicate by invading a living cell.
   A.Heat  B.Nucleolus  C.Adaptive Radiation  D.Viruses

113. B  Reacting molecules.
   A.Enzyme  B.Reactants  C.Photosynthesis  D.Refraction

114. A  A process in which bacteria absorb and incorporate pieces of DNA from their environment (usually from dead bacterial cells).
   A.Transformation  B.Epithelial Tissue  C.Meiosis  D.Electron Cloud

115. B  Carry impulses from body organs to the CNS.
   A.Somatic Sensory Nerve  B.Visceral Sensory Nerve  C.Endoplasmic Reticulum  D.Blood Tissue

116. C  Part of the brain that controls balance, equilibrium, and muscle coordination.
    A.Mitosis   B.Biogeography   C.Cerebellum   D.Ecology

117. A  Species that have internal backbones.
    A.Vertebrate   B.Sex Influenced Trait   C.Newtons Laws   D.Organic Compound

118. D  Carry impulses from body surface to the CNS.
    A.Immigration   B.Osmosis   C.Chlorophyll   D.Somatic Sensory Nerve

119. C  Instrumental in the storing, packaging, and shipping of proteins; also known as Golgi bodies or the Golgi complex.
    A.Society   B.Weight   C.Golgi Apparatus   D.Osmosis

120. B  Bond of attraction between positive and negative ions.
    A.Population   B.Ionic Bond   C.Osmosis   D.Differential Reproduction

121. D  Process of breaking down molecules and releasing stored energy.
    A.Ecology   B.Watson Crick Model   C.Heterozygous   D.Catabolism

122. B  Scientific model that proposes that adaptations of species arise suddenly and rapidly.
    A.Chlorophyll   B.Punctuated Equilibrium   C.Law of Dominance   D.Visceral Sensory Nerve

123. A  Occurs when two populations are geographically isolated from each other.
    A.Allopatric Speciation   B.Laws of Thermodynamics   C.Olfactory Lobe   D.Prophase

124. B  The force of gravity acting upon that object.
    A.Transduction   B.Weight   C.Immigration   D.Connective Tissue

125. B  Provides structural support to a cell.
    A.Atmospheric Pressure   B.Cytoskeleton   C.Active Transport   D.Sympatric Speciation

126. C  Forms the barrier between the environment and the interior of the body.
    A.Competition   B.Momentum   C.Epithelial Tissue   D.Reflection

127. B  Calculated by adding up the masses of the protons and neutrons.
    A.Cytoskeleton   B.Atomic Mass   C.Active Transport   D.Evaporation

128. D  Holds tissues and organs together, stabilizing the body structure.
    A.Independent Assortment   B.Circuit   C.Momentum   D.Connective Tissue

129. A  One gene is usually dominant over the other.
    A.Law of Dominance   B.Flower   C.Circulatory System   D.Evolution

130. D  The path that an electrical current follows.
    A.Atmospheric Pressure   B.Prokaryotic Cell   C.Somatic Sensory Nerve   D.Circuit

131. B  The actions in animals we call instincts; highly stereotyped.
    A.Olfactory Lobe   B.Innate Behaviors   C.Sperm   D.Habitat

132. B  A special process of diffusion that occurs when the water concentration inside the cell differs from the concentration outside the cell.
    A.Atmospheric Pressure   B.Osmosis   C.Allopatric Speciation   D.Population

133. C  The total number of a single species of organism found in an ecosystem.
    A.Sex Influenced Trait   B.Medulla Oblongata   C.Population   D.Circulatory System

134. C   Membrane-bound organelles containing digestive enzymes; digest unused material within the cell, damaged organelles, or materials absorbed by the cell for use.
    A.Atomic Weight   B.Society   C.Lysosome   D.Wavelength

135. A   Small round cases within the ovary that contain one or more egg cells.
    A.Ovules   B.Epithelial Tissue   C.Food Chain   D.Transduction

136. A   Poor conductors of electrical currents.
    A.Insulator   B.Evaporation   C.Digestive System   D.Organic Compound

137. C   Energy that flows from an object that is warm to an object that is cooler.
    A.Refraction   B.Sympatric Speciation   C.Heat   D.Krebs Cycle

138. B   The transfer or genetic material (portions of a bacterial chromosome) from one bacteria cell to another.
    A.Allopatric Speciation   B.Transduction   C.Genetic Drift   D.Habitat

139. A   Protein molecules that act as catalysts for organic reactions.
    A.Enzyme   B.Osmosis   C.Cerebellum   D.Olfactory Lobe

140. C   The average mass number.
    A.Absolute Zero   B.Adaptive Radiation   C.Atomic Weight   D.Golgi Apparatus

141. A   Explain the interaction between heat and work (energy) in the universe.
    A.Laws of Thermodynamics   B.Territory   C.Cell   D.Lysosome

142. B   The movement of mass over a distance.
    A.Ovules   B.Work   C.Territory   D.Biogeography

143. D   Populations that interact with each other in a ecosystem.
    A.Golgi Apparatus   B.Reactants   C.Cytoskeleton   D.Community

144. A   The study of how photosynthetic organisms and animals are distributed in a location plus the history of their distribution in the past.
    A.Biogeography   B.Society   C.Positron Decay   D.Heterozygous

145. A   Over time, a gene pool (particularly in a small population) may experience a change in frequency of particular genes simply due to change fluctuations.
    A.Genetic Drift   B.Translation   C.Evaporation   D.Territory

146. A   The precursor of the gut lining and various accessory structures.
    A.Endoderm   B.Law of Dominance   C.Watson Crick Model   D.Biogeography

147. B   An organization of individuals in a population in which tasks are divided for the group to work together.
    A.Punctuated Equilibrium   B.Society   C.Refraction   D.Chemistry

148. C   Genetically different members reproduce with each other, producing a population, which is separate from the original species.
    A.Sex Influenced Trait   B.Olfactory Lobe   C.Sympatric Speciation   D.Respiratory System

149. A   Individuals within a population that are most adapted to the environment and are also the most likely individuals to reproduce successfully.
    A.Differential Reproduction   B.Territory   C.Translation   D.Polar Molecule

© 2017 Network4Learning, Inc.

150. **B**   The first phase in mitosis.
   A. Law of Dominance   B. Prophase   C. Momentum   D. Ovules

151. **A**   Three-dimensional space where electrons travel freely; also known as an electron shell or orbital.
   A. Electron Cloud   B. Atmospheric Pressure   C. Endoderm   D. Prokaryotic Cell

152. **D**   Pressure that results from the total weight of the atmosphere exerting force on the Earth; can be measured with a barometer.
   A. Independent Assortment   B. Connective Tissue   C. Reactants   D. Atmospheric Pressure

153. **C**   Serves as a processing plant for ingested food.
   A. Habitat   B. Viruses   C. Digestive System   D. Cytoplasm

154. **A**   The change in direction of a wave as it passes from one medium to another.
   A. Refraction   B. Polar Molecule   C. Electron Cloud   D. Laws of Thermodynamics

155. **D**   Occurs when the nucleus emits a particle that degrades into a positron as it passes out of the atom.
   A. Laws of Thermodynamics   B. Adaptive Radiation   C. Law of Segregation   D. Positron Decay

156. **D**   Energy generally flows through the entire ecosystem in one direction from producers to consumers and on to decomposers.
   A. Transduction   B. Work   C. Digestive System   D. Food Chain

157. **B**   the process by which a cell distributes its duplicated chromosomes so that each daughter cell has a full set of chromosomes.
   A. Kidney   B. Mitosis   C. Community   D. Density

158. **A**   An area of land that lies within the home range that the individual will defend as his own.
   A. Territory   B. Meiosis   C. Evolution   D. Central Nervous System

159. **D**   The site of photosynthesis within plant cells.
   A. Independent Assortment   B. Sperm   C. Chemistry   D. Chloroplast

160. **A**   An individual of a species.
   A. Organism   B. Genetic Drift   C. Medulla Oblongata   D. Capillary

161. **D**   The measure of how much matter exists in a volume.
   A. Sympatric Speciation   B. Competition   C. Chemistry   D. Density

162. **C**   A learned behavior that develops in a critical or sensitive period of the animal's lifespan.
   A. Capillary   B. Vascular   C. Imprinting   D. Differential Reproduction

163. **D**   Permanent one-way movement into a new range.
   A. Golgi Apparatus   B. Genetic Drift   C. Organic Compound   D. Immigration

164. **D**   A single species can develop into several diverse species over time; over time a species will specially adapt to live more effectively in a new environment.
   A. Vertebrate   B. Immigration   C. Olfactory Lobe   D. Adaptive Radiation

165. **B**   Part of the brain that controls involuntary responses such as breathing and heartbeat.
   A. Connective Tissue   B. Medulla Oblongata   C. Enzyme   D. Biogeography

166. B   The conduit for delivering nutrients and gases to all cells and for removing waste products from them.
   A.Flower   B.Circulatory System   C.Laws of Thermodynamics   D.Reactants

167. B   Two main components, the brain and the spinal cord; which control all other organs and systems of the body.
   A.Golgi Apparatus   B.Central Nervous System   C.Chloroplast   D.Catabolism

168. B   Responsible for the intake and processing of gases required by an organism and for expelling gases produced as waste products.
   A.Osmosis   B.Respiratory System   C.Cytoplasm   D.Heat

169. A   Region between the nucleus and cell membrane.
   A.Cytoplasm   B.Laws of Thermodynamics   C.Population   D.Differential Reproduction

170. D   The distance from one crest (or top) of a wave to the next crest on the same side.
   A.Ovules   B.Pressure   C.Population   D.Wavelength

171. B   Phase of photosynthesis that requires a second type of RNA.
   A.Law of Segregation   B.Translation   C.Respiratory System   D.Olfactory Lobe

172. C   Short length of DNA wrapped around a core of small proteins.
   A.Evaporation   B.Sperm   C.Histone   D.Nucleolus

173. D   A learned behavior where the organism produces less and less response as a stimulus is repeated, without a subsequent negative or positive action.
   A.Chemistry   B.Immigration   C.Chlorophyll   D.Habituation

174. B   Named after scientists who discovered and modeled the structure of DNA.
   A.Circulatory System   B.Watson Crick Model   C.Chlorophyll   D.Lysosome

175. A   The gradual change of characteristics within a population, producing a change in a species over time.
   A.Evolution   B.Cell   C.Enzyme   D.Newtons Laws

176. B   The building blocks of all living things.
   A.Insulator   B.Organic Compound   C.Allopatric Speciation   D.Wavelength

177. D   The primary reproductive organ for a plant.
   A.Transformation   B.Digestive System   C.Cytoplasm   D.Flower

178. B   Molecule that has regions of partial change.
   A.Endoderm   B.Polar Molecule   C.Pressure   D.Independent Assortment

179. B   Results when two or more species living within the same area and that overlap niches both require a resource that is in limited supply.
   A.Reflection   B.Competition   C.Catabolism   D.Sympatric Speciation

180. B   Flows through the blood vessels and heart and is essential for carrying oxygen to cells, fighting infection, and carrying nutrients and wastes to and from cells.
   A.Vertebrate   B.Blood Tissue   C.Organism   D.Digestive System

181. A   Homologous chromosomes separate and independently sort in gamete formation.
   A.Independent Assortment   B.Lysosome   C.Reactants   D.Work

182. D  Behavior patterns that take into account other individuals.
    A.Habituation   B.Prophase   C.Sex Influenced Trait   D.Social Behavior

183. D  A crucial set of reactions that convert the light energy of the sun into chemical energy usable by living things.
    A.Ovules   B.Food Chain   C.Lysosome   D.Photosynthesis

184. D  The product of mass and velocity.
    A.Absolute Zero   B.Competition   C.Prophase   D.Momentum

185. B  When the two alleles for a given gene are different in an individual.
    A.Connective Tissue   B.Heterozygous   C.Pressure   D.Central Nervous System

186. C  A measure of the amount of force applied per unit of area.
    A.Kidney   B.Translation   C.Pressure   D.Endoderm

187. A  Three laws that form the basis of most of our understanding of things in motion.
    A.Newtons Laws   B.Adaptive Radiation   C.Meiosis   D.Blood Tissue

188. D  Theoretical temperature at which particle motion stops; also known as 0 Kelvin.
    A.Polar Molecule   B.Social Behavior   C.Medulla Oblongata   D.Absolute Zero

189. A  A rounded area within the nucleus of the cell where ribosomal RNA is synthesized.
    A.Nucleolus   B.Chloroplast   C.Transformation   D.Photosynthesis

190. A  The study of matter.
    A.Chemistry   B.Cerebellum   C.Respiratory System   D.Chlorophyll

191. A  traits are expressed from a pair of genes in the individual (on homologous chromosomes).
    A.Law of Segregation   B.Heat   C.Flower   D.Kidney

192. C  Large organization of folded membranes; responsible for the delivery of lipids and proteins to certain areas within the cytoplasm.
    A.Independent Assortment   B.Capillary   C.Endoplasmic Reticulum   D.Cytoskeleton

193. B  Pigment molecules that give the chloroplast their green color.
    A.Heat   B.Chlorophyll   C.Atomic Weight   D.Epithelial Tissue

194. C  Produced by the male gametophyte; also known as a male gamete.
    A.Insulator   B.Vascular   C.Sperm   D.Respiratory System

195. C  The physical place where a species lives.
    A.Evolution   B.Golgi Apparatus   C.Habitat   D.Epithelial Tissue

196. B  The first step in aerobic respiration that occurs in the matrix of a cell's mitochondria.
    A.Density   B.Krebs Cycle   C.Golgi Apparatus   D.Digestive System

197. A  The process of producing four daughter cells, each with single unduplicated chromosomes.
    A.Meiosis   B.Electron Cloud   C.Vascular   D.Laws of Thermodynamics

198. B  The smallest and most basic unit of most living things.
    A.Ionic Bond   B.Cell   C.Watson Crick Model   D.Territory

199. A  The study of how organisms interact with other organisms and how they influence or are influenced by their physical environment.
    A.Ecology  B.Wavelength  C.Organism  D.Differential Reproduction

200. C  Requires only one recessive gene to be expressed if there is no counteracting dominant gene.
    A.Respiratory System  B.Habitat  C.Sex Influenced Trait  D.Laws of Thermodynamics

*From the words provided for each clue, provide the letter of the word which best matches the clue.*

201. C  When one community completely replaces another over time in an area.
    A.Community  B.Transpiration  C.Succession  D.Osmosis

202. D  The number of individuals of a species living in an area.
    A.Embryo  B.Wavelength  C.Electron Transport  D.Population Density

203. D  Temporary movement out of one range into another and back.
    A.Refraction  B.Prokaryotic Cell  C.Allopatric Speciation  D.Migration

204. B  The path that an electrical current follows.
    A.Organelle  B.Circuit  C.Refraction  D.Adaptive Radiation

205. C  The first phase in mitosis.
    A.Krebs Cycle  B.Force  C.Prophase  D.Reactants

206. A  Pressure that results from the total weight of the atmosphere exerting force on the Earth; can be measured with a barometer.
    A.Atmospheric Pressure  B.Lysosome  C.Photosynthesis  D.Digestion

207. D  Two or more atoms held together by shared electrons (covalent bonds).
    A.Diffraction  B.Habitat  C.Protein  D.Molecule

208. A  The simplest unit of an element that retains the element's characteristics.
    A.Atom  B.Natural Selection  C.Immune System  D.Smooth Endoplasmic Reticulum

209. D  Tiny vessels that surround all tissues of the body and exchange carbon dioxide for oxygen.
    A.Cardiac Muscle  B.Diffraction  C.Connective Tissue  D.Capillary

210. A  One gene is usually dominant over the other.
    A.Law of Dominance  B.Electron Cloud  C.Olfactory Lobe  D.Neuron

211. D  The two identical strands of duplicated chromatin in a cell that is getting ready to divide.
    A.Molecule  B.Community  C.Dominant Allele  D.Chromatid

212. D  The study of how photosynthetic organisms and animals are distributed in a location plus the history of their distribution in the past.
    A.Hindbrain  B.Pressure  C.Natural Selection  D.Biogeography

213. D  The site of protein synthesis within cells.
    A.Capillary  B.Visceral Sensory Nerve  C.Weight  D.Ribosome

214. C   The introduction of new genes from an immigrant, which results in a change of the gene pool.
   A.Histone   B.Sympatric Speciation   C.Gene Migration   D.Diploid

215. A   Begin in bone marrow as stem cells and are collected and distributed via the lymph nodes.
   A.Lymphocyte   B.Protein   C.Habituation   D.Innate Behaviors

216. A   Occurs when the nucleus emits a beta particle that degrades into an electron as it passes out of the atom.
   A.Beta Decay   B.Friction   C.Atom   D.Cerebellum

217. A   A feature of population genetics that is the driving force behind evolution.
   A.Natural Selection   B.Cell Membrane   C.Chromatid   D.Lymphocyte

218. C   Tissue forming the walls of the heart with strength and electrical properties that are vital to the heart's ability to pump blood.
   A.Krebs Cycle   B.Eukaryotic Cell   C.Cardiac Muscle   D.Histone

219. A   A flow of electrons through a conductor.
   A.Electrical Current   B.Atom   C.Cerebellum   D.Eukaryotic Cell

220. D   The distance from one crest (or top) of a wave to the next crest on the same side.
   A.Histone   B.Photosynthesis   C.Lymphocyte   D.Wavelength

221. A   The parent cell that has a normal set of paired chromosomes.
   A.Diploid   B.Weight   C.Organelle   D.Biogeography

222. B   Occurs when two populations are geographically isolated from each other.
   A.Mitosis   B.Allopatric Speciation   C.Dominant Allele   D.Adaptive Radiation

223. D   Part of the brain that controls involuntary responses such as breathing and heartbeat.
   A.Competition   B.Genotype   C.Nuclear Membrane   D.Medulla Oblongata

224. A   The second step of aerobic respiration that captures the energy created by the release of electrons from the Krebs cycle.
   A.Electron Transport   B.Circuit   C.Cell Cycle   D.Histone

225. D   Cells that contain membrane-bound intracellular organelles, including a nucleus.
   A.Organelle   B.Exothermic   C.Prophase   D.Eukaryotic Cell

226. D   The physical place where a species lives.
   A.Weight   B.Atmospheric Pressure   C.Community   D.Habitat

227. D   Protein molecules that act as catalysts for organic reactions.
   A.Sympatric Speciation   B.Vein   C.Visceral Sensory Nerve   D.Enzyme

228. D   The rubbing force that acts against motion between two touching surfaces.
   A.Element   B.Catabolism   C.Taxonomy   D.Friction

229. D   An organization of individuals in a population in which tasks are divided for the group to work together.
   A.Succession   B.Element   C.Alpha Decay   D.Society

230. C   The formation of an RNA molecule, which corresponds to a gene.
   A.Protein   B.Mutation   C.Transcription   D.Wavelength

231. B  Thin-walled air sacs, which are the site of gas exchange.
    A.Alpha Decay   B.Alveoli   C.Reactants   D.Law of Dominance

232. C  What a zygote eventually grown into.
    A.Capillary   B.Cell Cycle   C.Embryo   D.Medulla Oblongata

233. D  Center of cellular respiration
    A.Circuit   B.Wavelength   C.Immune System   D.Mitochondria

234. C  The precursor of the gut lining and various accessory structures.
    A.Golgi Apparatus   B.Photosynthesis   C.Endoderm   D.Friction

235. C  Short length of DNA wrapped around a core of small proteins.
    A.Biogeography   B.Migration   C.Histone   D.Innate Behaviors

236. C  An allele that masks the effect of its partner allele.
    A.Transcription   B.Diffraction   C.Dominant Allele   D.Society

237. B  Membrane-bound organelles containing digestive enzymes; digest unused material within the cell, damaged organelles, or materials absorbed by the cell for use.
    A.Vein   B.Lysosome   C.Midbrain   D.Mutation

238. A  A process in which some water that has traveled up through the plant to the leaves is evaporated.
    A.Transpiration   B.Diploid   C.Natural Selection   D.Eukaryotic Cell

239. D  Present in every living cell, large un-branched chains of amino acids; may also be called polypeptides.
    A.Mitosis   B.Electron Transport   C.Enzyme   D.Protein

240. C  Vessels that carry blood toward the heart.
    A.Histone   B.Vertebrate   C.Vein   D.Golgi Apparatus

241. C  Requires only one recessive gene to be expressed if there is no counteracting dominant gene.
    A.Wavelength   B.Law of Dominance   C.Sex Influenced Trait   D.Beta Decay

242. A  Populations that interact with each other in a ecosystem.
    A.Community   B.Olfactory Lobe   C.Lysosome   D.Electron Cloud

243. B  A substance that cannot be broken down into any other substances.
    A.Pressure   B.Element   C.Energy Cycle   D.Visceral Sensory Nerve

244. A  Network of membranous channels; does not have attached ribosomes.
    A.Smooth Endoplasmic Reticulum   B.Allopatric Speciation   C.Cell Membrane   D.Dominant Allele

245. C  A measure of the amount of force applied per unit of area.
    A.Cell Cycle   B.Sympatric Speciation   C.Pressure   D.Biogeography

246. A  Explain the interaction between heat and work (energy) in the universe.
    A.Laws of Thermodynamics   B.Embryo   C.Endoderm   D.Frequency

247. C  Consists of the cerebellum and medulla oblongata.
    A.Nuclear Membrane   B.Electron Transport   C.Hindbrain   D.Refraction

© 2017 Network4Learning, Inc.

248. __A__  The boundary between the nucleus and the cytoplasm.
    A.Nuclear Membrane   B.Dominant Allele   C.Taxonomy   D.Digestion

249. __B__  Results when two or more species living within the same area and that overlap niches both require a resource that is in limited supply.
    A.Eukaryotic Cell   B.Competition   C.Exothermic   D.Refraction

250. __D__  Process of breaking down molecules and releasing stored energy.
    A.Allopatric Speciation   B.Reflex   C.Digestive System   D.Catabolism

251. __C__  A special process of diffusion that occurs when the water concentration inside the cell differs from the concentration outside the cell.
    A.Habitat   B.Cell Membrane   C.Osmosis   D.Catabolism

252. __D__  Reactions that release energy.
    A.Photosynthesis   B.Smooth Endoplasmic Reticulum   C.Osmosis   D.Exothermic

253. __A__  Carry impulses via electrochemical responses.
    A.Neuron   B.pH   C.Reflection   D.Cell Membrane

254. __A__  Provides the body with structure, stability, and the ability to move.
    A.Musculoskeletal System   B.Connective Tissue   C.Gene Migration   D.Nuclear Membrane

255. __D__  Cells with no nucleus or any other membrane-bound organelles.
    A.Cytoplasm   B.Connective Tissue   C.Weight   D.Prokaryotic Cell

256. __A__  the process by which a cell distributes its duplicated chromosomes so that each daughter cell has a full set of chromosomes.
    A.Mitosis   B.Electron Cloud   C.Ribosome   D.Enzyme

257. __C__  Responsible for the sense of smell.
    A.Eukaryotic Cell   B.Lysosome   C.Olfactory Lobe   D.Genotype

258. __D__  The bending of a light wave around an obstacle.
    A.Gene Pool   B.Prokaryotic Cell   C.Reflection   D.Diffraction

259. __A__  Three-dimensional space where electrons travel freely; also known as an electron shell or orbital.
    A.Electron Cloud   B.Law of Dominance   C.Cell Membrane   D.Krebs Cycle

260. __B__  A crucial set of reactions that convert the light energy of the sun into chemical energy usable by living things.
    A.Cardiac Muscle   B.Photosynthesis   C.Frequency   D.Digestive System

261. __D__  The combination of alleles that make a particular trait.
    A.Competition   B.Cell Membrane   C.Biogeography   D.Genotype

262. __C__  Occurs when the nucleus of an atom emits a package of two protons and two neutrons, called an alpha particle, which is equivalent to the nucleus of a helium atom.
    A.Diploid   B.Organelle   C.Alpha Decay   D.Reflex

263. __D__  Region between the nucleus and cell membrane.
    A.Atom   B.Vein   C.Neuron   D.Cytoplasm

© 2017 Network4Learning, Inc.

264. C   The entire collection of genes within a given population.
         A.Element  B.Immune System  C.Gene Pool  D.Alpha Decay

265. C   The push or pull exerted on an object.
         A.Chromatid  B.Cytoplasm  C.Force  D.Neuron

266. C   Structures that are similar because of their common function, although they do not share a common ancestry.
         A.Prophase  B.Mitosis  C.Analogous  D.Homozygous

267. A   Cells components that perform functions.
         A.Organelle  B.Diffraction  C.Lysosome  D.Eukaryotic Cell

268. D   A sequence of events ending in cell division, which produces two daughter cells.
         A.Analogous  B.Competition  C.Adaptive Radiation  D.Cell Cycle

269. A   The force of gravity acting upon that object.
         A.Weight  B.Cerebellum  C.Reactants  D.Atmospheric Pressure

270. A   Structure that encloses the cell and separates it from the environment; also known as the plasma membrane.
         A.Cell Membrane  B.Homozygous  C.Newtons Laws  D.Community

271. C   The change in direction of a wave as it passes from one medium to another.
         A.Exothermic  B.Digestive System  C.Refraction  D.Molecule

272. C   The bouncing of a wave of light off an object.
         A.Immune System  B.Force  C.Reflection  D.Homozygous

273. B   Arteries, veins, and capillaries.
         A.Competition  B.Vessel  C.Organelle  D.Electrical Current

274. D   When both alleles for a given gene are the same in an individual.
         A.Cerebellum  B.Genotype  C.Exothermic  D.Homozygous

275. B   A learned behavior where the organism produces less and less response as a stimulus is repeated, without a subsequent negative or positive action.
         A.Reactants  B.Habituation  C.Cytoplasm  D.Diffusion

276. A   The actions in animals we call instincts; highly stereotyped.
         A.Innate Behaviors  B.Digestive System  C.Law of Dominance  D.Smooth Endoplasmic Reticulum

277. B   Class of lymphocyte cell that emerge from the bone marrow mature and produce antibodies, which enter the bloodstream.
         A.Olfactory Lobe  B.B Cell  C.Atmospheric Pressure  D.Analogous

278. C   Functions to defend the body from infection by bacteria and viruses.
         A.Alpha Decay  B.Society  C.Immune System  D.Cytoplasm

279. D   Instrumental in the storing, packaging, and shipping of proteins; also known as Golgi bodies or the Golgi complex.
         A.Biogeography  B.Reflection  C.Gene Pool  D.Golgi Apparatus

280. D   The first step in aerobic respiration that occurs in the matrix of a cell's mitochondria.
         A.Alpha Decay  B.Alveoli  C.Habitat  D.Krebs Cycle

281. C  Three laws that form the basis of most of our understanding of things in motion.
    A.Force   B.Diffusion   C.Newtons Laws   D.Enzyme

282. D  A change of the DNA sequence of a gene, resulting in a change of the trait.
    A.Weight   B.Chromatid   C.B Cell   D.Mutation

283. B  Positive ion.
    A.Refraction   B.Cation   C.Atomic Weight   D.Hindbrain

284. C  Located between the forebrain and hindbrain; contains the optic lobes.
    A.Atom   B.Habituation   C.Midbrain   D.Digestive System

285. C  Holds tissues and organs together, stabilizing the body structure.
    A.Adaptive Radiation   B.Transpiration   C.Connective Tissue   D.Atom

286. A  Serves as a processing plant for ingested food.
    A.Digestive System   B.Dominant Allele   C.Musculoskeletal System   D.Organelle

287. C  The number of wavelengths that pass a point in a second.
    A.Immune System   B.Diploid   C.Frequency   D.Exothermic

288. A  Part of the brain that controls balance, equilibrium, and muscle coordination.
    A.Cerebellum   B.Innate Behaviors   C.Capillary   D.Connective Tissue

289. A  Study that organizes living things into groups based on morphology or, more recently, genetics.
    A.Taxonomy   B.Olfactory Lobe   C.Atomic Weight   D.Laws of Thermodynamics

290. B  The average mass number.
    A.Law of Dominance   B.Atomic Weight   C.Molecule   D.Neuron

291. C  Genetically different members reproduce with each other, producing a population, which is separate from the original species.
    A.Dominant Allele   B.Electron Transport   C.Sympatric Speciation   D.Olfactory Lobe

292. B  Supports life throughout the environment.
    A.Habitat   B.Energy Cycle   C.Reflex   D.Atomic Weight

293. B  Potential of hydrogen scale, which is a measurement of H+ ions in solutions.
    A.Exothermic   B.pH   C.Habitat   D.Medulla Oblongata

294. C  Species that have internal backbones.
    A.Lymphocyte   B.Adaptive Radiation   C.Vertebrate   D.Diploid

295. C  Reacting molecules.
    A.Krebs Cycle   B.Cation   C.Reactants   D.Diffusion

296. A  An automatic movement of a body part in response to a stimulus.
    A.Reflex   B.Prokaryotic Cell   C.Embryo   D.Eukaryotic Cell

297. A  Carry impulses from body organs to the CNS.
    A.Visceral Sensory Nerve   B.Enzyme   C.Lysosome   D.Law of Dominance

298. __D__  A single species can develop into several diverse species over time; over time a species will specially adapt to live more effectively in a new environment.
   A.Force  B.Sex Influenced Trait  C.Homozygous  D.Adaptive Radiation

299. __A__  The process whereby molecules and ions flow through the cell membrane from an area of higher concentration to an area of lower concentration; mixing of particles in a gas or liquid.
   A.Diffusion  B.Gene Migration  C.Frequency  D.Exothermic

300. __D__  Breakdown of ingested particles into molecules that can be absorbed by the body.
   A.Genotype  B.Diploid  C.Allopatric Speciation  D.Digestion

# Matching

*Provide the word that best matches each clue.*

1. _____ A communication network that connects the entire body of an organism and provides control over bodily functions.

2. _____ Carry impulses from body organs to the CNS.

3. _____ A substance that changes the speed of a reaction without being affected itself.

4. _____ The mass in grams of one mole of atoms.

5. _____ An organelle surrounded by two lipid bilayer membranes that is located near the center of the cell and contains chromosomes, nuclear pores, nucleoplasm, and nucleoli.

6. _____ traits are expressed from a pair of genes in the individual (on homologous chromosomes).

7. _____ Genetically different members reproduce with each other, producing a population, which is separate from the original species.

8. _____ Instrumental in the storing, packaging, and shipping of proteins; also known as Golgi bodies or the Golgi complex.

9. _____ Thin-walled air sacs, which are the site of gas exchange.

10. _____ Steps in the cellular respiration process that require oxygen.

11. _____ Structure that encloses the cell and separates it from the environment; also known as the plasma membrane.

12. _____ Study that organizes living things into groups based on morphology or, more recently, genetics.

13. _____ An area of land that lies within the home range that the individual will defend as his own.

14. _____ The measure of a substance's ability to retain energy.

15. _____ Projections of the cell extending from the cell membrane; increase the surface area of the cell membrane, increasing the area available to absorb nutrients.

A. Nucleus
B. Cell Membrane
C. Law of Segregation
D. Aerobic
E. Visceral Sensory Nerve
F. Nervous System
G. Specific Heat
H. Sympatric Speciation
I. Catalyst
J. Taxonomy
K. Molar Mass
L. Golgi Apparatus
M. Alveoli
N. Microvilli
O. Territory

© 2017 Network4Learning, Inc.

*Provide the word that best matches each clue.*

16. _____ Genes located on a gender chromosome.
17. _____ Carry impulses from body surface to the CNS.
18. _____ Located most anterior, it contains the olfactory lobes and cerebrum as well as the thalamus, hypothalamus, and pituitary gland.
19. _____ Charged atom
20. _____ The time it takes for 50 percent of an isotope to decay.
21. _____ RNA strand that migrates form the nucleus to the cytoplasm; also known as messenger RNA.
22. _____ Individuals within a population that are most adapted to the environment and are also the most likely individuals to reproduce successfully.
23. _____ Enzyme control that may occur when the product of the reaction is also an inhibitor to the reaction.
24. _____ What a zygote eventually grown into.
25. _____ Carry impulses to skeletal muscle from the CNS.
26. _____ The study of how photosynthetic organisms and animals are distributed in a location plus the history of their distribution in the past.
27. _____ Three-dimensional space where electrons travel freely; also known as an electron shell or orbital.
28. _____ When an object is placed in a fluid, the object will have a buoyant force equal to the weight of the displaced fluid.
29. _____ A communication network that connects the entire body of an organism and provides control over bodily functions.
30. _____ Studied the relationships between traits expressed in parents and offspring and the hereditary factors that caused expression of traits.

A. Biogeography
B. Archimedes Principle
C. Somatic Sensory Nerve
D. Differential Reproduction
E. Half Life
F. Sex Limited Trait
G. Ion
H. Nervous System
I. Gregor Mendel
J. Forebrain
K. Regulation
L. Embryo
M. Somatic Motor Nerve
N. mRNA
O. Electron Cloud

*Provide the word that best matches each clue.*

31. _____ A particle at rest will stay at rest and a particle in motion will stay in motion until acted upon by an outside force.

32. _____ The first step in aerobic respiration that occurs in the matrix of a cell's mitochondria.

33. _____ Responsible for collecting waste materials and transporting them to organs that expel them from the body.

34. _____ The parent cell that has a normal set of paired chromosomes.

35. _____ A chain of about 80 nucleotides that provide the link between the "language" of nucleotides (codon and anticodon) and the "language" of amino acids; also known as transfer RNA.

36. _____ Sum total of genetic information.

37. _____ Plants that produce flowers as reproductive organs.

38. _____ The study of things in motion.

39. _____ A learned behavior that develops in a critical or sensitive period of the animal's lifespan.

40. _____ The number of wavelengths that pass a point in a second.

41. _____ Reactions that require energy.

42. _____ Results when two or more species living within the same area and that overlap niches both require a resource that is in limited supply.

43. _____ The smallest and most basic unit of most living things.

44. _____ Energy generally flows through the entire ecosystem in one direction from producers to consumers and on to decomposers.

45. _____ Consists of the cerebellum and medulla oblongata.

A. tRNA                B. Hindbrain           C. Law of Inertia      D. Cell
E. Excretory System    F. Food Chain          G. Mechanics           H. Endothermic
I. Diploid             J. Genome              K. Angiosperm          L. Krebs Cycle
M. Imprinting          N. Frequency           O. Competition

*Provide the word that best matches each clue.*

46. _____ The formation of an RNA molecule, which corresponds to a gene.

47. _____ The movement of mass over a distance.

48. _____ Projections of the cell extending from the cell membrane; increase the surface area of the cell membrane, increasing the area available to absorb nutrients.

49. _____ Responsible for collecting waste materials and transporting them to organs that expel them from the body.

50. _____ Over time, a gene pool (particularly in a small population) may experience a change in frequency of particular genes simply due to change fluctuations.

51. _____ The number of protons found in the nucleus of an atom of that element.

52. _____ Carry impulses from body organs to the CNS.

53. _____ The first step in aerobic respiration that occurs in the matrix of a cell's mitochondria.

54. _____ Generated by the reproductive organs of the sporophyte through the process of meiosis.

55. _____ Has attached ribosomes; instrumental to protein synthesis.

56. _____ The process of producing four daughter cells, each with single unduplicated chromosomes.

57. _____ When both alleles for a given gene are the same in an individual.

58. _____ A sequence of events ending in cell division, which produces two daughter cells.

59. _____ Forms the barrier between the environment and the interior of the body.

60. _____ Pressure that results from the total weight of the atmosphere exerting force on the Earth; can be measured with a barometer.

A. Genetic Drift
B. Meiosis
C. Transcription
D. Atomic Number
E. Gametophyte
F. Krebs Cycle
G. Epithelial Tissue
H. Work
I. Atmospheric Pressure
J. Microvilli
K. Cell Cycle
L. Excretory System
M. Homozygous
N. Rough Endoplasmic Reticulum
O. Visceral Sensory Nerve

*Provide the word that best matches each clue.*

61. _____ Short length of DNA wrapped around a core of small proteins.

62. _____ Individuals within a population that are most adapted to the environment and are also the most likely individuals to reproduce successfully.

63. _____ Homologous chromosomes separate and independently sort in gamete formation.

64. _____ The measure of how much matter exists in a volume.

65. _____ a network of nerves throughout the body.

66. _____ The formation of an RNA molecule, which corresponds to a gene.

67. _____ A measure of the amount of force applied per unit of area.

68. _____ Carry impulses to skeletal muscle from the CNS.

69. _____ Tissue forming the walls of the heart with strength and electrical properties that are vital to the heart's ability to pump blood.

70. _____ The total number of a single species of organism found in an ecosystem.

71. _____ Calculated by adding up the masses of the protons and neutrons.

72. _____ Change of a gaseous substance to liquid form.

73. _____ Bond formed between the atoms when atoms share electrons.

74. _____ Cells components that perform functions.

75. _____ Named after scientists who discovered and modeled the structure of DNA.

A. Population
B. Organelle
C. Covalent Bond
D. Histone
E. Peripheral Nervous System
F. Atomic Mass
G. Independent Assortment
H. Cardiac Muscle
I. Condensation
J. Pressure
K. Transcription
L. Density
M. Differential Reproduction
N. Watson Crick Model
O. Somatic Motor Nerve

© 2017 Network4Learning, Inc.

*Provide the word that best matches each clue.*

76. _____ Serves as a processing plant for ingested food.
77. _____ An ecosystem that is generally defined by its climate characteristics.
78. _____ A chemical that donates proton (H+ ions) when dissolved in water.
79. _____ Reacting molecules
80. _____ Code proteins that form organs and structural characteristics.
81. _____ Attaches bones of the skeleton to each other and surrounding tissues, which enables voluntary movement.
82. _____ The process of producing four daughter cells, each with single unduplicated chromosomes.
83. _____ Network of membranous channels; does not have attached ribosomes.
84. _____ Smaller than even the smallest cells; survive and replicate by invading a living cell.
85. _____ The actions in animals we call instincts; highly stereotyped.
86. _____ Responsible for the intake and processing of gases required by an organism and for expelling gases produced as waste products.
87. _____ The study of matter.
88. _____ RNA strand that migrates form the nucleus to the cytoplasm; also known as messenger RNA.
89. _____ Protein molecules that act as catalysts for organic reactions.
90. _____ Tissue forming the walls of the heart with strength and electrical properties that are vital to the heart's ability to pump blood.

A. Acid
C. Chemistry
E. Digestive System
G. Reactants
I. mRNA

B. Enzyme
D. Cardiac Muscle
F. Skeletal Muscle
H. Viruses
J. Smooth Endoplasmic Reticulum

K. Structural Gene
M. Meiosis
O. Biome

L. Respiratory System
N. Innate Behaviors

*Provide the word that best matches each clue.*

91. _____ When the entire population of a particular species is eliminated.

92. _____ Calculated by adding up the masses of the protons and neutrons.

93. _____ The combination of DNA with histones.

94. _____ Enzyme control that may occur when the product of the reaction is also an inhibitor to the reaction.

95. _____ Code proteins that determine fictional or physiological events.

96. _____ The combination of alleles that make a particular trait.

97. _____ Attaches bones of the skeleton to each other and surrounding tissues, which enables voluntary movement.

98. _____ Filter metabolic waste from the blood and excrete them as urine

99. _____ traits are expressed from a pair of genes in the individual (on homologous chromosomes).

100. _____ the rate of change of an object's distance traveled.

101. _____ The first phase in mitosis.

102. _____ Cell that results when a sperm cell fertilizes an egg cell.

103. _____ Instrumental in the storing, packaging, and shipping of proteins; also known as Golgi bodies or the Golgi complex.

104. _____ A change of the DNA sequence of a gene, resulting in a change of the trait.

105. _____ Individuals within a population that are most adapted to the environment and are also the most likely individuals to reproduce successfully.

A. Mutation
B. Zygote
C. Skeletal Muscle

D. Extinction
G. Atomic Mass
J. Genotype
M. Kidney
E. Regulation
H. Prophase
K. Regulatory Genes
N. Speed
F. Law of Segregation
I. Golgi Apparatus
L. Chromatin
O. Differential Reproduction

*Provide the word that best matches each clue.*

106. _____ Requires only one recessive gene to be expressed if there is no counteracting dominant gene.

107. _____ Mathematical quantities that recognize both the size and direction of the dimension being considered.

108. _____ The actions in animals we call instincts; highly stereotyped.

109. _____ A feature of population genetics that is the driving force behind evolution.

110. _____ The trait expressed.

111. _____ Process of breaking down molecules and releasing stored energy.

112. _____ The rate of change of displacement; includes both speed and direction.

113. _____ Theoretical temperature at which particle motion stops; also known as 0 Kelvin.

114. _____ Potential of hydrogen scale, which is a measurement of H+ ions in solutions.

115. _____ Formed when two or more different atoms bond together chemically to form a unique substance.

116. _____ Cell that results when a sperm cell fertilizes an egg cell.

117. _____ Genetically different members reproduce with each other, producing a population, which is separate from the original species.

118. _____ Part of the Earth that includes all living things.

119. _____ A rounded area within the nucleus of the cell where ribosomal RNA is synthesized.

120. _____ Tiny vessels that surround all tissues of the body and exchange carbon dioxide for oxygen.

A. Zygote
D. Sympatric Speciation
G. Nucleolus
J. Velocity
B. pH
E. Compound
H. Natural Selection
K. Biosphere
C. Innate Behaviors
F. Catabolism
I. Capillary
L. Vector

© 2017 Network4Learning, Inc.

M. Absolute Zero     N. Phenotype     O. Sex Influenced Trait

*Provide the word that best matches each clue.*

121. _____ Studied the relationships between traits expressed in parents and offspring and the hereditary factors that caused expression of traits.

122. _____ The study of how photosynthetic organisms and animals are distributed in a location plus the history of their distribution in the past.

123. _____ Charged atom.

124. _____ A chain of about 80 nucleotides that provide the link between the "language" of nucleotides (codon and anticodon) and the "language" of amino acids; also known as transfer RNA.

125. _____ A process in which bacteria absorb and incorporate pieces of DNA from their environment (usually from dead bacterial cells).

126. _____ The two identical strands of duplicated chromatin in a cell that is getting ready to divide.

127. _____ Consists of the cerebellum and medulla oblongata.

128. _____ Short length of DNA wrapped around a core of small proteins.

129. _____ Those species having no internal backbone structure.

130. _____ Scientific model that proposes that adaptations of species arise suddenly and rapidly.

131. _____ The first phase in mitosis.

132. _____ Instrumental in the storing, packaging, and shipping of proteins; also known as Golgi bodies or the Golgi complex.

133. _____ A general term that includes all types of energy transformation processes, including photosynthesis, respiration, growth, movement, etc.

134. _____ Study that organizes living things into groups based on morphology or, more recently, genetics.

135. _____ Attaches bones of the skeleton to each other and surrounding tissues, which enables voluntary movement.

© 2017 Network4Learning, Inc.

A. Golgi Apparatus
B. Biogeography
C. Hindbrain
D. Cellular Metabolism
E. Punctuated Equilibrium
F. Skeletal Muscle
G. Taxonomy
H. Prophase
I. Histone
J. Transformation
K. Invertebrate
L. Chromatid
M. tRNA
N. Gregor Mendel
O. Ion

*Provide the word that best matches each clue.*

136. _____ Flows through the blood vessels and heart and is essential for carrying oxygen to cells, fighting infection, and carrying nutrients and wastes to and from cells.

137. _____ The export of substances from the cell.

138. _____ Thin-walled air sacs, which are the site of gas exchange.

139. _____ A substance that changes the speed of a reaction without being affected itself.

140. _____ the ability of a substance to produce a magnetic field.

141. _____ A rounded area within the nucleus of the cell where ribosomal RNA is synthesized.

142. _____ Some traits have no genes that are dominant and instead produce offspring that are a mix of the two parents.

143. _____ Populations that interact with each other in a ecosystem.

144. _____ Study that organizes living things into groups based on morphology or, more recently, genetics.

145. _____ Visual center connected to the eyes by the optic nerves.

146. _____ Carry substances produced within the cell to the cell membrane; packets of material packaged by the Golgi apparatus or endoplasmic reticulum.

147. _____ Located most anterior, it contains the olfactory lobes and cerebrum as well as the thalamus, hypothalamus, and pituitary gland.

148. _____ When one community completely replaces another over time in an area.

149. _____ Pigment molecules that give the chloroplast their green color.

150. _____ Supports life throughout the environment.

A. Nucleolus
B. Blood Tissue
C. Forebrain
D. Energy Cycle
E. Exocytosis
F. Optic Lobe

© 2017 Network4Learning, Inc.

G. Taxonomy
H. Magnetism
I. Succession
J. Secretory Vesicle
K. Catalyst
L. Community
M. Alveoli
N. Chlorophyll
O. Incomplete Dominance

*Provide the word that best matches each clue.*

151. __Phenotype__ — The trait expressed.

152. __Optic Lobe__ — Visual center connected to the eyes by the optic nerves.

153. __Learned Behavior__ — May have some basis in genetics, but they also require learning.

154. __Meiosis__ — The process of producing four daughter cells, each with single unduplicated chromosomes.

155. __Hydrogen Bond__ — Occurs when a hydrogen atom is involved with a polar intermolecular attraction to a more electronegative atom.

156. __Digestive System__ — Serves as a processing plant for ingested food.

157. __Stroma__ — The body of the chloroplast.

158. __Quantum Mechanic__ — Predicts the probabilities of an electron being in a certain area at a certain time.

159. __Secretory Vesicle__ — Carry substances produced within the cell to the cell membrane; packets of material packaged by the Golgi apparatus or endoplasmic reticulum.

160. __Polygenic Trait__ — Traits produced from integration of multiple sets of genes.

161. __Speed__ — the rate of change of an object's distance traveled.

162. __Evolution__ — The gradual change of characteristics within a population, producing a change in a species over time.

163. __Pascals Principle__ — The pressure exerted on any point of a confined fluid is transmitted unchanged throughout the fluid.

164. __Flower__ — The primary reproductive organ for a plant.

165. __Recessive Allele__ — The allele that does not produce its trait when present with a dominant allele.

A. Quantum Mechanic
B. Speed
C. Meiosis
D. Hydrogen Bond
E. Phenotype
F. Pascals Principle
G. Flower
H. Evolution
I. Secretory Vesicle
J. Optic Lobe
K. Recessive Allele
L. Learned Behavior
M. Polygenic Trait
N. Stoma
O. Digestive System

*Provide the word that best matches each clue.*

166. _____ The site of photosynthesis within plant cells.

167. _____ Carries impulses back from organs.

168. _____ Escape of individual particles of a substance into gaseous form.

169. _____ Requires only one recessive gene to be expressed if there is no counteracting dominant gene.

170. _____ Momentary force of attraction that exist between molecules and are much weaker than the forces of chemical bonding.

171. _____ Provides the body with structure, stability, and the ability to move.

172. _____ Change of a gaseous substance to liquid form.

173. _____ the period when the cell is active in carrying on its functions.

174. _____ Movement of energy by transfer from particle to particle; can only occur when objects are touching.

175. _____ Another name for anaerobic respiration, which breaks down the two pyruvic acid molecules (three carbons each) into end products (such as ethyl alcohol, or lactic acid), plus carbon dioxide.

176. _____ Plants that produce seeds without flowers.

177. _____ Class of lymphocyte cell that emerge from the bone marrow mature and produce antibodies, which enter the bloodstream.

178. _____ The process whereby cells build molecules and store energy.

179. _____ A particle at rest will stay at rest and a particle in motion will stay in motion until acted upon by an outside force.

© 2017 Network4Learning, Inc.

180. _____ Tissue forming the walls of the heart with strength and electrical properties that are vital to the heart's ability to pump blood.

- A. Law of Inertia
- B. Interphase
- C. Evaporation
- D. Condensation
- E. Chloroplast
- F. Cardiac Muscle
- G. Gymnosperm
- H. B Cell
- I. Conduction
- J. Parasympathetic Nervous System
- K. Fermentation
- L. Anabolism
- M. Musculoskeletal System
- N. Sex Influenced Trait
- O. Van der Waals Force

*Provide the word that best matches each clue.*

181. _____ Steps in the cellular respiration process that require oxygen.

182. _____ The export of substances from the cell.

183. _____ The trait expressed.

184. _____ Allows for the transfer of substances across the cell membrane with the help of specialized proteins.

185. _____ The intentional alteration of genetic material of a living organism.

186. _____ A substance that cannot be broken down into any other substances.

187. _____ Provides the body with structure, stability, and the ability to move.

188. _____ Instrumental in the storing, packaging, and shipping of proteins; also known as Golgi bodies or the Golgi complex.

189. _____ Reduces friction between bones and supports and connects them.

190. _____ Code proteins that determine fictional or physiological events.

191. _____ Mathematical quantities that recognize both the size and direction of the dimension being considered.

192. _____ Over time, a gene pool (particularly in a small population) may experience a change in frequency of particular genes simply due to change fluctuations.

193. _____ Predicts the probabilities of an electron being in a certain area at a certain time.

194. _____ Uses energy to move molecules across a cell membrane against a concentration gradient.

195. _____ The measure of a substance's ability to retain energy.

A. Genetic Engineering     B. Musculoskeletal System     C. Regulatory Genes
D. Quantum Mechanic        E. Exocytosis                 F. Genetic Drift
G. Element                 H. Active Transport           I. Phenotype
J. Facilitated Diffusion   K. Vector                     L. Cartilage Tissue
M. Specific Heat           N. Aerobic                    O. Golgi Apparatus

*Provide the word that best matches each clue.*

196. _____ A substance that cannot be broken down into any other substances.

197. _____ The electromotive force that pushes electrons through the circuit.

198. _____ Steps in the cellular respiration process that require oxygen.

199. _____ Occurs when the nucleus of an atom emits a package of two protons and two neutrons, called an alpha particle, which is equivalent to the nucleus of a helium atom.

200. _____ The path that an electrical current follows.

201. _____ A rounded area within the nucleus of the cell where ribosomal RNA is synthesized.

202. _____ The transfer or genetic material (portions of a bacterial chromosome) from one bacteria cell to another.

203. _____ The rate of change of displacement; includes both speed and direction.

204. _____ Movement of energy by transfer from particle to particle; can only occur when objects are touching.

205. _____ Carries impulses back from organs.

206. _____ Attaches bones of the skeleton to each other and surrounding tissues, which enables voluntary movement.

207. _____  The number of individuals of a species living in an area.

208. _____  The principal infection-fighting component of the immune system.

209. _____  Length of DNA that encodes a particular protein.

210. _____  Studied the relationships between traits expressed in parents and offspring and the hereditary factors that caused expression of traits.

A. Gregor Mendel
B. Aerobic
C. Parasympathetic Nervous System
D. Nucleolus
E. Gene
F. Transduction
G. Alpha Decay
H. Element
I. Lymphatic System
J. Population Density
K. Voltage
L. Skeletal Muscle
M. Velocity
N. Circuit
O. Conduction

*Provide the word that best matches each clue.*

211. _____  What a zygote eventually grown into.

212. _____  An ecosystem that is generally defined by its climate characteristics.

213. _____  The breaking down of the six-carbon sugar (glucose) into smaller carbon-containing molecules yielding ATP.

214. _____  Present in every living cell, large un-branched chains of amino acids; may also be called polypeptides.

215. _____  The push or pull exerted on an object.

216. _____  The building blocks of all living things.

217. _____  The process of producing four daughter cells, each with single unduplicated chromosomes.

218. _____  Part of the brain that controls involuntary responses such as breathing and heartbeat.

219. _____  Individuals within a population that are most adapted to the environment and are also the most likely individuals to reproduce successfully.

© 2017 Network4Learning, Inc.

220. _____ Located between the forebrain and hindbrain; contains the optic lobes.

221. _____ Uses energy to move molecules across a cell membrane against a concentration gradient.

222. _____ Classification category even more general than kingdoms.

223. _____ Named after scientists who discovered and modeled the structure of DNA.

224. _____ The measure of the average kinetic energy of a substance.

225. _____ Plants that produce seeds without flowers.

A. Domain
B. Midbrain
C. Active Transport
D. Protein
E. Force
F. Watson Crick Model
G. Differential Reproduction
H. Organic Compound
I. Medulla Oblongata
J. Biome
K. Embryo
L. Temperature
M. Meiosis
N. Gymnosperm
O. Glycolysis

*Provide the word that best matches each clue.*

226. _____ Temporary movement out of one range into another and back.

227. _____ Involved in hunger, thirst, blood pressure, body temperature, hostility, pain, pleasure, etc.

228. _____ Named after scientists who discovered and modeled the structure of DNA.

229. _____ Carry impulses from body surface to the CNS.

230. _____ Provides structural support to a cell.

231. _____ Mathematical quantities that recognize both the size and direction of the dimension being considered.

232. _____ Predicts the probabilities of an electron being in a certain area at a certain time.

233. _____ A feature of population genetics that is the driving force behind evolution.

234. _____ A flow of electrons through a conductor.

235. _____ Uses energy to move molecules across a cell membrane against a concentration gradient.

236. _____ The principal infection-fighting component of the immune system.

237. _____ The force of gravity acting upon that object.

238. _____ The conduit for delivering nutrients and gases to all cells and for removing waste products from them.

239. _____ The process whereby cells build molecules and store energy.

240. _____ Responsible for the intake and processing of gases required by an organism and for expelling gases produced as waste products.

A. Electrical Current
B. Hypothalamus
C. Vector
D. Anabolism
E. Cytoskeleton
F. Quantum Mechanic
G. Circulatory System
H. Migration
I. Somatic Sensory Nerve
J. Lymphatic System
K. Active Transport
L. Respiratory System
M. Weight
N. Natural Selection
O. Watson Crick Model

*Provide the word that best matches each clue.*

241. _____ Energy generally flows through the entire ecosystem in one direction from producers to consumers and on to decomposers.

242. _____ Formed when two or more different atoms bond together chemically to form a unique substance.

243. _____ Reacting molecules.

244. _____ Poor conductors of electrical currents.

245. _____ Cells with no nucleus or any other membrane-bound organelles.

246. _____ Carries impulses that stimulate organs.

247. _____ Structures that are similar because of their common function, although they do not share a common ancestry.

248. _____ The building blocks of all living things.

249. _____ Releases various hormones.

250. _____ Particular substance of an enzyme that fits within the active site.

251. _____ A learned behavior that develops in a critical or sensitive period of the animal's lifespan.

© 2017 Network4Learning, Inc.

252. _____ Involved in hunger, thirst, blood pressure, body temperature, hostility, pain, pleasure, etc.

253. _____ When an object is placed in a fluid, the object will have a buoyant force equal to the weight of the displaced fluid.

254. _____ The process by which characteristics pass from one generation to another.

255. _____ Permanent one-way movement into a new range.

A. Immigration
B. Reactants
C. Organic Compound
D. Insulator
E. Hypothalamus
F. Analogous
G. Inheritance
H. Pituitary Gland
I. Food Chain
J. Compound
K. Archimedes Principle
L. Prokaryotic Cell
M. Sympathetic Nervous System
N. Substrate
O. Imprinting

*Provide the word that best matches each clue.*

256. _____ Carries electrical and chemical impulses to and from organs and limbs to the brain.

257. _____ Step three in mitosis.

258. _____ Mature cells in the thymus gland that patrol the blood for antigens but are also equipped to destroy antigens themselves.

259. _____ Region between the nucleus and cell membrane.

260. _____ An area of land that lies within the home range that the individual will defend as his own.

261. _____ Sum total of genetic information.

262. _____ When one community completely replaces another over time in an area.

263. _____ Listing of elements by atomic number.

264. _____ Responsible for the intake and processing of gases required by an organism and for expelling gases produced as waste products.

265. _____ Class of lymphocyte cell that emerge from the bone marrow mature and produce antibodies, which enter the bloodstream.

266. _____ The rubbing force that acts against motion between two touching surfaces.

267. _____ Temperature at which a substance changes from solid to liquid form.

268. _____  Single unduplicated chromosomes.

269. _____  Provides structural support to a cell.

270. _____  Generated by the reproductive organs of the sporophyte through the process of meiosis.

A. B Cell          B. Gametophyte        C. Genome          D. Cytoskeleton
E. Respiratory System   F. T Cell         G. Nerve Tissue    H. Anaphase
I. Friction        J. Succession         K. Melting Point   L. Cytoplasm
M. Territory       N. Periodic Table     O. Haploid

*Provide the word that best matches each clue.*

271. _____  A general term that includes all types of energy transformation processes, including photosynthesis, respiration, growth, movement, etc.

272. _____  Permanent one-way movement out of the original range.

273. _____  Plants that have tissue organized in such a way as to conduct food and water throughout their structure.

274. _____  The measure of how much matter exists in a volume.

275. _____  The pressure exerted on any point of a confined fluid is transmitted unchanged throughout the fluid.

276. _____  A state of dynamic equilibrium, which balances forces tending toward change with forces acceptable for life functions.

277. _____  Distributes the remaining set of chromosomes in a mitosis-like process.

278. _____  the process by which a cell distributes its duplicated chromosomes so that each daughter cell has a full set of chromosomes.

279. _____  Sum total of genetic information.

280. _____  The entire collection of genes within a given population.

281. _____  A single species can develop into several diverse species over time; over time a species will specially adapt to live more effectively in a new environment.

282. _____  The physical place where a species lives.

283. _____  The study of things in motion.

284. _____ The process whereby molecules and ions flow through the cell membrane from an area of higher concentration to an area of lower concentration; mixing of particles in a gas or liquid.

285. _____ Protein molecules that act as catalysts for organic reactions.

| | | | |
|---|---|---|---|
| A. Mechanics | B. Division | C. Density | D. Genome |
| E. Gene Pool | F. Emigration | G. Cellular Metabolism | H. Diffusion |
| I. Pascal's Principle | J. Vasodilor | K. Habitat | L. Adaptive Radiation |
| M. Enzyme | N. Mitosis | O. Homeostasis | |

*Provide the word that best matches each clue.*

1. __NERVOUS SYSTEM__ — A communication network that connects the entire body of an organism and provides control over bodily functions.
2. __VISCERAL SENSORY NERVE__ — Carry impulses from body organs to the CNS.
3. __CATALYST__ — A substance that changes the speed of a reaction without being affected itself.
4. __MOLAR MASS__ — The mass in grams of one mole of atoms.
5. __NUCLEUS__ — An organelle surrounded by two lipid bilayer membranes that is located near the center of the cell and contains chromosomes, nuclear pores, nucleoplasm, and nucleoli.
6. __LAW OF SEGREGATION__ — traits are expressed from a pair of genes in the individual (on homologous chromosomes).
7. __SYMPATRIC SPECIATION__ — Genetically different members reproduce with each other, producing a population, which is separate from the original species.
8. __GOLGI APPARATUS__ — Instrumental in the storing, packaging, and shipping of proteins; also known as Golgi bodies or the Golgi complex.
9. __ALVEOLI__ — Thin-walled air sacs, which are the site of gas exchange.
10. __AEROBIC__ — Steps in the cellular respiration process that require oxygen.
11. __CELL MEMBRANE__ — Structure that encloses the cell and separates it from the environment; also known as the plasma membrane.
12. __TAXONOMY__ — Study that organizes living things into groups based on morphology or, more recently, genetics.
13. __TERRITORY__ — An area of land that lies within the home range that the individual will defend as his own.
14. __SPECIFIC HEAT__ — The measure of a substance's ability to retain energy.
15. __MICROVILLI__ — Projections of the cell extending from the cell membrane; increase the surface area of the cell membrane, increasing the area available to absorb nutrients.

A. Nucleus
B. Cell Membrane
C. Law of Segregation
D. Aerobic
E. Visceral Sensory Nerve
F. Nervous System
G. Specific Heat
H. Sympatric Speciation
I. Catalyst
J. Taxonomy
K. Molar Mass
L. Golgi Apparatus
M. Alveoli
N. Microvilli
O. Territory

*Provide the word that best matches each clue.*

| | | |
|---|---|---|
| 16. SEX LIMITED TRAIT | | Genes located on a gender chromosome. |
| 17. SOMATIC SENSORY NERVE | | Carry impulses from body surface to the CNS. |
| 18. FOREBRAIN | | Located most anterior, it contains the olfactory lobes and cerebrum as well as the thalamus, hypothalamus, and pituitary gland. |
| 19. ION | | Charged atom. |
| 20. HALF LIFE | | The time it takes for 50 percent of an isotope to decay. |
| 21. MRNA | | RNA strand that migrates form the nucleus to the cytoplasm; also known as messenger RNA. |
| 22. DIFFERENTIAL REPRODUCTION | | Individuals within a population that are most adapted to the environment and are also the most likely individuals to reproduce successfully. |
| 23. REGULATION | | Enzyme control that may occur when the product of the reaction is also an inhibitor to the reaction. |
| 24. EMBRYO | | What a zygote eventually grown into. |
| 25. SOMATIC MOTOR NERVE | | Carry impulses to skeletal muscle from the CNS. |
| 26. BIOGEOGRAPHY | | The study of how photosynthetic organisms and animals are distributed in a location plus the history of their distribution in the past. |
| 27. ELECTRON CLOUD | | Three-dimensional space where electrons travel freely; also known as an electron shell or orbital. |
| 28. ARCHIMEDES PRINCIPLE | | When an object is placed in a fluid, the object will have a buoyant force equal to the weight of the displaced fluid. |
| 29. NERVOUS SYSTEM | | A communication network that connects the entire body of an organism and provides control over bodily functions. |
| 30. GREGOR MENDEL | | Studied the relationships between traits expressed in parents and offspring and the hereditary factors that caused expression of traits. |

A. Biogeography
B. Archimedes Principle
C. Somatic Sensory Nerve
D. Differential Reproduction
E. Half Life
F. Sex Limited Trait
G. Ion
H. Nervous System
I. Gregor Mendel
J. Forebrain
K. Regulation
L. Embryo
M. Somatic Motor Nerve
N. mRNA
O. Electron Cloud

© 2017 Network4Learning, Inc.

*Provide the word that best matches each clue.*

31. **LAW OF INERTIA** — A particle at rest will stay at rest and a particle in motion will stay in motion until acted upon by an outside force.

32. **KREBS CYCLE** — The first step in aerobic respiration that occurs in the matrix of a cell's mitochondria.

33. **EXCRETORY SYSTEM** — Responsible for collecting waste materials and transporting them to organs that expel them from the body.

34. **DIPLOID** — The parent cell that has a normal set of paired chromosomes.

35. **TRNA** — A chain of about 80 nucleotides that provide the link between the "language" of nucleotides (codon and anticodon) and the "language" of amino acids; also known as transfer RNA.

36. **GENOME** — Sum total of genetic information.

37. **ANGIOSPERM** — Plants that produce flowers as reproductive organs.

38. **MECHANICS** — The study of things in motion.

39. **IMPRINTING** — A learned behavior that develops in a critical or sensitive period of the animal's lifespan.

40. **FREQUENCY** — The number of wavelengths that pass a point in a second.

41. **ENDOTHERMIC** — Reactions that require energy.

42. **COMPETITION** — Results when two or more species living within the same area and that overlap niches both require a resource that is in limited supply.

43. **CELL** — The smallest and most basic unit of most living things.

44. **FOOD CHAIN** — Energy generally flows through the entire ecosystem in one direction from producers to consumers and on to decomposers.

45. **HINDBRAIN** — Consists of the cerebellum and medulla oblongata.

A. tRNA  B. Hindbrain  C. Law of Inertia  D. Cell
E. Excretory System  F. Food Chain  G. Mechanics  H. Endothermic
I. Diploid  J. Genome  K. Angiosperm  L. Krebs Cycle
M. Imprinting  N. Frequency  O. Competition

*Provide the word that best matches each clue.*

46. **TRANSCRIPTION** — The formation of an RNA molecule, which corresponds to a gene.

47. **WORK** — The movement of mass over a distance.

© 2017 Network4Learning, Inc.

48. MICROVILLI _____ Projections of the cell extending from the cell membrane; increase the surface area of the cell membrane, increasing the area available to absorb nutrients.

49. EXCRETORY SYSTEM _____ Responsible for collecting waste materials and transporting them to organs that expel them from the body.

50. GENETIC DRIFT _____ Over time, a gene pool (particularly in a small population) may experience a change in frequency of particular genes simply due to change fluctuations.

51. ATOMIC NUMBER _____ The number of protons found in the nucleus of an atom of that element.

52. VISCERAL SENSORY NERVE _____ Carry impulses from body organs to the CNS.

53. KREBS CYCLE _____ The first step in aerobic respiration that occurs in the matrix of a cell's mitochondria.

54. GAMETOPHYTE _____ Generated by the reproductive organs of the sporophyte through the process of meiosis.

55. ROUGH ENDOPLASMIC RETICULUM _____ Has attached ribosomes; instrumental to protein synthesis.

56. MEIOSIS _____ The process of producing four daughter cells, each with single unduplicated chromosomes.

57. HOMOZYGOUS _____ When both alleles for a given gene are the same in an individual.

58. CELL CYCLE _____ A sequence of events ending in cell division, which produces two daughter cells.

59. EPITHELIAL TISSUE _____ Forms the barrier between the environment and the interior of the body.

60. ATMOSPHERIC PRESSURE _____ Pressure that results from the total weight of the atmosphere exerting force on the Earth; can be measured with a barometer.

A. Genetic Drift
C. Transcription
E. Gametophyte
G. Epithelial Tissue
I. Atmospheric Pressure
K. Cell Cycle
M. Homozygous
O. Visceral Sensory Nerve

B. Meiosis
D. Atomic Number
F. Krebs Cycle
H. Work
J. Microvilli
L. Excretory System
N. Rough Endoplasmic Reticulum

© 2017 Network4Learning, Inc.

*Provide the word that best matches each clue.*

| # | Answer | Clue |
|---|---|---|
| 61. | HISTONE | Short length of DNA wrapped around a core of small proteins. |
| 62. | DIFFERENTIAL REPRODUCTION | Individuals within a population that are most adapted to the environment and are also the most likely individuals to reproduce successfully. |
| 63. | INDEPENDENT ASSORTMENT | Homologous chromosomes separate and independently sort in gamete formation. |
| 64. | DENSITY | The measure of how much matter exists in a volume. |
| 65. | PERIPHERAL NERVOUS SYSTEM | a network of nerves throughout the body. |
| 66. | TRANSCRIPTION | The formation of an RNA molecule, which corresponds to a gene. |
| 67. | PRESSURE | A measure of the amount of force applied per unit of area. |
| 68. | SOMATIC MOTOR NERVE | Carry impulses to skeletal muscle from the CNS. |
| 69. | CARDIAC MUSCLE | Tissue forming the walls of the heart with strength and electrical properties that are vital to the heart's ability to pump blood. |
| 70. | POPULATION | The total number of a single species of organism found in an ecosystem. |
| 71. | ATOMIC MASS | Calculated by adding up the masses of the protons and neutrons. |
| 72. | CONDENSATION | Change of a gaseous substance to liquid form. |
| 73. | COVALENT BOND | Bond formed between the atoms when atoms share electrons. |
| 74. | ORGANELLE | Cells components that perform functions. |
| 75. | WATSON CRICK MODEL | Named after scientists who discovered and modeled the structure of DNA. |

A. Population
B. Organelle
C. Covalent Bond
D. Histone
E. Peripheral Nervous System
F. Atomic Mass
G. Independent Assortment
H. Cardiac Muscle
I. Condensation
J. Pressure
K. Transcription
L. Density
M. Differential Reproduction
N. Watson Crick Model
O. Somatic Motor Nerve

*Provide the word that best matches each clue.*

76. DIGESTIVE SYSTEM — Serves as a processing plant for ingested food.

77. BIOME — An ecosystem that is generally defined by its climate characteristics.

78. ACID — A chemical that donates proton (H+ ions) when dissolved in water.

79. REACTANTS — Reacting molecules

80. STRUCTURAL GENE — Code proteins that form organs and structural characteristics.

81. SKELETAL MUSCLE — Attaches bones of the skeleton to each other and surrounding tissues, which enables voluntary movement.

82. MEIOSIS — The process of producing four daughter cells, each with single unduplicated chromosomes.

83. SMOOTH ENDOPLASMIC RETICULUM — Network of membranous channels; does not have attached ribosomes.

84. VIRUSES — Smaller than even the smallest cells; survive and replicate by invading a living cell.

85. INNATE BEHAVIORS — The actions in animals we call instincts; highly stereotyped.

86. RESPIRATORY SYSTEM — Responsible for the intake and processing of gases required by an organism and for expelling gases produced as waste products.

87. CHEMISTRY — The study of matter.

88. MRNA — RNA strand that migrates form the nucleus to the cytoplasm; also known as messenger RNA.

89. ENZYME — Protein molecules that act as catalysts for organic reactions.

90. CARDIAC MUSCLE — Tissue forming the walls of the heart with strength and electrical properties that are vital to the heart's ability to pump blood.

A. Acid
B. Enzyme
C. Chemistry
D. Cardiac Muscle
E. Digestive System
F. Skeletal Muscle
G. Reactants
H. Viruses
I. mRNA
J. Smooth Endoplasmic Reticulum

© 2017 Network4Learning, Inc.

K. Structural Gene
M. Meiosis
O. Biome

L. Respiratory System
N. Innate Behaviors

*Provide the word that best matches each clue.*

91. EXTINCTION — When the entire population of a particular species is eliminated.

92. ATOMIC MASS — Calculated by adding up the masses of the protons and neutrons.

93. CHROMATIN — The combination of DNA with histones.

94. REGULATION — Enzyme control that may occur when the product of the reaction is also an inhibitor to the reaction.

95. REGULATORY GENES — Code proteins that determine fictional or physiological events.

96. GENOTYPE — The combination of alleles that make a particular trait.

97. SKELETAL MUSCLE — Attaches bones of the skeleton to each other and surrounding tissues, which enables voluntary movement.

98. KIDNEY — Filter metabolic waste from the blood and excrete them as urine

99. LAW OF SEGREGATION — traits are expressed from a pair of genes in the individual (on homologous chromosomes).

100. SPEED — the rate of change of an object's distance traveled.

101. PROPHASE — The first phase in mitosis.

102. ZYGOTE — Cell that results when a sperm cell fertilizes an egg cell.

103. GOLGI APPARATUS — Instrumental in the storing, packaging, and shipping of proteins; also known as Golgi bodies or the Golgi complex.

104. MUTATION — A change of the DNA sequence of a gene, resulting in a change of the trait.

105. DIFFERENTIAL REPRODUCTION — Individuals within a population that are most adapted to the environment and are also the most likely individuals to reproduce successfully.

A. Mutation     B. Zygote     C. Skeletal Muscle

© 2017 Network4Learning, Inc.

D. Extinction
G. Atomic Mass
J. Genotype
M. Kidney

E. Regulation
H. Prophase
K. Regulatory Genes
N. Speed

F. Law of Segregation
I. Golgi Apparatus
L. Chromatin
O. Differential Reproduction

*Provide the word that best matches each clue.*

106. SEX INFLUENCED TRAIT — Requires only one recessive gene to be expressed if there is no counteracting dominant gene.

107. VECTOR — Mathematical quantities that recognize both the size and direction of the dimension being considered.

108. INNATE BEHAVIORS — The actions in animals we call instincts; highly stereotyped.

109. NATURAL SELECTION — A feature of population genetics that is the driving force behind evolution.

110. PHENOTYPE — The trait expressed.

111. CATABOLISM — Process of breaking down molecules and releasing stored energy.

112. VELOCITY — The rate of change of displacement; includes both speed and direction.

113. ABSOLUTE ZERO — Theoretical temperature at which particle motion stops; also known as 0 Kelvin.

114. PH — Potential of hydrogen scale, which is a measurement of H+ ions in solutions.

115. COMPOUND — Formed when two or more different atoms bond together chemically to form a unique substance.

116. ZYGOTE — Cell that results when a sperm cell fertilizes an egg cell.

117. SYMPATRIC SPECIATION — Genetically different members reproduce with each other, producing a population, which is separate from the original species.

118. BIOSPHERE — Part of the Earth that includes all living things.

119. NUCLEOLUS — A rounded area within the nucleus of the cell where ribosomal RNA is synthesized.

120. CAPILLARY — Tiny vessels that surround all tissues of the body and exchange carbon dioxide for oxygen.

A. Zygote
D. Sympatric Speciation
G. Nucleolus
J. Velocity

B. pH
E. Compound
H. Natural Selection
K. Biosphere

C. Innate Behaviors
F. Catabolism
I. Capillary
L. Vector

© 2017 Network4Learning, Inc.

M. Absolute Zero      N. Phenotype      O. Sex Influenced Trait

*Provide the word that best matches each clue.*

| # | Term | Clue |
|---|---|---|
| 121. | GREGOR MENDEL | Studied the relationships between traits expressed in parents and offspring and the hereditary factors that caused expression of traits. |
| 122. | BIOGEOGRAPHY | The study of how photosynthetic organisms and animals are distributed in a location plus the history of their distribution in the past. |
| 123. | ION | Charged atom. |
| 124. | TRNA | A chain of about 80 nucleotides that provide the link between the "language" of nucleotides (codon and anticodon) and the "language" of amino acids; also known as transfer RNA. |
| 125. | TRANSFORMATION | A process in which bacteria absorb and incorporate pieces of DNA from their environment (usually from dead bacterial cells). |
| 126. | CHROMATID | The two identical strands of duplicated chromatin in a cell that is getting ready to divide. |
| 127. | HINDBRAIN | Consists of the cerebellum and medulla oblongata. |
| 128. | HISTONE | Short length of DNA wrapped around a core of small proteins. |
| 129. | INVERTEBRATE | Those species having no internal backbone structure. |
| 130. | PUNCTUATED EQUILIBRIUM | Scientific model that proposes that adaptations of species arise suddenly and rapidly. |
| 131. | PROPHASE | The first phase in mitosis. |
| 132. | GOLGI APPARATUS | Instrumental in the storing, packaging, and shipping of proteins; also known as Golgi bodies or the Golgi complex. |
| 133. | CELLULAR METABOLISM | A general term that includes all types of energy transformation processes, including photosynthesis, respiration, growth, movement, etc. |
| 134. | TAXONOMY | Study that organizes living things into groups based on morphology or, more recently, genetics. |
| 135. | SKELETAL MUSCLE | Attaches bones of the skeleton to each other and surrounding tissues, which enables voluntary movement. |

A. Golgi Apparatus
B. Biogeography
C. Hindbrain
D. Cellular Metabolism
E. Punctuated Equilibrium
F. Skeletal Muscle
G. Taxonomy
H. Prophase
I. Histone
J. Transformation
K. Invertebrate
L. Chromatid
M. tRNA
N. Gregor Mendel
O. Ion

*Provide the word that best matches each clue.*

136. BLOOD TISSUE — Flows through the blood vessels and heart and is essential for carrying oxygen to cells, fighting infection, and carrying nutrients and wastes to and from cells.

137. EXOCYTOSIS — The export of substances from the cell.

138. ALVEOLI — Thin-walled air sacs, which are the site of gas exchange.

139. CATALYST — A substance that changes the speed of a reaction without being affected itself.

140. MAGNETISM — the ability of a substance to produce a magnetic field.

141. NUCLEOLUS — A rounded area within the nucleus of the cell where ribosomal RNA is synthesized.

142. INCOMPLETE DOMINANCE — Some traits have no genes that are dominant and instead produce offspring that are a mix of the two parents.

143. COMMUNITY — Populations that interact with each other in a ecosystem.

144. TAXONOMY — Study that organizes living things into groups based on morphology or, more recently, genetics.

145. OPTIC LOBE — Visual center connected to the eyes by the optic nerves.

146. SECRETORY VESICLE — Carry substances produced within the cell to the cell membrane; packets of material packaged by the Golgi apparatus or endoplasmic reticulum.

147. FOREBRAIN — Located most anterior, it contains the olfactory lobes and cerebrum as well as the thalamus, hypothalamus, and pituitary gland.

148. SUCCESSION — When one community completely replaces another over time in an area.

149. CHLOROPHYLL — Pigment molecules that give the chloroplast their green color.

150. ENERGY CYCLE — Supports life throughout the environment.

A. Nucleolus
B. Blood Tissue
C. Forebrain
D. Energy Cycle
E. Exocytosis
F. Optic Lobe

G. Taxonomy
H. Magnetism
I. Succession
J. Secretory Vesicle
K. Catalyst
L. Community
M. Alveoli
N. Chlorophyll
O. Incomplete Dominance

*Provide the word that best matches each clue.*

151. <u>PHENOTYPE</u> — The trait expressed.

152. <u>OPTIC LOBE</u> — Visual center connected to the eyes by the optic nerves.

153. <u>LEARNED BEHAVIOR</u> — May have some basis in genetics, but they also require learning.

154. <u>MEIOSIS</u> — The process of producing four daughter cells, each with single unduplicated chromosomes.

155. <u>HYDROGEN BOND</u> — Occurs when a hydrogen atom is involved with a polar intermolecular attraction to a more electronegative atom.

156. <u>DIGESTIVE SYSTEM</u> — Serves as a processing plant for ingested food.

157. <u>STOMA</u> — The body of the chloroplast.

158. <u>QUANTUM MECHANIC</u> — Predicts the probabilities of an electron being in a certain area at a certain time.

159. <u>SECRETORY VESICLE</u> — Carry substances produced within the cell to the cell membrane; packets of material packaged by the Golgi apparatus or endoplasmic reticulum.

160. <u>POLYGENIC TRAIT</u> — Traits produced from integration of multiple sets of genes.

161. <u>SPEED</u> — the rate of change of an object's distance traveled.

162. <u>EVOLUTION</u> — The gradual change of characteristics within a population, producing a change in a species over time.

163. <u>PASCALS PRINCIPLE</u> — The pressure exerted on any point of a confined fluid is transmitted unchanged throughout the fluid.

164. <u>FLOWER</u> — The primary reproductive organ for a plant.

165. <u>RECESSIVE ALLELE</u> — The allele that does not produce its trait when present with a dominant allele.

A. Quantum Mechanic
B. Speed
C. Meiosis
D. Hydrogen Bond
E. Phenotype
F. Pascals Principle
G. Flower
H. Evolution
I. Secretory Vesicle
J. Optic Lobe
K. Recessive Allele
L. Learned Behavior
M. Polygenic Trait
N. Stoma
O. Digestive System

© 2017 Network4Learning, Inc.

*Provide the word that best matches each clue.*

166. CHLOROPLAST — The site of photosynthesis within plant cells.

167. PARASYMPATHETIC NERVOUS SYSTEM — Carries impulses back from organs.

168. EVAPORATION — Escape of individual particles of a substance into gaseous form.

169. SEX INFLUENCED TRAIT — Requires only one recessive gene to be expressed if there is no counteracting dominant gene.

170. VAN DER WAALS FORCE — Momentary force of attraction that exist between molecules and are much weaker than the forces of chemical bonding.

171. MUSCULOSKELETAL SYSTEM — Provides the body with structure, stability, and the ability to move.

172. CONDENSATION — Change of a gaseous substance to liquid form.

173. INTERPHASE — the period when the cell is active in carrying on its functions.

174. CONDUCTION — Movement of energy by transfer from particle to particle; can only occur when objects are touching.

175. FERMENTATION — Another name for anaerobic respiration, which breaks down the two pyruvic acid molecules (three carbons each) into end products (such as ethyl alcohol, or lactic acid), plus carbon dioxide.

176. GYMNOSPERM — Plants that produce seeds without flowers.

177. B CELL — Class of lymphocyte cell that emerge from the bone marrow mature and produce antibodies, which enter the bloodstream.

178. ANABOLISM — The process whereby cells build molecules and store energy.

179. LAW OF INERTIA — A particle at rest will stay at rest and a particle in motion will stay in motion until acted upon by an outside force.

180. CARDIAC MUSCLE — Tissue forming the walls of the heart with strength and electrical properties that are vital to the heart's ability to pump blood.

A. Law of Inertia
B. Interphase
C. Evaporation
D. Condensation
E. Chloroplast
F. Cardiac Muscle
G. Gymnosperm
H. B Cell
I. Conduction
J. Parasympathetic Nervous System
K. Fermentation
L. Anabolism
M. Musculoskeletal System
N. Sex Influenced Trait
O. Van der Waals Force

*Provide the word that best matches each clue.*

181. AEROBIC — Steps in the cellular respiration process that require oxygen.

182. EXOCYTOSIS — The export of substances from the cell.

183. PHENOTYPE — The trait expressed.

184. FACILITATED DIFFUSION — Allows for the transfer of substances across the cell membrane with the help of specialized proteins.

185. GENETIC ENGINEERING — The intentional alteration of genetic material of a living organism.

186. ELEMENT — A substance that cannot be broken down into any other substances.

187. MUSCULOSKELETAL SYSTEM — Provides the body with structure, stability, and the ability to move.

188. GOLGI APPARATUS — Instrumental in the storing, packaging, and shipping of proteins; also known as Golgi bodies or the Golgi complex.

189. CARTILAGE TISSUE — Reduces friction between bones and supports and connects them.

190. REGULATORY GENES — Code proteins that determine fictional or physiological events.

191. VECTOR — Mathematical quantities that recognize both the size and direction of the dimension being considered.

192. GENETIC DRIFT — Over time, a gene pool (particularly in a small population) may experience a change in frequency of particular genes simply due to change fluctuations.

© 2017 Network4Learning, Inc.

193. <u>QUANTUM MECHANIC</u>    Predicts the probabilities of an electron being in a certain area at a certain time.

194. <u>ACTIVE TRANSPORT</u>    Uses energy to move molecules across a cell membrane against a concentration gradient.

195. <u>SPECIFIC HEAT</u>    The measure of a substance's ability to retain energy.

| | | |
|---|---|---|
| A. Genetic Engineering | B. Musculoskeletal System | C. Regulatory Genes |
| D. Quantum Mechanic | E. Exocytosis | F. Genetic Drift |
| G. Element | H. Active Transport | I. Phenotype |
| J. Facilitated Diffusion | K. Vector | L. Cartilage Tissue |
| M. Specific Heat | N. Aerobic | O. Golgi Apparatus |

*Provide the word that best matches each clue.*

196. <u>ELEMENT</u>    A substance that cannot be broken down into any other substances.

197. <u>VOLTAGE</u>    The electromotive force that pushes electrons through the circuit.

198. <u>AEROBIC</u>    Steps in the cellular respiration process that require oxygen.

199. <u>ALPHA DECAY</u>    Occurs when the nucleus of an atom emits a package of two protons and two neutrons, called an alpha particle, which is equivalent to the nucleus of a helium atom.

200. <u>CIRCUIT</u>    The path that an electrical current follows.

201. <u>NUCLEOLUS</u>    A rounded area within the nucleus of the cell where ribosomal RNA is synthesized.

202. <u>TRANSDUCTION</u>    The transfer or genetic material (portions of a bacterial chromosome) from one bacteria cell to another.

203. <u>VELOCITY</u>    The rate of change of displacement; includes both speed and direction.

204. <u>CONDUCTION</u>    Movement of energy by transfer from particle to particle; can only occur when objects are touching.

205. <u>PARASYMPATHETIC NERVOUS SYSTEM</u>    Carries impulses back from organs.

206. <u>SKELETAL MUSCLE</u>    Attaches bones of the skeleton to each other and surrounding tissues, which enables voluntary movement.

© 2017 Network4Learning, Inc.

207. POPULATION DENSITY — The number of individuals of a species living in an area.

208. LYMPHATIC SYSTEM — The principal infection-fighting component of the immune system.

209. GENE — Length of DNA that encodes a particular protein.

210. GREGOR MENDEL — Studied the relationships between traits expressed in parents and offspring and the hereditary factors that caused expression of traits.

A. Gregor Mendel
B. Aerobic
C. Parasympathetic Nervous System
D. Nucleolus
E. Gene
F. Transduction
G. Alpha Decay
H. Element
I. Lymphatic System
J. Population Density
K. Voltage
L. Skeletal Muscle
M. Velocity
N. Circuit
O. Conduction

*Provide the word that best matches each clue.*

211. EMBRYO — What a zygote eventually grown into.

212. BIOME — An ecosystem that is generally defined by its climate characteristics.

213. GLYCOLYSIS — The breaking down of the six-carbon sugar (glucose) into smaller carbon-containing molecules yielding ATP.

214. PROTEIN — Present in every living cell, large un-branched chains of amino acids; may also be called polypeptides.

215. FORCE — The push or pull exerted on an object.

216. ORGANIC COMPOUND — The building blocks of all living things.

217. MEIOSIS — The process of producing four daughter cells, each with single unduplicated chromosomes.

218. MEDULLA OBLONGATA — Part of the brain that controls involuntary responses such as breathing and heartbeat.

219. DIFFERENTIAL REPRODUCTION — Individuals within a population that are most adapted to the environment and are also the most likely individuals to reproduce successfully.

| | | |
|---|---|---|
| 220. MIDBRAIN | | Located between the forebrain and hindbrain; contains the optic lobes. |
| 221. ACTIVE TRANSPORT | | Uses energy to move molecules across a cell membrane against a concentration gradient. |
| 222. DOMAIN | | Classification category even more general than kingdoms. |
| 223. WATSON CRICK MODEL | | Named after scientists who discovered and modeled the structure of DNA |
| 224. TEMPERATURE | | The measure of the average kinetic energy of a substance. |
| 225. GYMNOSPERM | | Plants that produce seeds without flowers. |

| | | |
|---|---|---|
| A. Domain | B. Midbrain | C. Active Transport |
| D. Protein | E. Force | F. Watson Crick Model |
| G. Differential Reproduction | H. Organic Compound | I. Medulla Oblongata |
| J. Biome | K. Embryo | L. Temperature |
| M. Meiosis | N. Gymnosperm | O. Glycolysis |

*Provide the word that best matches each clue.*

| | |
|---|---|
| 226. MIGRATION | Temporary movement out of one range into another and back. |
| 227. HYPOTHALAMUS | Involved in hunger, thirst, blood pressure, body temperature, hostility, pain, pleasure, etc. |
| 228. WATSON CRICK MODEL | Named after scientists who discovered and modeled the structure of DNA. |
| 229. SOMATIC SENSORY NERVE | Carry impulses from body surface to the CNS. |
| 230. CYTOSKELETON | Provides structural support to a cell. |
| 231. VECTOR | Mathematical quantities that recognize both the size and direction of the dimension being considered. |
| 232. QUANTUM MECHANIC | Predicts the probabilities of an electron being in a certain area at a certain time. |
| 233. NATURAL SELECTION | A feature of population genetics that is the driving force behind evolution. |
| 234. ELECTRICAL CURRENT | A flow of electrons through a conductor. |
| 235. ACTIVE TRANSPORT | Uses energy to move molecules across a cell membrane against a concentration gradient. |

236. LYMPHATIC SYSTEM          The principal infection-fighting component of the immune system.

237. WEIGHT                    The force of gravity acting upon that object.

238. CIRCULATORY SYSTEM        The conduit for delivering nutrients and gases to all cells and for removing waste products from them.

239. ANABOLISM                 The process whereby cells build molecules and store energy.

240. RESPIRATORY SYSTEM        Responsible for the intake and processing of gases required by an organism and for expelling gases produced as waste products.

| | | |
|---|---|---|
| A. Electrical Current | B. Hypothalamus | C. Vector |
| D. Anabolism | E. Cytoskeleton | F. Quantum Mechanic |
| G. Circulatory System | H. Migration | I. Somatic Sensory Nerve |
| J. Lymphatic System | K. Active Transport | L. Respiratory System |
| M. Weight | N. Natural Selection | O. Watson Crick Model |

*Provide the word that best matches each clue.*

241. FOOD CHAIN                Energy generally flows through the entire ecosystem in one direction from producers to consumers and on to decomposers.

242. COMPOUND                  Formed when two or more different atoms bond together chemically to form a unique substance.

243. REACTANTS                 Reacting molecules.

244. INSULATOR                 Poor conductors of electrical currents.

245. PROKARYOTIC CELL          Cells with no nucleus or any other membrane-bound organelles.

246. SYMPATHETIC NERVOUS SYSTEM   Carries impulses that stimulate organs.

247. ANALOGOUS                 Structures that are similar because of their common function, although they do not share a common ancestry.

248. ORGANIC COMPOUND          The building blocks of all living things.

249. PITUITARY GLAND           Releases various hormones.

250. SUBSTRATE                 Particular substance of an enzyme that fits within the active site.

251. IMPRINTING                A learned behavior that develops in a critical or sensitive period of the animal's lifespan.

© 2017 Network4Learning, Inc.

252. HYPOTHALAMUS — Involved in hunger, thirst, blood pressure, body temperature, hostility, pain, pleasure, etc.

253. ARCHIMEDES PRINCIPLE — When an object is placed in a fluid, the object will have a buoyant force equal to the weight of the displaced fluid.

254. INHERITANCE — The process by which characteristics pass from one generation to another.

255. IMMIGRATION — Permanent one-way movement into a new range.

A. Immigration  B. Reactants  C. Organic Compound
D. Insulator  E. Hypothalamus  F. Analogous
G. Inheritance  H. Pituitary Gland  I. Food Chain
J. Compound  K. Archimedes Principle  L. Prokaryotic Cell
M. Sympathetic Nervous System  N. Substrate  O. Imprinting

*Provide the word that best matches each clue.*

256. NERVE TISSUE — Carries electrical and chemical impulses to and from organs and limbs to the brain.

257. ANAPHASE — Step three in mitosis.

258. T CELL — Mature cells in the thymus gland that patrol the blood for antigens but are also equipped to destroy antigens themselves.

259. CYTOPLASM — Region between the nucleus and cell membrane.

260. TERRITORY — An area of land that lies within the home range that the individual will defend as his own.

261. GENOME — Sum total of genetic information.

262. SUCCESSION — When one community completely replaces another over time in an area.

263. PERIODIC TABLE — Listing of elements by atomic number.

264. RESPIRATORY SYSTEM — Responsible for the intake and processing of gases required by an organism and for expelling gases produced as waste products.

265. B CELL — Class of lymphocyte cell that emerge from the bone marrow mature and produce antibodies, which enter the bloodstream.

266. FRICTION — The rubbing force that acts against motion between two touching surfaces.

267. MELTING POINT — Temperature at which a substance changes from solid to liquid form.

268. **HAPLOID** — Single unduplicated chromosomes.
269. **CYTOSKELETON** — Provides structural support to a cell.
270. **GAMETOPHYTE** — Generated by the reproductive organs of the sporophyte through the process of meiosis.

| | | | |
|---|---|---|---|
| A. B Cell | B. Gametophyte | C. Genome | D. Cytoskeleton |
| E. Respiratory System | F. T Cell | G. Nerve Tissue | H. Anaphase |
| I. Friction | J. Succession | K. Melting Point | L. Cytoplasm |
| M. Territory | N. Periodic Table | O. Haploid | |

*Provide the word that best matches each clue.*

271. **CELLULAR METABOLISM** — A general term that includes all types of energy transformation processes, including photosynthesis, respiration, growth, movement, etc.
272. **EMIGRATION** — Permanent one-way movement out of the original range.
273. **VASCULAR** — Plants that have tissue organized in such a way as to conduct food and water throughout their structure.
274. **DENSITY** — The measure of how much matter exists in a volume.
275. **PASCALS PRINCIPLE** — The pressure exerted on any point of a confined fluid is transmitted unchanged throughout the fluid.
276. **HOMEOSTASIS** — A state of dynamic equilibrium, which balances forces tending toward change with forces acceptable for life functions.
277. **DIVISION** — Distributes the remaining set of chromosomes in a mitosis-like process.
278. **MITOSIS** — the process by which a cell distributes its duplicated chromosomes so that each daughter cell has a full set of chromosomes.
279. **GENOME** — Sum total of genetic information.
280. **GENE POOL** — The entire collection of genes within a given population.
281. **ADAPTIVE RADIATION** — A single species can develop into several diverse species over time; over time a species will specially adapt to live more effectively in a new environment.
282. **HABITAT** — The physical place where a species lives.
283. **MECHANICS** — The study of things in motion.

284. DIFFUSION _____  The process whereby molecules and ions flow through the cell membrane from an area of higher concentration to an area of lower concentration; mixing of particles in a gas or liquid.

285. ENZYME _____  Protein molecules that act as catalysts for organic reactions.

A. Mechanics
B. Division
C. Density
D. Genome
E. Gene Pool
F. Emigration
G. Cellular Metabolism
H. Diffusion
I. Pascals Principle
J. Vascular
K. Habitat
L. Adaptive Radiation
M. Enzyme
N. Mitosis
O. Homeostasis

# Word Search

1. *Find the hidden words. The words have been placed horizontally, vertically, or diagonally. When you locate a word, draw a circle around it.*

| S | Y | M | P | A | T | R | I | C | S | P | E | C | I | A | T | I | O | N | B |
|---|---|---|---|---|---|---|---|---|---|---|---|---|---|---|---|---|---|---|---|
| A | Q | L | Y | M | P | H | A | T | I | C | S | Y | S | T | E | M | W | N | A |
| N | E | A | O | Q | Y | F | Y | H | A | B | I | T | U | A | T | I | O | N | F |
| G | C | N | S | P | R | O | P | H | A | S | E | D | I | P | L | O | I | D | O |
| I | G | A | M | E | T | O | P | H | Y | T | E | W | O | R | K | Q | U | K | S |
| O | K | B | O | K | E | S | M | O | O | T | H | M | U | S | C | L | E | E | T |
| S | Z | O | S | V | A | N | D | E | R | W | A | A | L | S | F | O | R | C | E |
| P | K | L | I | G | R | H | E | N | D | O | T | H | E | R | M | I | C | B | K |
| E | F | I | S | E | H | E | C | A | R | D | I | A | C | M | U | S | C | L | E |
| R | A | S | P | U | Y | P | I | N | U | C | L | E | U | S | L | B | D | S | J |
| M | A | M | B | M | R | S | P | E | R | M | P | A | Q | A | I | S | N | I | Q |
| A | D | A | P | T | I | V | E | R | A | D | I | A | T | I | O | N | L | G | I |

1. Makes up the walls of internal organs and functions in involuntary movement. (breathing, etc.)
2. The principal infection-fighting component of the immune system.
3. The parent cell that has a normal set of paired chromosomes.
4. Produced by the male gametophyte; also known as a male gamete.
5. The process whereby cells build molecules and store energy.
6. A learned behavior where the organism produces less and less response as a stimulus is repeated, without a subsequent negative or positive action.
7. An organelle surrounded by two lipid bilayer membranes that is located near the center of the cell and contains chromosomes, nuclear pores, nucleoplasm, and nucleoli.
8. Genetically different members reproduce with each other, producing a population, which is separate from the original species.
9. Generated by the reproductive organs of the sporophyte through the process of meiosis.
10. Momentary force of attraction that exist between molecules and are much weaker than the forces of chemical bonding.
11. A special process of diffusion that occurs when the water concentration inside the cell differs from the concentration outside the cell.
12. Reactions that require energy.
13. A single species can develop into several diverse species over time; over time a species will specially adapt to live more effectively in a new environment.
14. Plants that produce flowers as reproductive organs.
15. Tissue forming the walls of the heart with strength and electrical properties that are vital to the heart's ability to pump blood.
16. The boundary between the nucleus and the cytoplasm.
17. The movement of mass over a distance.
18. The first phase in mitosis.
19. Notation that allow us to easily predict the results of a genetic cross.

A. Habituation
B. Diploid
C. Endothermic
D. Work
E. Punnett Square
F. Nuclear Membrane
G. Sperm
H. Anabolism
I. Nucleus
J. Sympatric Speciation
K. Smooth Muscle
L. Cardiac Muscle
M. Adaptive Radiation
N. Osmosis
O. Lymphatic System
P. Gametophyte
Q. Prophase
R. Angiosperm
S. Van der Waals Force

© 2017 Network4Learning, Inc.

2. *Find the hidden words. The words have been placed horizontally, vertically, or diagonally. When you locate a word, draw a circle around it.*

| W | A | V | E | L | E | N | G | T | H | X | M | O | M | E | N | T | U | M | P |
|---|---|---|---|---|---|---|---|---|---|---|---|---|---|---|---|---|---|---|---|
| N | Z | U | X | Y | I | O | N | C | O | V | A | L | E | N | T | B | O | N | D |
| E | C | O | L | O | G | Y | N | A | Z | O | R | G | A | N | E | L | L | E | L |
| F | R | E | Q | U | E | N | C | Y | Z | Y | G | O | T | E | D | B | Y | C | A |
| B | O | K | F | D | I | G | E | S | T | I | V | E | S | Y | S | T | E | M |   |
| P | L | K | P | D | Z | C | Y | T | O | S | K | E | L | E | T | O | N | M | M |
| P | O | P | U | L | A | T | I | O | N | D | E | N | S | I | T | Y | H | D | N |
| A | L | L | O | P | A | T | R | I | C | S | P | E | C | I | A | T | I | O | N |
| I | A | O | M | Q | S | P | C | D | I | F | F | U | S | I | O | N | C | Z | Q |
| N | U | C | L | E | O | L | U | S | B | E | T | A | D | E | C | A | Y | P | O |
| N | Y | J | P | C | O | N | D | I | T | I | O | N | I | N | G | N | G | A | A |
| N | A | T | U | R | A | L | S | E | L | E | C | T | I | O | N | B | D | H | D |

1. Provides structural support to a cell.
2. The number of individuals of a species living in an area.
3. Cell that results when a sperm cell fertilizes an egg cell.
4. The product of mass and velocity.
5. Cells components that perform functions.
6. Occurs when two populations are geographically isolated from each other.
7. Charged atom.
8. The process whereby molecules and ions flow through the cell membrane from an area of higher concentration to an area of lower concentration; mixing of particles in a gas or liquid.
9. Occurs when the nucleus emits a beta particle that degrades into an electron as it passes out of the atom.
10. Involves learning to apply an old response to a new stimulus.
11. The number of wavelengths that pass a point in a second.
12. Serves as a processing plant for ingested food.
13. Bond formed between the atoms when atoms share electrons.
14. A feature of population genetics that is the driving force behind evolution.
15. A rounded area within the nucleus of the cell where ribosomal RNA is synthesized.
16. Within a given area, there is a maximum level the population may reach at which it will continue to thrive.
17. The study of how organisms interact with other organisms and how they influence or are influenced by their physical environment.
18. The distance from one crest (or top) of a wave to the next crest on the same side.

A. Nucleolus
B. Covalent Bond
C. Cytoskeleton
D. Diffusion
E. Natural Selection
F. Wavelength
G. Ion
H. Ecology
I. Conditioning
J. Carrying Capacity
K. Digestive System
L. Population Density
M. Momentum
N. Allopatric Speciation
O. Beta Decay
P. Zygote
Q. Frequency
R. Organelle

© 2017 Network4Learning, Inc.

3. *Find the hidden words. The words have been placed horizontally, vertically, or diagonally. When you locate a word, draw a circle around it.*

| D | K | Q | Y | D | I | G | E | S | T | I | V | E | S | Y | S | T | E | M | M |
|---|---|---|---|---|---|---|---|---|---|---|---|---|---|---|---|---|---|---|---|
| A | T | V | N | U | C | L | E | A | R | M | E | M | B | R | A | N | E | F | D |
| C | E | L | L | C | Y | C | L | E | Y | U | B | K | I | M | Q | J | M | O | I |
| O | C | H | L | O | R | O | P | L | A | S | T | I | O | E | A | H | O | R | F |
| M | V | A | L | E | N | C | E | S | H | E | L | L | N | T | C | F | M | E | F |
| P | Z | W | W | M | I | T | O | S | I | S | B | F | I | A | P | W | E | B | U |
| O | Z | A | D | O | P | T | I | C | L | O | B | E | C | P | M | H | N | R | S |
| U | H | O | M | O | Z | Y | G | O | U | S | W | G | B | H | I | M | T | A | I |
| N | I | Z | D | I | V | I | S | I | O | N | D | Q | O | A | Z | X | U | I | O |
| D | S | P | E | C | I | F | I | C | H | E | A | T | N | S | T | P | M | N | N |
| T | X | Z | C | O | N | D | U | C | T | I | O | N | D | E | B | I | O | M | E |
| A | R | C | H | I | M | E | D | E | S | P | R | I | N | C | I | P | L | E | Z |

1. Visual center connected to the eyes by the optic nerves.
2. Step two of mitosis; occurs when the spindle fibers pull the chromosomes into alignment along the equatorial plane of the cell, creating the metaphase plate.
3. Distributes the remaining set of chromosomes in a mitosis-like process.
4. Movement of energy by transfer from particle to particle; can only occur when objects are touching.
5. The outermost occupied energy level of an element.
6. The site of photosynthesis within plant cells.
7. When an object is placed in a fluid, the object will have a buoyant force equal to the weight of the displaced fluid.
8. The measure of a substance's ability to retain energy.
9. Serves as a processing plant for ingested food.
10. The process whereby molecules and ions flow through the cell membrane from an area of higher concentration to an area of lower concentration; mixing of particles in a gas or liquid.
11. Located most anterior, it contains the olfactory lobes and cerebrum as well as the thalamus, hypothalamus, and pituitary gland.
12. The boundary between the nucleus and the cytoplasm.
13. A sequence of events ending in cell division, which produces two daughter cells.
14. the process by which a cell distributes its duplicated chromosomes so that each daughter cell has a full set of chromosomes.
15. When both alleles for a given gene are the same in an individual.
16. Bond of attraction between positive and negative ions.
17. An ecosystem that is generally defined by its climate characteristics.
18. The product of mass and velocity.
19. Formed when two or more different atoms bond together chemically to form a unique substance.

A. Ionic Bond
B. Valence Shell
C. Nuclear Membrane
D. Mitosis
E. Digestive System
F. Metaphase
G. Conduction
H. Diffusion
I. Biome
J. Forebrain
K. Cell Cycle
L. Specific Heat
M. Compound
N. Chloroplast
O. Optic Lobe
P. Homozygous
Q. Division
R. Momentum
S. Archimedes Principle

© 2017 Network4Learning, Inc.

4. *Find the hidden words. The words have been placed horizontally, vertically, or diagonally. When you locate a word, draw a circle around it.*

| C | A | T | I | O | N | D | O | Y | N | E | R | V | E | T | I | S | S | U | E |
|---|---|---|---|---|---|---|---|---|---|---|---|---|---|---|---|---|---|---|---|
| Z | S | Y | X | I | H | H | P | J | H | A | B | I | T | U | A | T | I | O | N |
| K | J | P | A | S | S | L | T | M | F | D | H | X | A | B | E | M | G | B | C |
| G | I | I | P | X | W | C | I | H | O | M | O | L | O | G | O | U | S | F | T |
| F | T | J | Y | Y | B | F | C | Z | O | U | A | Y | V | E | B | D | G | O | A |
| A | L | V | E | O | L | I | L | R | W | O | R | G | A | N | I | S | M | U | A |
| E | R | G | X | X | O | L | O | R | G | E | A | A | S | C | U | S | E | D | O |
| M | Q | N | R | D | G | E | B | G | S | B | N | K | C | L | I | X | B | C | N |
| B | C | B | Q | S | F | Q | E | E | G | F | X | H | U | R | W | E | Y | H | O |
| R | A | T | O | M | I | C | N | U | M | B | E | R | L | L | Z | I | T | A | M |
| Y | O | N | L | C | L | R | K | N | V | K | E | A | A | I | J | D | Y | I | Y |
| O | Z | C | H | E | M | I | S | T | R | Y | M | B | R | M | O | L | G | N | M |

1. Study that organizes living things into groups based on morphology or, more recently, genetics.
2. Visual center connected to the eyes by the optic nerves.
3. An individual of a species.
4. Plants that have tissue organized in such a way as to conduct food and water throughout their structure.
5. The number of protons found in the nucleus of an atom of that element.
6. Positive ion.
7. A learned behavior where the organism produces less and less response as a stimulus is repeated, without a subsequent negative or positive action.
8. Thin-walled air sacs, which are the site of gas exchange.
9. What a zygote eventually grown into.
10. The allele that does not produce its trait when present with a dominant allele.
11. Momentary force of attraction that exist between molecules and are much weaker than the forces of chemical bonding.
12. Carry substances produced within the cell to the cell membrane; packets of material packaged by the Golgi apparatus or endoplasmic reticulum.
13. Structures that exist in two different species because they share a common ancestry.
14. Cells with no nucleus or any other membrane-bound organelles.
15. Energy generally flows through the entire ecosystem in one direction from producers to consumers and on to decomposers.
16. The study of matter.
17. The intentional alteration of genetic material of a living organism.
18. Carries electrical and chemical impulses to and from organs and limbs to the brain.

A. Embryo
B. Organism
C. Food Chain
D. Nerve Tissue
E. Secretory Vesicle
F. Vascular
G. Optic Lobe
H. Cation
I. Habituation
J. Homologous
K. Atomic Number
L. Van der Waals Force
M. Alveoli
N. Chemistry
O. Genetic Engineering
P. Recessive Allele
Q. Prokaryotic Cell
R. Taxonomy

5. *Find the hidden words. The words have been placed horizontally, vertically, or diagonally. When you locate a word, draw a circle around it.*

| A | L | L | O | P | A | T | R | I | C | S | P | E | C | I | A | T | I | O | N |
|---|---|---|---|---|---|---|---|---|---|---|---|---|---|---|---|---|---|---|---|
| F | Y | M | K | C | A | P | I | L | L | A | R | Y | N | D | B | K | D | O | J |
| N | Q | Z | E | A | E | V | O | L | U | T | I | O | N | H | V | C | J | T | B |
| W | A | X | G | E | N | E | M | I | G | R | A | T | I | O | N | Y | L | E | I |
| I | E | L | E | C | T | R | O | N | C | L | O | U | D | R | T | G | Y | L | O |
| Y | Z | X | T | R | A | N | S | L | A | T | I | O | N | M | V | F | S | O | S |
| C | R | A | C | T | I | V | E | T | R | A | N | S | P | O | R | T | O | P | P |
| G | E | E | N | D | O | T | H | E | R | M | I | C | Z | N | W | M | S | H | H |
| F | F | C | E | L | L | M | E | M | B | R | A | N | E | E | P | H | O | A | E |
| A | L | Z | M | R | N | A | S | I | T | W | U | Z | P | S | H | A | M | S | R |
| H | E | B | R | M | C | H | A | L | F | L | I | F | E | K | L | I | E | E | E |
| A | X | D | Q | H | C | E | L | L | D | I | V | I | S | I | O | N | E | B | M |

1. The introduction of new genes from an immigrant, which results in a change of the gene pool.
2. Potential of hydrogen scale, which is a measurement of H+ ions in solutions.
3. Reactions that require energy.
4. Occurs when two populations are geographically isolated from each other.
5. Chemicals produced in the endocrine glands of an organism which modify metabolic activities.
6. The process of cell reproduction that centers on the replication and separation of strands of DNA.
7. An automatic movement of a body part in response to a stimulus.
8. Step four in mitosis; occurs as nuclear membranes form around the chromosomes and disperse through the new nucleoplasm; spindle fibers also disappear.
9. Tiny vessels that surround all tissues of the body and exchange carbon dioxide for oxygen.
10. The time it takes for 50 percent of an isotope to decay.
11. Structure that encloses the cell and separates it from the environment; also known as the plasma membrane.
12. Part of the Earth that includes all living things.
13. Uses energy to move molecules across a cell membrane against a concentration gradient.
14. Phase of photosynthesis that requires a second type of RNA.
15. Membrane-bound organelles containing digestive enzymes; digest unused material within the cell, damaged organelles, or materials absorbed by the cell for use.
16. RNA strand that migrates form the nucleus to the cytoplasm; also known as messenger RNA.
17. Three-dimensional space where electrons travel freely; also known as an electron shell or orbital.
18. The gradual change of characteristics within a population, producing a change in a species over time.

A. Endothermic
B. Electron Cloud
C. Active Transport
D. Telophase
E. Translation
F. Cell Division
G. Gene Migration
H. Allopatric Speciation
I. pH
J. Cell Membrane
K. Evolution
L. mRNA
M. Half Life
N. Reflex
O. Hormones
P. Biosphere
Q. Capillary
R. Lysosome

© 2017 Network4Learning, Inc.

6. *Find the hidden words. The words have been placed horizontally, vertically, or diagonally. When you locate a word, draw a circle around it.*

| I | I | C | V | A | N | D | E | R | W | A | A | L | S | F | O | R | C | E | G |
|---|---|---|---|---|---|---|---|---|---|---|---|---|---|---|---|---|---|---|---|
| E | G | O | R | C | S | V | E | U | E | X | T | I | N | C | T | I | O | N | C |
| N | C | N | Q | N | H | A | N | E | J | B | I | O | S | P | H | E | R | E | D |
| D | H | D | D | Y | Y | S | D | M | U | T | A | T | I | O | N | W | D | T | A |
| O | P | U | O | W | N | O | O | M | B | W | A | V | E | L | E | N | G | T | H |
| T | O | C | M | J | S | N | C | G | H | O | C | A | P | I | L | L | A | R | Y |
| H | M | T | A | L | T | I | Y | D | I | F | F | U | S | I | O | N | P | X | P |
| E | A | I | I | F | W | K | T | L | W | E | H | V | I | R | U | S | E | S | W |
| R | T | O | N | L | A | W | O | F | S | E | G | R | E | G | A | T | I | O | N |
| M | I | N | U | M | J | F | S | A | T | O | M | I | C | N | U | M | B | E | R |
| I | N | J | P | E | P | F | I | K | O | R | G | A | N | E | L | L | E | E | N |
| C | F | U | K | J | C | H | S | Z | M | S | P | U | O | V | A | R | Y | I | A |

1. The process whereby large molecules are taken up into a pocket of membrane; the pocket pinches off, delivering the molecules, still inside a membrane sack into the cytoplasm.
2. ___ traits are expressed from a pair of genes in the individual (on homologous chromosomes).
3. The hollow, bulb-shaped structure in the lower interior of the pistil.
4. Movement of energy by transfer from particle to particle; can only occur when objects are touching.
5. A change of the DNA sequence of a gene, resulting in a change of the trait.
6. The number of protons found in the nucleus of an atom of that element.
7. Smaller than even the smallest cells; survive and replicate by invading a living cell.
8. The distance from one crest (or top) of a wave to the next crest on the same side.
9. Cells components that perform functions.
10. Part of the Earth that includes all living things.
11. The process whereby molecules and ions flow through the cell membrane from an area of higher concentration to an area of lower concentration; mixing of particles in a gas or liquid.
12. Momentary force of attraction that exist between molecules and are much weaker than the forces of chemical bonding.
13. Tiny vessels that surround all tissues of the body and exchange carbon dioxide for oxygen.
14. The combination of DNA with histones.
15. A crucial set of reactions that convert the light energy of the sun into chemical energy usable by living things.
16. When the entire population of a particular species is eliminated.
17. Classification category even more general than kingdoms.
18. Reactions that require energy.

A. Chromatin
B. Endocytosis
C. Extinction
D. Atomic Number
E. Domain
F. Photosynthesis
G. Van der Waals Force
H. Wavelength
I. Conduction
J. Diffusion
K. Law of Segregation
L. Capillary
M. Viruses
N. Mutation
O. Organelle
P. Biosphere
Q. Ovary
R. Endothermic

7. *Find the hidden words. The words have been placed horizontally, vertically, or diagonally. When you locate a word, draw a circle around it.*

| C | R | G | I | P | A | N | A | B | O | L | I | S | M | A | I | G | Q | G | X |
|---|---|---|---|---|---|---|---|---|---|---|---|---|---|---|---|---|---|---|---|
| J | I | W | R | J | P | H | E | N | O | T | Y | P | E | V | N | Y | L | K | I |
| R | E | C | E | S | S | I | V | E | A | L | L | E | L | E | K | L | M | A | M |
| I | A | T | O | M | P | E | I | M | M | U | N | E | S | Y | S | T | E | M | P |
| U | D | F | S | A | E | V | E | I | N | F | R | E | Q | U | E | N | C | Y | R |
| H | E | L | E | C | T | R | O | N | C | L | O | U | D | Y | Y | G | Q | J | I |
| V | E | P | I | T | H | E | L | I | A | L | T | I | S | S | U | E | H | P | N |
| N | N | H | E | M | O | G | L | O | B | I | N | M | I | T | O | S | I | S | T |
| A | U | K | I | D | O | R | G | A | N | I | S | M | W | C | V | W | Q | S | I |
| F | U | I | G | W | A | V | E | L | E | N | G | T | H | K | E | L | M | B | N |
| P | O | P | U | L | A | T | I | O | N | D | E | N | S | I | T | Y | E | I | G |
| D | P | D | I | S | P | L | A | C | E | M | E | N | T | S | L | P | W | O | Q |

1. Functions to defend the body from infection by bacteria and viruses.
2. The trait expressed.
3. A learned behavior that develops in a critical or sensitive period of the animal's lifespan.
4. Forms the barrier between the environment and the interior of the body.
5. The number of individuals of a species living in an area.
6. Measures the change in position of an object, using the starting point and ending point and noting the direction.
7. Vessels that carry blood toward the heart.
8. The number of wavelengths that pass a point in a second.
9. The measure of how much matter exists in a volume.
10. The distance from one crest (or top) of a wave to the next crest on the same side.
11. Component of blood responsible for carrying oxygen.
12. Three-dimensional space where electrons travel freely; also known as an electron shell or orbital.
13. the process by which a cell distributes its duplicated chromosomes so that each daughter cell has a full set of chromosomes.
14. The allele that does not produce its trait when present with a dominant allele.
15. The simplest unit of an element that retains the element's characteristics.
16. An individual of a species.
17. The process whereby cells build molecules and store energy.
18. A rounded area within the nucleus of the cell where ribosomal RNA is synthesized.

A. Frequency　　B. Mitosis　　C. Nucleolus　　D. Hemoglobin　　E. Atom
F. Phenotype　　G. Population Density　　H. Epithelial Tissue　　I. Imprinting　　J. Density
K. Vein　　L. Electron Cloud　　M. Immune System　　N. Anabolism　　O. Displacement
P. Recessive Allele　　Q. Wavelength　　R. Organism

8. *Find the hidden words. The words have been placed horizontally, vertically, or diagonally. When you locate a word, draw a circle around it.*

| C | C | D | O | U | X | W | E | L | E | C | T | R | O | N | C | L | O | U | D |
|---|---|---|---|---|---|---|---|---|---|---|---|---|---|---|---|---|---|---|---|
| Y | Y | O | V | Z | N | E | F | O | R | E | B | R | A | I | N | E | W | R | H |
| T | C | M | A | C | W | I | D | N | P | T | C | A | T | I | O | N | D | Y | K |
| O | Y | I | R | Y | Q | G | V | C | M | I | S | G | E | N | O | T | Y | P | E |
| U | T | M | Y | R | V | H | O | I | N | V | E | R | T | E | B | R | A | T | E |
| K | O | A | C | R | H | T | F | G | A | L | P | H | A | D | E | C | A | Y | I |
| E | P | N | I | A | R | T | E | R | Y | H | I | N | D | B | R | A | I | N | N |
| L | L | C | R | X | H | D | I | F | F | R | A | C | T | I | O | N | V | J | T |
| E | A | E | C | G | C | O | N | D | U | C | T | I | O | N | I | T | E | Y | I |
| T | S | E | U | P | A | Z | H | V | I | R | U | S | E | S | Q | M | Q | Z | H |
| O | M | S | I | I | M | M | U | N | E | S | Y | S | T | E | M | L | P | G | W |
| N | J | F | T | A | A | W | P | X | C | O | M | P | E | T | I | T | I | O | N |

1. Provides structural support to a cell.
2. Consists of the cerebellum and medulla oblongata.
3. Region between the nucleus and cell membrane.
4. Movement of energy by transfer from particle to particle; can only occur when objects are touching.
5. Results when two or more species living within the same area and that overlap niches both require a resource that is in limited supply.
6. The hollow, bulb-shaped structure in the lower interior of the pistil.
7. Occurs when the nucleus of an atom emits a package of two protons and two neutrons, called an alpha particle, which is equivalent to the nucleus of a helium atom.
8. Occurs when older, more established individuals compete for status within the community.
9. The force of gravity acting upon that object.
10. The path that an electrical current follows.
11. The bending of a light wave around an obstacle.
12. The combination of alleles that make a particular trait.
13. Smaller than even the smallest cells; survive and replicate by invading a living cell.
14. Three-dimensional space where electrons travel freely; also known as an electron shell or orbital.
15. Functions to defend the body from infection by bacteria and viruses.
16. Larger vessels that carry blood away from the heart.
17. Positive ion.
18. Those species having no internal backbone structure.
19. Located most anterior, it contains the olfactory lobes and cerebrum as well as the thalamus, hypothalamus, and pituitary gland.

A. Forebrain
B. Viruses
C. Electron Cloud
D. Cytoplasm
E. Weight
F. Dominance
G. Immune System
H. Circuit
I. Ovary
J. Competition
K. Hindbrain
L. Artery
M. Cytoskeleton
N. Diffraction
O. Invertebrate
P. Genotype
Q. Alpha Decay
R. Cation
S. Conduction

9. *Find the hidden words. The words have been placed horizontally, vertically, or diagonally. When you locate a word, draw a circle around it.*

| O | V | A | R | Y | U | Y | V | P | V | G | E | N | E | P | O | O | L | W | Y |
|---|---|---|---|---|---|---|---|---|---|---|---|---|---|---|---|---|---|---|---|
| X | P | D | I | F | F | U | S | I | O | N | I | O | N | I | C | B | O | N | D |
| B | A | K | Y | B | L | T | R | A | N | S | C | R | I | P | T | I | O | N | J |
| M | H | D | K | E | V | H | I | N | D | B | R | A | I | N | E | E | C | U | B |
| P | L | C | W | A | T | S | O | N | C | R | I | C | K | M | O | D | E | L | C |
| R | P | S | M | I | T | O | C | H | O | N | D | R | I | A | D | Y | N | L | I |
| Q | N | U | C | L | E | O | L | U | S | R | P | M | E | I | O | S | I | S | R |
| F | D | I | V | I | S | I | O | N | N | Y | X | I | S | O | T | O | P | E | C |
| S | D | E | V | O | L | U | T | I | O | N | A | J | N | H | W | V | D | D | U |
| Z | Z | T | Q | N | E | R | V | O | U | S | S | Y | S | T | E | M | M | A | I |
| I | N | N | A | T | E | B | E | H | A | V | I | O | R | S | U | I | L | M | T |
| J | K | A | C | T | I | V | E | T | R | A | N | S | P | O | R | T | S | V | C |

1. Named after scientists who discovered and modeled the structure of DNA.
2. A rounded area within the nucleus of the cell where ribosomal RNA is synthesized.
3. Uses energy to move molecules across a cell membrane against a concentration gradient.
4. Atoms with the same number of protons by different numbers of neutrons.
5. The path that an electrical current follows.
6. The formation of an RNA molecule, which corresponds to a gene.
7. Center of cellular respiration
8. Consists of the cerebellum and medulla oblongata.
9. The hollow, bulb-shaped structure in the lower interior of the pistil.
10. Bond of attraction between positive and negative ions.
11. Distributes the remaining set of chromosomes in a mitosis-like process.
12. The entire collection of genes within a given population.
13. The actions in animals we call instincts; highly stereotyped.
14. The gradual change of characteristics within a population, producing a change in a species over time.
15. A communication network that connects the entire body of an organism and provides control over bodily functions.
16. The process whereby molecules and ions flow through the cell membrane from an area of higher concentration to an area of lower concentration; mixing of particles in a gas or liquid.
17. The process of producing four daughter cells, each with single unduplicated chromosomes.
18. Momentary force of attraction that exist between molecules and are much weaker than the forces of chemical bonding.

A. Van der Waals Force
B. Innate Behaviors
C. Transcription
D. Active Transport
E. Gene Pool
F. Ovary
G. Nucleolus
H. Evolution
I. Mitochondria
J. Diffusion
K. Circuit
L. Nervous System
M. Ionic Bond
N. Isotope
O. Hindbrain
P. Meiosis
Q. Division
R. Watson Crick Model

© 2017 Network4Learning, Inc.

10. *Find the hidden words. The words have been placed horizontally, vertically, or diagonally. When you locate a word, draw a circle around it.*

| F | O | R | E | B | R | A | I | N | C | A | T | A | B | O | L | I | S | M | Y |
|---|---|---|---|---|---|---|---|---|---|---|---|---|---|---|---|---|---|---|---|
| Y | W | T | E | M | P | E | R | A | T | U | R | E | P | N | F | R | W | H | L |
| C | Z | T | S | C | E | G | A | T | P | V | M | P | E | Z | T | U | E | Q | V |
| H | W | C | L | D | O | L | F | A | C | T | O | R | Y | L | O | B | E | N | I |
| R | L | A | W | O | F | S | E | G | R | E | G | A | T | I | O | N | L | F | G |
| O | P | J | A | M | F | Q | Y | Z | Y | G | O | T | E | I | B | C | E | L | L |
| M | C | M | E | A | N | H | C | G | G | M | I | T | O | S | I | S | G | O | Y |
| A | D | R | D | I | F | C | E | L | L | M | E | M | B | R | A | N | E | D | R |
| T | Z | S | I | N | O | N | E | R | V | O | U | S | S | Y | S | T | E | M | K |
| I | N | E | U | R | O | N | C | E | R | E | B | E | L | L | U | M | U | D | O |
| D | O | L | M | V | G | P | V | Q | O | R | G | A | N | E | L | L | E | W | W |
| V | E | I | N | V | I | L | L | I | G | Q | A | N | A | P | H | A | S | E | R |

1. Structure that encloses the cell and separates it from the environment; also known as the plasma membrane.
2. Protrusions out into the lumen of the intestine that provide a large surface area for absorption of nutrients.
3. Classification category even more general than kingdoms.
4. Step three in mitosis.
5. Energy currency of cellular activity; consists of a nitrogenous base (adenine), a simple sugar (ribose), and three phosphate groups.
6. Carry impulses via electrochemical responses.
7. Part of the brain that controls balance, equilibrium, and muscle coordination.
8. A communication network that connects the entire body of an organism and provides control over bodily functions.
9. Vessels that carry blood toward the heart.
10. Cell that results when a sperm cell fertilizes an egg cell.
11. Located most anterior, it contains the olfactory lobes and cerebrum as well as the thalamus, hypothalamus, and pituitary gland.
12. Process of breaking down molecules and releasing stored energy.
13. Cells components that perform functions.
14. the process by which a cell distributes its duplicated chromosomes so that each daughter cell has a full set of chromosomes.
15. The two identical strands of duplicated chromatin in a cell that is getting ready to divide.
16. Class of lymphocyte cell that emerge from the bone marrow mature and produce antibodies, which enter the bloodstream.
17. The measure of the average kinetic energy of a substance.
18. traits are expressed from a pair of genes in the individual (on homologous chromosomes).
19. Responsible for the sense of smell.

A. ATP
B. Forebrain
C. Catabolism
D. Temperature
E. Nervous System
F. Cell Membrane
G. Neuron
H. Domain
I. Organelle
J. Mitosis
K. Anaphase
L. Law of Segregation
M. Cerebellum
N. Zygote
O. Villi
P. B Cell
Q. Olfactory Lobe
R. Vein
S. Chromatid

© 2017 Network4Learning, Inc.

11. *Find the hidden words. The words have been placed horizontally, vertically, or diagonally. When you locate a word, draw a circle around it.*

| J | T | Q | C | E | L | L | M | E | M | B | R | A | N | E | R | V | I | F | Z |
|---|---|---|---|---|---|---|---|---|---|---|---|---|---|---|---|---|---|---|---|
| M | I | T | O | S | I | S | J | H | N | D | K | F | I | G | E | H | N | G | E |
| E | V | A | P | O | R | A | T | I | O | N | P | X | P | T | F | I | T | A | X |
| H | A | B | I | T | U | A | T | I | O | N | R | R | A | L | S | E | M | T |   |
| Z | S | O | R | G | A | N | E | L | L | E | E | Q | T | K | E | T | R | E | I |
| E | N | E | R | G | Y | C | Y | C | L | E | S | Z | Y | C | C | O | P | T | N |
| M | A | C | T | I | V | E | T | R | A | N | S | P | O | R | T | N | H | O | C |
| U | G | Y | N | A | P | Z | S | S | F | V | U | U | G | A | I | E | A | P | T |
| I | C | Q | X | G | E | N | E | M | I | G | R | A | T | I | O | N | S | H | I |
| J | W | O | R | K | Y | B | D | E | P | P | E | S | Q | D | N | W | E | Y | O |
| L | P | H | O | T | O | S | Y | N | T | H | E | S | I | S | F | B | G | T | N |
| U | E | L | E | C | T | R | O | N | T | R | A | N | S | P | O | R | T | E | T |

1. Generated by the reproductive organs of the sporophyte through the process of meiosis.
2. the process by which a cell distributes its duplicated chromosomes so that each daughter cell has a full set of chromosomes.
3. A measure of the amount of force applied per unit of area.
4. The introduction of new genes from an immigrant, which results in a change of the gene pool.
5. The movement of mass over a distance.
6. The second step of aerobic respiration that captures the energy created by the release of electrons from the Krebs cycle.
7. Escape of individual particles of a substance into gaseous form.
8. Supports life throughout the environment.
9. The bouncing of a wave of light off an object.
10. Cells components that perform functions.
11. A crucial set of reactions that convert the light energy of the sun into chemical energy usable by living things.
12. When the entire population of a particular species is eliminated.
13. A learned behavior where the organism produces less and less response as a stimulus is repeated, without a subsequent negative or positive action.
14. Uses energy to move molecules across a cell membrane against a concentration gradient.
15. Short length of DNA wrapped around a core of small proteins.
16. Structure that encloses the cell and separates it from the environment; also known as the plasma membrane.
17. A single species can develop into several diverse species over time; over time a species will specially adapt to live more effectively in a new environment.
18. the period when the cell is active in carrying on its functions.

A. Evaporation  
B. Energy Cycle  
C. Work  
D. Electron Transport  
E. Extinction  
F. Photosynthesis  
G. Active Transport  
H. Histone  
I. Interphase  
J. Organelle  
K. Mitosis  
L. Adaptive Radiation  
M. Pressure  
N. Gene Migration  
O. Cell Membrane  
P. Gametophyte  
Q. Reflection  
R. Habituation  

© 2017 Network4Learning, Inc.

**12.** *Find the hidden words. The words have been placed horizontally, vertically, or diagonally. When you locate a word, draw a circle around it.*

| W | L | S | I | R | Y | X | A | I | M | W | M | E | C | H | A | N | I | C | S |
|---|---|---|---|---|---|---|---|---|---|---|---|---|---|---|---|---|---|---|---|
| G | S | S | W | A | T | S | O | N | C | R | I | C | K | M | O | D | E | L | H |
| C | O | N | N | E | C | T | I | V | E | T | I | S | S | U | E | R | U | R | C |
| O | E | L | E | P | I | T | H | E | L | I | A | L | T | I | S | S | U | E | R |
| U | J | Y | I | Y | V | V | H | R | Z | H | O | R | M | O | N | E | S | F | U |
| N | L | H | M | Q | X | P | A | T | O | M | I | C | M | A | S | S | K | K | L |
| D | C | R | S | I | Z | Y | V | E | F | Q | D | M | B | J | B | T | C | A | U |
| Z | S | C | C | S | N | C | T | B | M | E | T | A | P | H | A | S | E | C | G |
| K | U | A | W | M | I | M | P | R | I | N | T | I | N | G | X | F | H | T | P |
| K | Q | S | K | E | L | E | T | A | L | M | U | S | C | L | E | P | I | I | Z |
| E | N | Z | Y | M | E | Z | P | T | R | C | E | L | L | W | A | L | L | O | W |
| A | R | T | E | R | Y | I | L | E | R | E | A | C | T | A | N | T | S | N | C |

1. Those species having no internal backbone structure.
2. The change in direction of a wave as it passes from one medium to another.
3. Holds tissues and organs together, stabilizing the body structure.
4. Reacting molecules.
5. The study of things in motion.
6. Carry impulses from body surface to the CNS.
7. Carry impulses to skeletal muscle from the CNS.
8. Forms the barrier between the environment and the interior of the body.
9. Named after scientists who discovered and modeled the structure of DNA.
10. Calculated by adding up the masses of the protons and neutrons.
11. Chemicals produced in the endocrine glands of an organism which modify metabolic activities.
12. Protein molecules that act as catalysts for organic reactions.
13. A learned behavior that develops in a critical or sensitive period of the animal's lifespan.
14. Made of cellulose and lignin, they enclose the cell membrane providing strength and protection for the cell.
15. Makes up the walls of internal organs and functions in involuntary movement. (breathing, etc.)
16. Larger vessels that carry blood away from the heart.
17. Attaches bones of the skeleton to each other and surrounding tissues, which enables voluntary movement.
18. Within a given area, there is a maximum level the population may reach at which it will continue to thrive.
19. Step two of mitosis; occurs when the spindle fibers pull the chromosomes into alignment along the equatorial plane of the cell, creating the metaphase plate.

A. Invertebrate
B. Refraction
C. Cell Wall
D. Atomic Mass
E. Enzyme
F. Imprinting
G. Metaphase
H. Skeletal Muscle
I. Carrying Capacity
J. Epithelial Tissue
K. Connective Tissue
L. Artery
M. Hormones
N. Reactants
O. Watson Crick Model
P. Mechanics
Q. Somatic Motor Nerve
R. Smooth Muscle
S. Somatic Sensory Nerve

13. *Find the hidden words. The words have been placed horizontally, vertically, or diagonally. When you locate a word, draw a circle around it.*

| G | D | E | N | S | I | T | Y | S | N | D | P | E | N | D | O | D | E | R | M |
|---|---|---|---|---|---|---|---|---|---|---|---|---|---|---|---|---|---|---|---|
| C | A | R | D | I | A | C | M | U | S | C | L | E | Z | W | B | J | E | Q | L |
| H | V | D | I | V | I | S | I | O | N | M | O | L | A | R | M | A | S | S | Y |
| A | A | E | L | E | C | T | R | I | C | A | L | C | U | R | R | E | N | T | S |
| L | S | P | T | O | B | F | T | Q | V | E | R | T | E | B | R | A | T | E | O |
| F | C | A | D | I | P | O | S | E | T | I | S | S | U | E | P | W | C | M | S |
| L | U | J | M | P | E | R | I | O | D | I | C | T | A | B | L | E | E | Q | O |
| I | L | S | C | M | P | O | S | I | T | R | O | N | D | E | C | A | Y | B | M |
| F | A | R | L | A | W | O | F | I | N | E | R | T | I | A | U | H | E | E | E |
| E | R | B | M | T | C | Y | T | O | S | K | E | L | E | T | O | N | W | X | J |
| A | E | R | O | B | I | C | G | R | E | G | O | R | M | E | N | D | E | L | F |
| F | F | T | R | A | N | S | L | A | T | I | O | N | B | C | E | L | L | Z | A |

1. A particle at rest will stay at rest and a particle in motion will stay in motion until acted upon by an outside force.
2. The precursor of the gut lining and various accessory structures.
3. Distributes the remaining set of chromosomes in a mitosis-like process.
4. Species that have internal backbones.
5. Occurs when the nucleus emits a particle that degrades into a positron as it passes out of the atom.
6. Listing of elements by atomic number.
7. Steps in the cellular respiration process that require oxygen.
8. Tissue forming the walls of the heart with strength and electrical properties that are vital to the heart's ability to pump blood.
9. The measure of how much matter exists in a volume.
10. Studied the relationships between traits expressed in parents and offspring and the hereditary factors that caused expression of traits.
11. Phase of photosynthesis that requires a second type of RNA.
12. A flow of electrons through a conductor.
13. Found beneath the skin and around organs, providing cushioning, insulation, and fat storage.
14. The time it takes for 50 percent of an isotope to decay.
15. Provides structural support to a cell.
16. Plants that have tissue organized in such a way as to conduct food and water throughout their structure.
17. The mass in grams of one mole of atoms.
18. Membrane-bound organelles containing digestive enzymes; digest unused material within the cell, damaged organelles, or materials absorbed by the cell for use.
19. Class of lymphocyte cell that emerge from the bone marrow mature and produce antibodies, which enter the bloodstream.

A. Cytoskeleton
B. Vertebrate
C. Half Life
D. Lysosome
E. Aerobic
F. Cardiac Muscle
G. Vascular
H. Division
I. Endoderm
J. Law of Inertia
K. B Cell
L. Gregor Mendel
M. Molar Mass
N. Electrical Current
O. Adipose Tissue
P. Density
Q. Positron Decay
R. Translation
S. Periodic Table

© 2017 Network4Learning, Inc.

14. *Find the hidden words. The words have been placed horizontally, vertically, or diagonally. When you locate a word, draw a circle around it.*

| A | T | M | O | S | P | H | E | R | I | C | P | R | E | S | S | U | R | E | P |
|---|---|---|---|---|---|---|---|---|---|---|---|---|---|---|---|---|---|---|---|
| L | Y | K | Y | F | S | A | P | C | E | L | L | D | I | V | I | S | I | O | N |
| S | A | U | J | A | Z | N | Z | C | O | V | A | L | E | N | T | B | O | N | D |
| Y | H | P | O | L | Y | G | E | N | I | C | T | R | A | I | T | G | T | P | C |
| M | A | I | N | W | H | I | L | A | W | O | F | I | N | E | R | T | I | A | H |
| B | L | O | J | A | T | O | M | A | M | E | T | A | P | H | A | S | E | J | R |
| I | F | Z | T | R | N | S | V | H | O | M | E | O | S | T | A | S | I | S | O |
| O | L | W | G | D | N | P | E | D | E | N | D | O | D | E | R | M | A | H | M |
| S | I | E | C | C | M | E | I | B | D | I | P | L | O | I | D | S | D | K | A |
| I | F | R | L | T | X | R | N | H | A | P | L | O | I | D | R | Q | Q | W | T |
| S | E | S | D | T | A | M | C | M | U | T | A | T | I | O | N | Y | R | Y | I |
| L | B | C | D | N | F | N | W | Y | Z | O | M | F | B | V | P | K | Z | I | D |

1. Vessels that carry blood toward the heart.
2. When two species interact with each other within the same range.
3. Single unduplicated chromosomes.
4. Plants that produce flowers as reproductive organs.
5. Traits produced from integration of multiple sets of genes.
6. Bond formed between the atoms when atoms share electrons.
7. The two identical strands of duplicated chromatin in a cell that is getting ready to divide.
8. A particle at rest will stay at rest and a particle in motion will stay in motion until acted upon by an outside force.
9. The parent cell that has a normal set of paired chromosomes.
10. The simplest unit of an element that retains the element's characteristics.
11. The time it takes for 50 percent of an isotope to decay.
12. A state of dynamic equilibrium, which balances forces tending toward change with forces acceptable for life functions.
13. Step two of mitosis; occurs when the spindle fibers pull the chromosomes into alignment along the equatorial plane of the cell, creating the metaphase plate.
14. The process of cell reproduction that centers on the replication and separation of strands of DNA.
15. Pressure that results from the total weight of the atmosphere exerting force on the Earth; can be measured with a barometer.
16. A change of the DNA sequence of a gene, resulting in a change of the trait.
17. Temperature at which a substance changes from liquid to solid.
18. The precursor of the gut lining and various accessory structures.

A. Atmospheric Pressure
B. Angiosperm
C. Homeostasis
D. Endoderm
E. Atom
F. Diploid
G. Symbiosis
H. Metaphase
I. Freezing Point
J. Covalent Bond
K. Mutation
L. Polygenic Trait
M. Chromatid
N. Haploid
O. Law of Inertia
P. Half Life
Q. Cell Division
R. Vein

15. *Find the hidden words. The words have been placed horizontally, vertically, or diagonally. When you locate a word, draw a circle around it.*

| R | G | G | W | S | P | E | C | I | F | I | C | H | E | A | T | Z | W | G | K |
|---|---|---|---|---|---|---|---|---|---|---|---|---|---|---|---|---|---|---|---|
| A | K | K | F | R | E | E | Z | I | N | G | P | O | I | N | T | T | K | Z | F |
| D | G | K | E | A | T | R | A | N | S | L | A | T | I | O | N | E | C | Z | Q |
| I | V | A | W | M | Y | X | B | I | O | S | P | H | E | R | E | L | E | Z | A |
| A | A | S | T | R | U | C | T | U | R | A | L | G | E | N | E | O | L | S | N |
| T | S | B | D | Q | R | H | P | H | E | N | O | T | Y | P | E | P | L | D | A |
| I | C | P | C | C | O | N | D | E | N | S | A | T | I | O | N | H | C | Q | P |
| O | U | G | L | Y | C | O | L | Y | S | I | S | L | S | O | C | A | Y | G | H |
| N | L | A | E | R | O | B | I | C | F | X | D | V | D | L | Y | S | C | E | A |
| U | A | O | L | F | A | C | T | O | R | Y | L | O | B | E | I | E | L | N | S |
| C | R | B | A | N | E | U | R | O | N | I | S | O | T | O | P | E | E | E | E |
| C | E | N | T | R | A | L | N | E | R | V | O | U | S | S | Y | S | T | E | M |

1. Plants that have tissue organized in such a way as to conduct food and water throughout their structure.
2. Atoms with the same number of protons by different numbers of neutrons.
3. Steps in the cellular respiration process that require oxygen.
4. The breaking down of the six-carbon sugar (glucose) into smaller carbon-containing molecules yielding ATP.
5. Length of DNA that encodes a particular protein.
6. Part of the Earth that includes all living things.
7. A sequence of events ending in cell division, which produces two daughter cells.
8. Phase of photosynthesis that requires a second type of RNA.
9. Code proteins that form organs and structural characteristics.
10. The measure of a substance's ability to retain energy.
11. Carry impulses via electrochemical responses.
12. Two main components, the brain and the spinal cord; which control all other organs and systems of the body.
13. Responsible for the sense of smell.
14. The trait expressed.
15. Step three in mitosis.
16. Change of a gaseous substance to liquid form.
17. Temperature at which a substance changes from liquid to solid.
18. The transfer of energy via waves.
19. Step four in mitosis; occurs as nuclear membranes form around the chromosomes and disperse through the new nucleoplasm; spindle fibers also disappear.

A. Olfactory Lobe
B. Condensation
C. Translation
D. Cell Cycle
E. Glycolysis
F. Freezing Point
G. Neuron
H. Central Nervous System
I. Gene
J. Isotope
K. Vascular
L. Telophase
M. Phenotype
N. Structural Gene
O. Radiation
P. Specific Heat
Q. Aerobic
R. Biosphere
S. Anaphase

© 2017 Network4Learning, Inc.

1. *Find the hidden words. The words have been placed horizontally, vertically, or diagonally. When you locate a word, draw a circle around it.*

| S | Y | M | P | A | T | R | I | C | S | P | E | C | I | A | T | I | O | N | B |
|---|---|---|---|---|---|---|---|---|---|---|---|---|---|---|---|---|---|---|---|
| A | Q | L | Y | M | P | H | A | T | I | C | S | Y | S | T | E | M | W | N | A |
| N | E | A | O | Q | Y | F | Y | H | A | B | I | T | U | A | T | I | O | N | F |
| G | C | N | S | P | R | O | P | H | A | S | E | D | I | P | L | O | I | D | O |
| I | G | A | M | E | T | O | P | H | Y | T | E | W | O | R | K | Q | U | K | S |
| O | K | B | O | K | E | S | M | O | O | T | H | M | U | S | C | L | E | E | I |
| S | Z | O | S | V | A | N | D | E | R | W | A | A | L | S | F | O | R | C | E |
| P | K | L | I | G | R | H | E | N | D | O | T | H | E | R | M | I | C | B | K |
| E | F | I | S | E | H | E | C | A | R | D | I | A | C | M | U | S | C | L | E |
| R | A | S | P | U | Y | P | I | N | U | C | L | E | U | S | L | B | D | S | J |
| M | A | M | B | M | R | S | P | E | R | M | P | A | Q | A | I | S | N | I | Q |
| A | D | A | P | T | I | V | E | R | A | D | I | A | T | I | O | N | L | G | I |

1. Makes up the walls of internal organs and functions in involuntary movement. (breathing, etc.)
2. The principal infection-fighting component of the immune system.
3. The parent cell that has a normal set of paired chromosomes.
4. Produced by the male gametophyte; also known as a male gamete.
5. The process whereby cells build molecules and store energy.
6. A learned behavior where the organism produces less and less response as a stimulus is repeated, without a subsequent negative or positive action.
7. An organelle surrounded by two lipid bilayer membranes that is located near the center of the cell and contains chromosomes, nuclear pores, nucleoplasm, and nucleoli.
8. Genetically different members reproduce with each other, producing a population, which is separate from the original species.
9. Generated by the reproductive organs of the sporophyte through the process of meiosis.
10. Momentary force of attraction that exist between molecules and are much weaker than the forces of chemical bonding.
11. A special process of diffusion that occurs when the water concentration inside the cell differs from the concentration outside the cell.
12. Reactions that require energy.
13. A single species can develop into several diverse species over time; over time a species will specially adapt to live more effectively in a new environment.
14. Plants that produce flowers as reproductive organs.
15. Tissue forming the walls of the heart with strength and electrical properties that are vital to the heart's ability to pump blood.
16. The boundary between the nucleus and the cytoplasm.
17. The movement of mass over a distance.
18. The first phase in mitosis.
19. Notation that allow us to easily predict the results of a genetic cross.

A. Habituation
B. Diploid
C. Endothermic
D. Work
E. Punnett Square
F. Nuclear Membrane
G. Sperm
H. Anabolism
I. Nucleus
J. Sympatric Speciation
K. Smooth Muscle
L. Cardiac Muscle
M. Adaptive Radiation
N. Osmosis
O. Lymphatic System
P. Gametophyte
Q. Prophase
R. Angiosperm
S. Van der Waals Force

2. *Find the hidden words. The words have been placed horizontally, vertically, or diagonally. When you locate a word, draw a circle around it.*

| W | A | V | E | L | E | N | G | T | H | X | M | O | M | E | N | T | U | M | P |
|---|---|---|---|---|---|---|---|---|---|---|---|---|---|---|---|---|---|---|---|
| N | Z | U | X | Y | I | O | N | C | O | V | A | L | E | N | T | B | O | N | D |
| E | C | O | L | O | G | Y | N | A | Z | O | R | G | A | N | E | L | L | E | L |
| F | R | E | Q | U | E | N | C | Y | Z | Y | G | O | T | E | D | B | Y | C | A |
| B | Q | K | F | F | D | I | G | E | S | T | I | V | E | S | Y | S | T | E | M |
| P | L | K | P | D | Z | C | Y | T | O | S | K | E | L | E | T | O | N | M | N |
| P | O | P | U | L | A | T | I | O | N | D | E | N | S | I | T | Y | H | D | N |
| A | L | L | O | P | A | T | R | I | C | S | P | E | C | I | A | T | I | O | N |
| I | A | O | M | Q | S | P | C | D | I | F | F | U | S | I | O | N | C | Z | Q |
| N | U | C | L | E | O | L | U | S | B | E | T | A | D | E | C | A | Y | P | O |
| N | Y | J | P | C | O | N | D | I | T | I | O | N | I | N | G | N | G | A | A |
| N | A | T | U | R | A | L | S | E | L | E | C | T | I | O | N | B | D | H | D |

1. Provides structural support to a cell.
2. The number of individuals of a species living in an area.
3. Cell that results when a sperm cell fertilizes an egg cell.
4. The product of mass and velocity.
5. Cells components that perform functions.
6. Occurs when two populations are geographically isolated from each other.
7. Charged atom.
8. The process whereby molecules and ions flow through the cell membrane from an area of higher concentration to an area of lower concentration; mixing of particles in a gas or liquid.
9. Occurs when the nucleus emits a beta particle that degrades into an electron as it passes out of the atom.
10. Involves learning to apply an old response to a new stimulus.
11. The number of wavelengths that pass a point in a second.
12. Serves as a processing plant for ingested food.
13. Bond formed between the atoms when atoms share electrons.
14. A feature of population genetics that is the driving force behind evolution.
15. A rounded area within the nucleus of the cell where ribosomal RNA is synthesized.
16. Within a given area, there is a maximum level the population may reach at which it will continue to thrive.
17. The study of how organisms interact with other organisms and how they influence or are influenced by their physical environment.
18. The distance from one crest (or top) of a wave to the next crest on the same side.

A. Nucleolus
B. Covalent Bond
C. Cytoskeleton
D. Diffusion
E. Natural Selection
F. Wavelength
G. Ion
H. Ecology
I. Conditioning
J. Carrying Capacity
K. Digestive System
L. Population Density
M. Momentum
N. Allopatric Speciation
O. Beta Decay
P. Zygote
Q. Frequency
R. Organelle

© 2017 Network4Learning, Inc.

3. *Find the hidden words. The words have been placed horizontally, vertically, or diagonally. When you locate a word, draw a circle around it.*

| D | K | Q | Y | D | I | G | E | S | T | I | V | E | S | Y | S | T | E | M | M |
|---|---|---|---|---|---|---|---|---|---|---|---|---|---|---|---|---|---|---|---|
| A | T | V | N | U | C | L | E | A | R | M | E | M | B | R | A | N | E | F | D |
| C | E | L | L | C | Y | C | L | E | Y | U | B | K | I | M | Q | J | M | O | I |
| O | C | H | L | O | R | O | P | L | A | S | T | I | O | E | A | H | O | R | F |
| M | V | A | L | E | N | C | E | S | H | E | L | L | N | T | C | F | M | E | F |
| P | Z | W | W | M | I | T | O | S | I | S | B | F | I | A | P | W | E | B | U |
| O | Z | A | D | O | P | T | I | C | L | O | B | E | C | P | M | H | N | R | S |
| U | H | O | M | O | Z | Y | G | O | U | S | W | G | B | H | I | M | T | A | I |
| N | I | Z | D | I | V | I | S | I | O | N | D | Q | O | A | Z | X | U | I | O |
| D | S | P | E | C | I | F | I | C | H | E | A | T | N | S | T | P | M | N | N |
| T | X | Z | C | O | N | D | U | C | T | I | O | N | D | E | B | I | O | M | E |
| A | R | C | H | I | M | E | D | E | S | P | R | I | N | C | I | P | L | E | Z |

1. Visual center connected to the eyes by the optic nerves.
2. Step two of mitosis; occurs when the spindle fibers pull the chromosomes into alignment along the equatorial plane of the cell, creating the metaphase plate.
3. Distributes the remaining set of chromosomes in a mitosis-like process.
4. Movement of energy by transfer from particle to particle; can only occur when objects are touching.
5. The outermost occupied energy level of an element.
6. The site of photosynthesis within plant cells.
7. When an object is placed in a fluid, the object will have a buoyant force equal to the weight of the displaced fluid.
8. The measure of a substance's ability to retain energy.
9. Serves as a processing plant for ingested food.
10. The process whereby molecules and ions flow through the cell membrane from an area of higher concentration to an area of lower concentration; mixing of particles in a gas or liquid.
11. Located most anterior, it contains the olfactory lobes and cerebrum as well as the thalamus, hypothalamus, and pituitary gland.
12. The boundary between the nucleus and the cytoplasm.
13. A sequence of events ending in cell division, which produces two daughter cells.
14. the process by which a cell distributes its duplicated chromosomes so that each daughter cell has a full set of chromosomes.
15. When both alleles for a given gene are the same in an individual.
16. Bond of attraction between positive and negative ions.
17. An ecosystem that is generally defined by its climate characteristics.
18. The product of mass and velocity.
19. Formed when two or more different atoms bond together chemically to form a unique substance.

A. Ionic Bond
B. Valence Shell
C. Nuclear Membrane
D. Mitosis
E. Digestive System
F. Metaphase
G. Conduction
H. Diffusion
I. Biome
J. Forebrain
K. Cell Cycle
L. Specific Heat
M. Compound
N. Chloroplast
O. Optic Lobe
P. Homozygous
Q. Division
R. Momentum
S. Archimedes Principle

4. *Find the hidden words. The words have been placed horizontally, vertically, or diagonally. When you locate a word, draw a circle around it.*

| C | A | T | I | O | N | D | O | Y | N | E | R | V | E | T | I | S | S | U | E |
|---|---|---|---|---|---|---|---|---|---|---|---|---|---|---|---|---|---|---|---|
| Z | S | Y | X | I | H | H | P | J | H | A | B | I | T | U | A | T | I | O | N |
| K | J | P | A | S | S | L | T | M | F | D | H | X | A | B | E | M | G | B | C |
| G | I | I | P | X | W | C | I | H | O | M | O | L | O | G | O | U | S | F | T |
| E | T | J | Y | Y | B | F | C | Z | O | U | A | Y | V | E | B | D | G | O | A |
| A | L | V | E | O | L | I | L | R | W | O | R | G | A | N | I | S | M | O | X |
| E | R | G | X | X | O | L | O | R | G | E | A | A | S | C | U | S | E | D | O |
| M | Q | N | R | D | G | E | B | G | S | B | N | K | C | L | I | X | B | C | N |
| B | C | B | Q | S | F | Q | E | E | G | F | X | H | U | R | W | E | Y | H | O |
| R | A | T | O | M | I | C | N | U | M | B | E | R | L | L | Z | I | T | A | M |
| Y | O | N | L | C | L | R | K | N | V | K | E | A | A | I | J | D | Y | I | Y |
| O | Z | C | H | E | M | I | S | T | R | Y | M | B | R | M | O | L | G | N | M |

1. Study that organizes living things into groups based on morphology or, more recently, genetics.
2. Visual center connected to the eyes by the optic nerves.
3. An individual of a species.
4. Plants that have tissue organized in such a way as to conduct food and water throughout their structure.
5. The number of protons found in the nucleus of an atom of that element.
6. Positive ion.
7. A learned behavior where the organism produces less and less response as a stimulus is repeated, without a subsequent negative or positive action.
8. Thin-walled air sacs, which are the site of gas exchange.
9. What a zygote eventually grown into.
10. The allele that does not produce its trait when present with a dominant allele.
11. Momentary force of attraction that exist between molecules and are much weaker than the forces of chemical bonding.
12. Carry substances produced within the cell to the cell membrane; packets of material packaged by the Golgi apparatus or endoplasmic reticulum.
13. Structures that exist in two different species because they share a common ancestry.
14. Cells with no nucleus or any other membrane-bound organelles.
15. Energy generally flows through the entire ecosystem in one direction from producers to consumers and on to decomposers.
16. The study of matter.
17. The intentional alteration of genetic material of a living organism.
18. Carries electrical and chemical impulses to and from organs and limbs to the brain.

A. Embryo
B. Organism
C. Food Chain
D. Nerve Tissue
E. Secretory Vesicle
F. Vascular
G. Optic Lobe
H. Cation
I. Habituation
J. Homologous
K. Atomic Number
L. Van der Waals Force
M. Alveoli
N. Chemistry
O. Genetic Engineering
P. Recessive Allele
Q. Prokaryotic Cell
R. Taxonomy

© 2017 Network4Learning, Inc.

5. *Find the hidden words. The words have been placed horizontally, vertically, or diagonally. When you locate a word, draw a circle around it.*

| A | L | L | O | P | A | T | R | I | C | S | P | E | C | I | A | T | I | O | N |
|---|---|---|---|---|---|---|---|---|---|---|---|---|---|---|---|---|---|---|---|
| F | Y | M | K | C | A | P | I | L | L | A | R | Y | N | D | B | K | D | O | J |
| N | Q | Z | E | A | E | V | O | L | U | T | I | O | N | H | V | C | J | T | B |
| W | A | X | G | E | N | E | M | I | G | R | A | T | I | O | N | Y | L | E | I |
| I | E | L | E | C | T | R | O | N | C | L | O | U | D | R | T | G | Y | L | O |
| Y | Z | X | T | R | A | N | S | L | A | T | I | O | N | M | V | F | S | O | C |
| C | R | A | C | T | I | V | E | T | R | A | N | S | P | O | R | T | O | P | P |
| G | E | E | N | D | O | T | H | E | R | M | I | C | Z | N | W | M | S | H | H |
| F | F | C | E | L | L | M | E | M | B | R | A | N | E | E | P | H | O | A | E |
| A | L | Z | M | R | N | A | S | I | T | W | U | Z | P | S | H | A | M | S | R |
| H | E | B | R | M | C | H | A | L | F | L | I | F | E | K | L | I | E | E | E |
| A | X | D | Q | H | C | E | L | L | D | I | V | I | S | I | O | N | E | B | M |

1. The introduction of new genes from an immigrant, which results in a change of the gene pool.
2. Potential of hydrogen scale, which is a measurement of H+ ions in solutions.
3. Reactions that require energy.
4. Occurs when two populations are geographically isolated from each other.
5. Chemicals produced in the endocrine glands of an organism which modify metabolic activities.
6. The process of cell reproduction that centers on the replication and separation of strands of DNA.
7. An automatic movement of a body part in response to a stimulus.
8. Step four in mitosis; occurs as nuclear membranes form around the chromosomes and disperse through the new nucleoplasm; spindle fibers also disappear.
9. Tiny vessels that surround all tissues of the body and exchange carbon dioxide for oxygen.
10. The time it takes for 50 percent of an isotope to decay.
11. Structure that encloses the cell and separates it from the environment; also known as the plasma membrane.
12. Part of the Earth that includes all living things.
13. Uses energy to move molecules across a cell membrane against a concentration gradient.
14. Phase of photosynthesis that requires a second type of RNA.
15. Membrane-bound organelles containing digestive enzymes; digest unused material within the cell, damaged organelles, or materials absorbed by the cell for use.
16. RNA strand that migrates form the nucleus to the cytoplasm; also known as messenger RNA.
17. Three-dimensional space where electrons travel freely; also known as an electron shell or orbital.
18. The gradual change of characteristics within a population, producing a change in a species over time.

A. Endothermic  B. Electron Cloud  C. Active Transport  D. Telophase
E. Translation  F. Cell Division  G. Gene Migration  H. Allopatric Speciation
I. pH  J. Cell Membrane  K. Evolution  L. mRNA
M. Half Life  N. Reflex  O. Hormones  P. Biosphere
Q. Capillary  R. Lysosome

© 2017 Network4Learning, Inc.

6. *Find the hidden words. The words have been placed horizontally, vertically, or diagonally. When you locate a word, draw a circle around it.*

|   |   |   |   |   |   |   |   |   |   |   |   |   |   |   |   |
|---|---|---|---|---|---|---|---|---|---|---|---|---|---|---|---|
| I | I | C | V | A | N | D | E | R | W | A | A | L | S | F | O | R | C | E | G |
| E | G | O | R | C | S | V | E | U | E | X | T | I | N | C | T | I | O | N | C |
| N | C | N | Q | N | H | A | N | E | J | B | I | O | S | P | H | E | R | E | D |
| D | H | D | D | Y | Y | S | D | M | U | T | A | T | I | O | N | W | D | T | A |
| O | R | U | O | W | N | O | O | M | B | W | A | V | E | L | E | N | G | T | H |
| T | O | C | M | J | S | N | C | G | H | O | C | A | P | I | L | L | A | R | Y |
| H | M | T | A | L | T | I | Y | D | I | F | F | U | S | I | O | N | P | X | P |
| E | A | I | I | F | W | K | T | L | W | E | H | V | I | R | U | S | E | S | W |
| R | T | O | N | L | A | W | O | F | S | E | G | R | E | G | A | T | I | O | N |
| M | I | N | U | M | J | F | S | A | T | O | M | I | C | N | U | M | B | E | R |
| I | N | J | P | E | P | F | I | K | O | R | G | A | N | E | L | L | E | E | N |
| C | F | U | K | J | C | H | S | Z | M | S | P | U | O | V | A | R | Y | I | A |

1. The process whereby large molecules are taken up into a pocket of membrane; the pocket pinches off, delivering the molecules, still inside a membrane sack into the cytoplasm.
2. traits are expressed from a pair of genes in the individual (on homologous chromosomes).
3. The hollow, bulb-shaped structure in the lower interior of the pistil.
4. Movement of energy by transfer from particle to particle; can only occur when objects are touching.
5. A change of the DNA sequence of a gene, resulting in a change of the trait.
6. The number of protons found in the nucleus of an atom of that element.
7. Smaller than even the smallest cells; survive and replicate by invading a living cell.
8. The distance from one crest (or top) of a wave to the next crest on the same side.
9. Cells components that perform functions.
10. Part of the Earth that includes all living things.
11. The process whereby molecules and ions flow through the cell membrane from an area of higher concentration to an area of lower concentration; mixing of particles in a gas or liquid.
12. Momentary force of attraction that exist between molecules and are much weaker than the forces of chemical bonding.
13. Tiny vessels that surround all tissues of the body and exchange carbon dioxide for oxygen.
14. The combination of DNA with histones.
15. A crucial set of reactions that convert the light energy of the sun into chemical energy usable by living things.
16. When the entire population of a particular species is eliminated.
17. Classification category even more general than kingdoms.
18. Reactions that require energy.

A. Chromatin
B. Endocytosis
C. Extinction
D. Atomic Number
E. Domain
F. Photosynthesis
G. Van der Waals Force
H. Wavelength
I. Conduction
J. Diffusion
K. Law of Segregation
L. Capillary
M. Viruses
N. Mutation
O. Organelle
P. Biosphere
Q. Ovary
R. Endothermic

© 2017 Network4Learning, Inc.

7. *Find the hidden words. The words have been placed horizontally, vertically, or diagonally. When you locate a word, draw a circle around it.*

| C | R | G | I | P | A | N | A | B | O | L | I | S | M | A | I | G | Q | G | X |
|---|---|---|---|---|---|---|---|---|---|---|---|---|---|---|---|---|---|---|---|
| J | I | W | R | J | P | H | E | N | O | T | Y | P | E | V | N | Y | L | K | I |
| R | E | C | E | S | S | I | V | E | A | L | L | E | L | E | K | L | M | A | M |
| I | A | T | O | M | P | E | I | M | M | U | N | E | S | Y | S | T | E | M | P |
| U | D | L | S | A | F | V | E | I | N | F | R | E | Q | U | E | N | C | Y | R |
| H | E | L | E | C | T | R | O | N | C | L | O | U | D | Y | Y | G | Q | J | I |
| V | E | P | I | T | H | E | L | I | A | L | T | I | S | S | U | E | H | P | N |
| N | N | H | E | M | O | G | L | O | B | I | N | M | I | T | O | S | I | S | T |
| A | U | K | I | D | O | R | G | A | N | I | S | M | W | C | V | W | Q | S | I |
| F | U | I | G | W | A | V | E | L | E | N | G | T | H | K | E | L | M | B | N |
| P | O | P | U | L | A | T | I | O | N | D | E | N | S | I | T | Y | E | I | G |
| D | P | D | I | S | P | L | A | C | E | M | E | N | T | S | L | P | W | O | Q |

1. Functions to defend the body from infection by bacteria and viruses.
2. The trait expressed.
3. A learned behavior that develops in a critical or sensitive period of the animal's lifespan.
4. Forms the barrier between the environment and the interior of the body.
5. The number of individuals of a species living in an area.
6. Measures the change in position of an object, using the starting point and ending point and noting the direction.
7. Vessels that carry blood toward the heart.
8. The number of wavelengths that pass a point in a second.
9. The measure of how much matter exists in a volume.
10. The distance from one crest (or top) of a wave to the next crest on the same side.
11. Component of blood responsible for carrying oxygen.
12. Three-dimensional space where electrons travel freely; also known as an electron shell or orbital.
13. the process by which a cell distributes its duplicated chromosomes so that each daughter cell has a full set of chromosomes.
14. The allele that does not produce its trait when present with a dominant allele.
15. The simplest unit of an element that retains the element's characteristics.
16. An individual of a species.
17. The process whereby cells build molecules and store energy.
18. A rounded area within the nucleus of the cell where ribosomal RNA is synthesized.

A. Frequency  
B. Mitosis  
C. Nucleolus  
D. Hemoglobin  
E. Atom  
F. Phenotype  
G. Population Density  
H. Epithelial Tissue  
I. Imprinting  
J. Density  
K. Vein  
L. Electron Cloud  
M. Immune System  
N. Anabolism  
O. Displacement  
P. Recessive Allele  
Q. Wavelength  
R. Organism

8. *Find the hidden words. The words have been placed horizontally, vertically, or diagonally. When you locate a word, draw a circle around it.*

| C | C | D | O | U | X | W | E | L | E | C | T | R | O | N | C | L | O | U | D |
|---|---|---|---|---|---|---|---|---|---|---|---|---|---|---|---|---|---|---|---|
| Y | Y | O | V | Z | N | E | F | O | R | E | B | R | A | I | N | E | W | R | H |
| T | C | M | A | C | W | I | D | N | P | T | C | A | T | I | O | N | D | Y | K |
| O | Y | I | R | Y | Q | G | V | C | M | I | S | G | E | N | O | T | Y | P | E |
| S | T | N | Y | R | V | H | Q | I | N | V | E | R | T | E | B | R | A | T | E |
| K | O | A | C | R | H | T | F | G | A | L | P | H | A | D | E | C | A | Y | F |
| E | P | N | I | A | R | T | E | R | Y | H | I | N | D | B | R | A | I | N | N |
| L | L | C | R | X | H | D | I | F | F | R | A | C | T | I | O | N | V | J | T |
| E | A | E | C | G | C | O | N | D | U | C | T | I | O | N | I | T | E | Y | I |
| T | S | E | U | P | A | Z | H | V | I | R | U | S | E | S | Q | M | Q | Z | H |
| O | M | S | I | I | M | M | U | N | E | S | Y | S | T | E | M | L | P | G | W |
| N | J | F | T | A | A | W | P | X | C | O | M | P | E | T | I | T | I | O | N |

1. Provides structural support to a cell.
2. Consists of the cerebellum and medulla oblongata.
3. Region between the nucleus and cell membrane.
4. Movement of energy by transfer from particle to particle; can only occur when objects are touching.
5. Results when two or more species living within the same area and that overlap niches both require a resource that is in limited supply.
6. The hollow, bulb-shaped structure in the lower interior of the pistil.
7. Occurs when the nucleus of an atom emits a package of two protons and two neutrons, called an alpha particle, which is equivalent to the nucleus of a helium atom.
8. Occurs when older, more established individuals compete for status within the community.
9. The force of gravity acting upon that object.
10. The path that an electrical current follows.
11. The bending of a light wave around an obstacle.
12. The combination of alleles that make a particular trait.
13. Smaller than even the smallest cells; survive and replicate by invading a living cell.
14. Three-dimensional space where electrons travel freely; also known as an electron shell or orbital.
15. Functions to defend the body from infection by bacteria and viruses.
16. Larger vessels that carry blood away from the heart.
17. Positive ion.
18. Those species having no internal backbone structure.
19. Located most anterior, it contains the olfactory lobes and cerebrum as well as the thalamus, hypothalamus, and pituitary gland.

A. Forebrain
B. Viruses
C. Electron Cloud
D. Cytoplasm
E. Weight
F. Dominance
G. Immune System
H. Circuit
I. Ovary
J. Competition
K. Hindbrain
L. Artery
M. Cytoskeleton
N. Diffraction
O. Invertebrate
P. Genotype
Q. Alpha Decay
R. Cation
S. Conduction

© 2017 Network4Learning, Inc.

9. *Find the hidden words. The words have been placed horizontally, vertically, or diagonally. When you locate a word, draw a circle around it.*

| O | V | A | R | Y | U | Y | V | P | V | G | E | N | E | P | O | O | L | W | Y |
|---|---|---|---|---|---|---|---|---|---|---|---|---|---|---|---|---|---|---|---|
| X | P | D | I | F | F | U | S | I | O | N | I | O | N | I | C | B | O | N | D |
| B | A | K | Y | B | L | T | R | A | N | S | C | R | I | P | T | I | O | N | J |
| M | H | D | K | E | V | H | I | N | D | B | R | A | I | N | E | E | C | U | B |
| P | L | C | W | A | T | S | O | N | C | R | I | C | K | M | O | D | E | L | C |
| R | P | S | M | I | T | O | C | H | O | N | D | R | I | A | D | Y | N | L | I |
| Q | N | U | C | L | E | O | L | U | S | R | P | M | E | I | O | S | I | S | R |
| F | D | I | V | I | S | I | O | N | N | Y | X | I | S | O | T | O | P | E | C |
| S | D | E | V | O | L | U | T | I | O | N | A | J | N | H | W | V | D | D | U |
| Z | Z | T | Q | N | E | R | V | O | U | S | S | Y | S | T | E | M | M | A | I |
| I | N | N | A | T | E | B | E | H | A | V | I | O | R | S | U | I | L | M | T |
| J | K | A | C | T | I | V | E | T | R | A | N | S | P | O | R | T | S | V | C |

1. Named after scientists who discovered and modeled the structure of DNA.
2. A rounded area within the nucleus of the cell where ribosomal RNA is synthesized.
3. Uses energy to move molecules across a cell membrane against a concentration gradient.
4. Atoms with the same number of protons by different numbers of neutrons.
5. The path that an electrical current follows.
6. The formation of an RNA molecule, which corresponds to a gene.
7. Center of cellular respiration
8. Consists of the cerebellum and medulla oblongata.
9. The hollow, bulb-shaped structure in the lower interior of the pistil.
10. Bond of attraction between positive and negative ions.
11. Distributes the remaining set of chromosomes in a mitosis-like process.
12. The entire collection of genes within a given population.
13. The actions in animals we call instincts; highly stereotyped.
14. The gradual change of characteristics within a population, producing a change in a species over time.
15. A communication network that connects the entire body of an organism and provides control over bodily functions.
16. The process whereby molecules and ions flow through the cell membrane from an area of higher concentration to an area of lower concentration; mixing of particles in a gas or liquid.
17. The process of producing four daughter cells, each with single unduplicated chromosomes.
18. Momentary force of attraction that exist between molecules and are much weaker than the forces of chemical bonding.

A. Van der Waals Force
B. Innate Behaviors
C. Transcription
D. Active Transport
E. Gene Pool
F. Ovary
G. Nucleolus
H. Evolution
I. Mitochondria
J. Diffusion
K. Circuit
L. Nervous System
M. Ionic Bond
N. Isotope
O. Hindbrain
P. Meiosis
Q. Division
R. Watson Crick Model

© 2017 Network4Learning, Inc.

10. *Find the hidden words. The words have been placed horizontally, vertically, or diagonally. When you locate a word, draw a circle around it.*

| F | O | R | E | B | R | A | I | N | C | A | T | A | B | O | L | I | S | M | Y |
|---|---|---|---|---|---|---|---|---|---|---|---|---|---|---|---|---|---|---|---|
| Y | W | T | E | M | P | E | R | A | T | U | R | E | P | N | F | R | W | H | L |
| C | Z | T | S | C | E | G | A | T | P | V | M | P | E | Z | T | U | E | Q | V |
| H | W | C | L | D | O | L | F | A | C | T | O | R | Y | L | O | B | E | N | I |
| R | L | A | W | O | F | S | E | G | R | E | G | A | T | I | O | N | L | F | G |
| O | P | J | A | M | F | Q | Y | Z | Y | G | O | T | E | I | B | C | E | L | L |
| M | C | M | E | A | N | H | C | G | G | M | I | T | O | S | I | S | G | O | Y |
| A | D | R | D | I | F | C | E | L | L | M | E | M | B | R | A | N | E | D | R |
| T | Z | S | I | N | O | N | E | R | V | O | U | S | S | Y | S | T | E | M | K |
| I | N | E | U | R | O | N | C | E | R | E | B | E | L | L | U | M | U | D | O |
| D | O | L | M | V | G | P | V | Q | O | R | G | A | N | E | L | L | E | W | W |
| V | E | I | N | V | I | L | L | I | G | Q | A | N | A | P | H | A | S | E | R |

1. Structure that encloses the cell and separates it from the environment; also known as the plasma membrane.
2. Protrusions out into the lumen of the intestine that provide a large surface area for absorption of nutrients.
3. Classification category even more general than kingdoms.
4. Step three in mitosis.
5. Energy currency of cellular activity; consists of a nitrogenous base (adenine), a simple sugar (ribose), and three phosphate groups.
6. Carry impulses via electrochemical responses.
7. Part of the brain that controls balance, equilibrium, and muscle coordination.
8. A communication network that connects the entire body of an organism and provides control over bodily functions.
9. Vessels that carry blood toward the heart.
10. Cell that results when a sperm cell fertilizes an egg cell.
11. Located most anterior, it contains the olfactory lobes and cerebrum as well as the thalamus, hypothalamus, and pituitary gland.
12. Process of breaking down molecules and releasing stored energy.
13. Cells components that perform functions.
14. the process by which a cell distributes its duplicated chromosomes so that each daughter cell has a full set of chromosomes.
15. The two identical strands of duplicated chromatin in a cell that is getting ready to divide.
16. Class of lymphocyte cell that emerge from the bone marrow mature and produce antibodies, which enter the bloodstream.
17. The measure of the average kinetic energy of a substance.
18. traits are expressed from a pair of genes in the individual (on homologous chromosomes).
19. Responsible for the sense of smell.

A. ATP
B. Forebrain
C. Catabolism
D. Temperature
E. Nervous System
F. Cell Membrane
G. Neuron
H. Domain
I. Organelle
J. Mitosis
K. Anaphase
L. Law of Segregation
M. Cerebellum
N. Zygote
O. Villi
P. B Cell
Q. Olfactory Lobe
R. Vein
S. Chromatid

© 2017 Network4Learning, Inc.

**11.** *Find the hidden words. The words have been placed horizontally, vertically, or diagonally. When you locate a word, draw a circle around it.*

| J | T | Q | C | E | L | L | M | E | M | B | R | A | N | E | R | V | I | F | Z |
|---|---|---|---|---|---|---|---|---|---|---|---|---|---|---|---|---|---|---|---|
| | M | I | T | O | S | I | S | J | H | N | D | K | F | I | G | E | H | N | G | E |
| E | V | A | P | O | R | A | T | I | O | N | P | X | P | T | F | I | T | A | X |
| H | A | B | I | T | U | A | T | I | O | N | R | R | A | L | S | E | M | T |
| 7 | S | O | R | G | A | N | E | L | L | E | E | Q | T | K | E | T | R | E | I |
| E | N | E | R | G | Y | C | Y | C | L | E | S | Z | Y | C | C | O | P | T | N |
| M | A | C | T | I | V | E | T | R | A | N | S | P | O | R | T | N | H | O | C |
| U | G | Y | N | A | P | Z | S | S | F | V | U | U | G | A | I | E | A | P | T |
| I | C | Q | X | G | E | N | E | M | I | G | R | A | T | I | O | N | S | H | I |
| J | W | O | R | K | Y | B | D | E | P | P | E | S | Q | D | N | W | E | Y | O |
| L | P | H | O | T | O | S | Y | N | T | H | E | S | I | S | F | B | G | T | N |
| U | E | L | E | C | T | R | O | N | T | R | A | N | S | P | O | R | T | E | T |

1. Generated by the reproductive organs of the sporophyte through the process of meiosis.
2. the process by which a cell distributes its duplicated chromosomes so that each daughter cell has a full set of chromosomes.
3. A measure of the amount of force applied per unit of area.
4. The introduction of new genes from an immigrant, which results in a change of the gene pool.
5. The movement of mass over a distance.
6. The second step of aerobic respiration that captures the energy created by the release of electrons from the Krebs cycle.
7. Escape of individual particles of a substance into gaseous form.
8. Supports life throughout the environment.
9. The bouncing of a wave of light off an object.
10. Cells components that perform functions.
11. A crucial set of reactions that convert the light energy of the sun into chemical energy usable by living things.
12. When the entire population of a particular species is eliminated.
13. A learned behavior where the organism produces less and less response as a stimulus is repeated, without a subsequent negative or positive action.
14. Uses energy to move molecules across a cell membrane against a concentration gradient.
15. Short length of DNA wrapped around a core of small proteins.
16. Structure that encloses the cell and separates it from the environment; also known as the plasma membrane.
17. A single species can develop into several diverse species over time; over time a species will specially adapt to live more effectively in a new environment.
18. the period when the cell is active in carrying on its functions.

A. Evaporation
B. Energy Cycle
C. Work
D. Electron Transport
E. Extinction
F. Photosynthesis
G. Active Transport
H. Histone
I. Interphase
J. Organelle
K. Mitosis
L. Adaptive Radiation
M. Pressure
N. Gene Migration
O. Cell Membrane
P. Gametophyte
Q. Reflection
R. Habituation

12. *Find the hidden words. The words have been placed horizontally, vertically, or diagonally. When you locate a word, draw a circle around it.*

| W | L | S | I | R | Y | X | A | I | M | W | M | E | C | H | A | N | I | C | S |
|---|---|---|---|---|---|---|---|---|---|---|---|---|---|---|---|---|---|---|---|
| G | S | S | W | A | T | S | O | N | C | R | I | C | K | M | O | D | E | L | H |
| C | O | N | N | E | C | T | I | V | E | T | I | S | S | U | E | R | U | R | C |
| O | E | L | E | P | I | T | H | E | L | I | A | L | T | I | S | S | U | E | R |
| C | J | Y | I | V | V | H | R | Z | H | O | R | M | O | N | E | S | F | U |
| N | L | H | M | Q | X | P | A | T | O | M | I | C | M | A | S | S | R | R | Z |
| D | C | R | S | I | Z | Y | V | E | F | Q | D | M | B | J | B | T | C | A | U |
| Z | S | C | C | S | N | C | T | B | M | E | T | A | P | H | A | S | E | C | G |
| K | U | A | W | M | I | M | P | R | I | N | T | I | N | G | X | F | H | T | P |
| K | Q | S | K | E | L | E | T | A | L | M | U | S | C | L | E | P | I | I | Z |
| E | N | Z | Y | M | E | Z | P | T | R | C | E | L | L | W | A | L | L | O | W |
| A | R | T | E | R | Y | I | L | E | R | E | A | C | T | A | N | T | S | N | C |

1. Those species having no internal backbone structure.
2. The change in direction of a wave as it passes from one medium to another.
3. Holds tissues and organs together, stabilizing the body structure.
4. Reacting molecules.
5. The study of things in motion.
6. Carry impulses from body surface to the CNS.
7. Carry impulses to skeletal muscle from the CNS.
8. Forms the barrier between the environment and the interior of the body.
9. Named after scientists who discovered and modeled the structure of DNA.
10. Calculated by adding up the masses of the protons and neutrons.
11. Chemicals produced in the endocrine glands of an organism which modify metabolic activities.
12. Protein molecules that act as catalysts for organic reactions.
13. A learned behavior that develops in a critical or sensitive period of the animal's lifespan.
14. Made of cellulose and lignin, they enclose the cell membrane providing strength and protection for the cell.
15. Makes up the walls of internal organs and functions in involuntary movement. (breathing, etc.)
16. Larger vessels that carry blood away from the heart.
17. Attaches bones of the skeleton to each other and surrounding tissues, which enables voluntary movement.
18. Within a given area, there is a maximum level the population may reach at which it will continue to thrive.
19. Step two of mitosis; occurs when the spindle fibers pull the chromosomes into alignment along the equatorial plane of the cell, creating the metaphase plate.

A. Invertebrate
B. Refraction
C. Cell Wall
D. Atomic Mass
E. Enzyme
F. Imprinting
G. Metaphase
H. Skeletal Muscle
I. Carrying Capacity
J. Epithelial Tissue
K. Connective Tissue
L. Artery
M. Hormones
N. Reactants
O. Watson Crick Model
P. Mechanics
Q. Somatic Motor Nerve
R. Smooth Muscle
S. Somatic Sensory Nerve

13. *Find the hidden words. The words have been placed horizontally, vertically, or diagonally. When you locate a word, draw a circle around it.*

| G | D | E | N | S | I | T | Y | S | N | D | P | E | N | D | O | D | E | R | M |
|---|---|---|---|---|---|---|---|---|---|---|---|---|---|---|---|---|---|---|---|
| C | A | R | D | I | A | C | M | U | S | C | L | E | Z | W | B | J | E | Q | L |
| H | V | D | I | V | I | S | I | O | N | M | O | L | A | R | M | A | S | S | Y |
| A | A | E | L | E | C | T | R | I | C | A | L | C | U | R | R | E | N | T | S |
| L | S | P | T | O | B | F | T | Q | V | E | R | T | E | B | R | A | T | E | O |
| F | C | A | D | I | P | O | S | E | T | I | S | S | U | E | P | W | C | M | S |
| L | U | J | M | P | E | R | I | O | D | I | C | T | A | B | L | E | Q | O |
| I | L | S | C | M | P | O | S | I | T | R | O | N | D | E | C | A | Y | B | M |
| F | A | R | L | A | W | O | F | I | N | E | R | T | I | A | U | H | E | E | E |
| E | R | B | M | T | C | Y | T | O | S | K | E | L | E | T | O | N | W | X | J |
| A | E | R | O | B | I | C | G | R | E | G | O | R | M | E | N | D | E | L | F |
| F | F | T | R | A | N | S | L | A | T | I | O | N | B | C | E | L | L | Z | A |

1. A particle at rest will stay at rest and a particle in motion will stay in motion until acted upon by an outside force.
2. The precursor of the gut lining and various accessory structures.
3. Distributes the remaining set of chromosomes in a mitosis-like process.
4. Species that have internal backbones.
5. Occurs when the nucleus emits a particle that degrades into a positron as it passes out of the atom.
6. Listing of elements by atomic number.
7. Steps in the cellular respiration process that require oxygen.
8. Tissue forming the walls of the heart with strength and electrical properties that are vital to the heart's ability to pump blood.
9. The measure of how much matter exists in a volume.
10. Studied the relationships between traits expressed in parents and offspring and the hereditary factors that caused expression of traits.
11. Phase of photosynthesis that requires a second type of RNA.
12. A flow of electrons through a conductor.
13. Found beneath the skin and around organs, providing cushioning, insulation, and fat storage.
14. The time it takes for 50 percent of an isotope to decay.
15. Provides structural support to a cell.
16. Plants that have tissue organized in such a way as to conduct food and water throughout their structure.
17. The mass in grams of one mole of atoms.
18. Membrane-bound organelles containing digestive enzymes; digest unused material within the cell, damaged organelles, or materials absorbed by the cell for use.
19. Class of lymphocyte cell that emerge from the bone marrow mature and produce antibodies, which enter the bloodstream.

A. Cytoskeleton
B. Vertebrate
C. Half Life
D. Lysosome
E. Aerobic
F. Cardiac Muscle
G. Vascular
H. Division
I. Endoderm
J. Law of Inertia
K. B Cell
L. Gregor Mendel
M. Molar Mass
N. Electrical Current
O. Adipose Tissue
P. Density
Q. Positron Decay
R. Translation
S. Periodic Table

© 2017 Network4Learning, Inc.

14. *Find the hidden words. The words have been placed horizontally, vertically, or diagonally. When you locate a word, draw a circle around it.*

| A | T | M | O | S | P | H | E | R | I | C | P | R | E | S | S | U | R | E | P |
|---|---|---|---|---|---|---|---|---|---|---|---|---|---|---|---|---|---|---|---|
| L | Y | K | Y | F | S | A | P | C | E | L | L | D | I | V | I | S | I | O | N |
| S | A | U | J | A | Z | N | Z | C | O | V | A | L | E | N | T | B | O | N | D |
| Y | H | P | O | L | Y | G | E | N | I | C | T | R | A | I | T | G | T | P | C |
| M | A | I | N | W | H | I | L | A | W | O | F | I | N | E | R | T | I | A | H |
| B | L | O | J | A | T | O | M | A | M | E | T | A | P | H | A | S | E | S | R |
| I | F | Z | T | R | N | S | V | H | O | M | E | O | S | T | A | S | I | S | O |
| O | L | W | G | D | N | P | E | D | E | N | D | O | D | E | R | M | A | H | M |
| S | I | E | C | C | M | E | I | B | D | I | P | L | O | I | D | S | D | K | A |
| I | F | R | L | T | X | R | N | H | A | P | L | O | I | D | R | Q | Q | W | T |
| S | E | S | D | T | A | M | C | M | U | T | A | T | I | O | N | Y | R | Y | I |
| L | B | C | D | N | F | N | W | Y | Z | O | M | F | B | V | P | K | Z | I | D |

1. Vessels that carry blood toward the heart.
2. When two species interact with each other within the same range.
3. Single unduplicated chromosomes.
4. Plants that produce flowers as reproductive organs.
5. Traits produced from integration of multiple sets of genes.
6. Bond formed between the atoms when atoms share electrons.
7. The two identical strands of duplicated chromatin in a cell that is getting ready to divide.
8. A particle at rest will stay at rest and a particle in motion will stay in motion until acted upon by an outside force.
9. The parent cell that has a normal set of paired chromosomes.
10. The simplest unit of an element that retains the element's characteristics.
11. The time it takes for 50 percent of an isotope to decay.
12. A state of dynamic equilibrium, which balances forces tending toward change with forces acceptable for life functions.
13. Step two of mitosis; occurs when the spindle fibers pull the chromosomes into alignment along the equatorial plane of the cell, creating the metaphase plate.
14. The process of cell reproduction that centers on the replication and separation of strands of DNA.
15. Pressure that results from the total weight of the atmosphere exerting force on the Earth; can be measured with a barometer.
16. A change of the DNA sequence of a gene, resulting in a change of the trait.
17. Temperature at which a substance changes from liquid to solid.
18. The precursor of the gut lining and various accessory structures.

A. Atmospheric Pressure
B. Angiosperm
C. Homeostasis
D. Endoderm
E. Atom
F. Diploid
G. Symbiosis
H. Metaphase
I. Freezing Point
J. Covalent Bond
K. Mutation
L. Polygenic Trait
M. Chromatid
N. Haploid
O. Law of Inertia
P. Half Life
Q. Cell Division
R. Vein

© 2017 Network4Learning, Inc.

15. *Find the hidden words. The words have been placed horizontally, vertically, or diagonally. When you locate a word, draw a circle around it.*

| R | G | G | W | S | P | E | C | I | F | I | C | H | E | A | T | Z | W | G | K |
|---|---|---|---|---|---|---|---|---|---|---|---|---|---|---|---|---|---|---|---|
| A | K | K | F | R | E | E | Z | I | N | G | P | O | I | N | T | T | K | Z | F |
| D | G | K | E | A | T | R | A | N | S | L | A | T | I | O | N | E | C | Z | Q |
| I | V | A | W | M | Y | X | B | I | O | S | P | H | E | R | E | L | E | Z | A |
| A | A | S | T | R | U | C | T | U | R | A | L | G | E | N | E | O | L | S | N |
| T | S | B | D | Q | R | H | P | H | E | N | O | T | Y | P | E | P | L | U | A |
| I | C | P | C | O | N | D | E | N | S | A | T | I | O | N | H | C | Q | P |
| O | U | G | L | Y | C | O | L | Y | S | I | S | L | S | O | C | A | Y | G | H |
| N | L | A | E | R | O | B | I | C | F | X | D | V | D | L | Y | S | C | E | A |
| U | A | O | L | F | A | C | T | O | R | Y | L | O | B | E | I | E | L | N | S |
| C | R | B | A | N | E | U | R | O | N | I | S | O | T | O | P | E | E | E | E |
| C | E | N | T | R | A | L | N | E | R | V | O | U | S | S | Y | S | T | E | M |

1. Plants that have tissue organized in such a way as to conduct food and water throughout their structure.
2. Atoms with the same number of protons by different numbers of neutrons.
3. Steps in the cellular respiration process that require oxygen.
4. The breaking down of the six-carbon sugar (glucose) into smaller carbon-containing molecules yielding ATP.
5. Length of DNA that encodes a particular protein.
6. Part of the Earth that includes all living things.
7. A sequence of events ending in cell division, which produces two daughter cells.
8. Phase of photosynthesis that requires a second type of RNA.
9. Code proteins that form organs and structural characteristics.
10. The measure of a substance's ability to retain energy.
11. Carry impulses via electrochemical responses.
12. Two main components, the brain and the spinal cord; which control all other organs and systems of the body.
13. Responsible for the sense of smell.
14. The trait expressed.
15. Step three in mitosis.
16. Change of a gaseous substance to liquid form.
17. Temperature at which a substance changes from liquid to solid.
18. The transfer of energy via waves.
19. Step four in mitosis; occurs as nuclear membranes form around the chromosomes and disperse through the new nucleoplasm; spindle fibers also disappear.

A. Olfactory Lobe
B. Condensation
C. Translation
D. Cell Cycle
E. Glycolysis
F. Freezing Point
G. Neuron
H. Central Nervous System
I. Gene
J. Isotope
K. Vascular
L. Telophase
M. Phenotype
N. Structural Gene
O. Radiation
P. Specific Heat
Q. Aerobic
R. Biosphere
S. Anaphase

© 2017 Network4Learning, Inc.

# Glossary

Acid: A chemical that donates proton (H+ ions) when dissolved in water.

Active Transport: Uses energy to move molecules across a cell membrane against a concentration gradient.

Adaptive Radiation: A single species can develop into several diverse species over time; over time a species will specially adapt to live more effectively in a new environment.

Adipose Tissue: Found beneath the skin and around organs, providing cushioning, insulation, and fat storage.

Aerobic: Steps in the cellular respiration process that require oxygen.

Allopatric Speciation: Occurs when two populations are geographically isolated from each other.

Alpha Decay: Occurs when the nucleus of an atom emits a package of two protons and two neutrons, called an alpha particle, which is equivalent to the nucleus of a helium atom.

Alveoli: Thin-walled air sacs, which are the site of gas exchange.

Anabolism: The process whereby cells build molecules and store energy.

Anaerobic: Steps in the cellular respiration process that do not require oxygen.

Analogous: Structures that are similar because of their common function, although they do not share a common ancestry.

Anaphase: Step three in mitosis.

Angiosperm: Plants that produce flowers as reproductive organs.

Anion: Negative ion.

Archimedes Principle: When an object is placed in a fluid, the object will have a buoyant force equal to the weight of the displaced fluid.

Artery: Larger vessels that carry blood away from the heart.

Atmospheric Pressure: Pressure that results from the total weight of the atmosphere exerting force on the Earth; can be measured with a barometer.

Atom: The simplest unit of an element that retains the element's characteristics.

Atomic Mass: Calculated by adding up the masses of the protons and neutrons.

Atomic Number : The number of protons found in the nucleus of an atom of that element.

Atomic Weight: The average mass number.

ATP: Energy currency of cellular activity; consists of a nitrogenous base (adenine), a simple sugar (ribose), and three phosphate groups.

B Cell: Class of lymphocyte cell that emerge from the bone marrow mature and produce antibodies, which enter the bloodstream.

Base: A chemical that accepts protons (H+ ions) when dissolved in water.

Beta Decay: Occurs when the nucleus emits a beta particle that degrades into an electron as it passes out of the atom.

Biogeography: The study of how photosynthetic organisms and animals are distributed in a particular location plus the history of their distribution in the past.

Biome: An ecosystem that is generally defined by its climate characteristics.

Biosphere: Part of the Earth that includes all living things.

Blood Tissue: Flows through the blood vessels and heart and is essential for carrying oxygen to cells, fighting infection, and carrying nutrients and wastes to and from cells.

Boiling Point: Temperature at which a substance changes from liquid to gas.

Capillary: Tiny vessels that surround all tissues of the body and exchange carbon dioxide for oxygen.

Cardiac Muscle: Tissue forming the walls of the heart with strength and electrical properties that are vital to the heart's ability to pump blood.

Carrying Capacity: Within a given area, there is a maximum level the population may reach at which it will continue to thrive.

Cartilage Tissue: Reduces friction between bones and supports and connects them.

Catabolism: Process of breaking down molecules and releasing stored energy.

Catalyst: A substance that changes the speed of a reaction without being affected itself.

Cation: Positive ion.

Cell: The smallest and most basic unit of most living things.

Cell Cycle: A particular sequence of events ending in cell division, which produces two daughter cells.

Cell Division: The process of cell reproduction that centers on the replication and separation of strands of DNA.

Cell Membrane: Structure that encloses the cell and separates it from the environment; also known as the plasma membrane.

Cell Wall: Made of cellulose and lignin, they enclose the cell membrane providing strength and protection for the cell.

Cellular Metabolism: A general term that includes all types of energy transformation processes, including photosynthesis, respiration, growth, movement, etc.

Central Nervous System : Two main components, the brain and the spinal cord; which control all other organs and systems of the body.

Cerebellum: Part of the brain that controls balance, equilibrium, and muscle coordination.

Cerebrum: Part of the brain that controls sensory and motor responses, memory, speech, and most factors of intelligence.

Chemistry: The study of matter.

Chlorophyll: Pigment molecules that give the chloroplast their green color.

Chloroplast: The site of photosynthesis within plant cells.

Chromatid: The two identical strands of duplicated chromatin in a cell that is getting ready to divide.

Chromatin: The combination of DNA with histones.

Circuit The path that an electrical current follows.

Circulatory System: The conduit for delivering nutrients and gases to all cells and for removing waste products from them.

Community: Populations that interact with each other in a particular ecosystem.

Competition: Results when two or more species living within the same area and that overlap niches both require a resource that is in limited supply.

Compound: Formed when two or more different atoms bond together chemically to form a unique substance.

Condensation: Change of a gaseous substance to liquid form.

Conditioning: Involves learning to apply an old response to a new stimulus.

Conduction: Movement of energy by transfer from particle to particle; can only occur when objects are touching.

Connective Tissue: Holds tissues and organs together, stabilizing the body structure.

Cortex: A ring inside the epidermis that is made up of large parenchyma cells.

Covalent Bond: Bond formed between the atoms when atoms share electrons.

Cytoplasm: Region between the nucleus and cell membrane.

Cytoskeleton: Provides structural support to a cell.

Density: The measure of how much matter exists in a given volume.

Differential Reproduction: Individuals within a population that are most adapted to the environment and are also the most likely individuals to reproduce successfully.

Diffraction: The bending of a light wave around an obstacle.

Diffusion: The process whereby molecules and ions flow through the cell membrane from an area of higher concentration to an area of lower concentration; mixing of particles in a gas or liquid.

Digestion: Breakdown of ingested particles into molecules that can be absorbed by the body.

Digestive System: Serves as a processing plant for ingested food.

Diploid: The parent cell that has a normal set of paired chromosomes.

Dispersion: Process in which a species may move in or out of a particular area over the course of time.

Displacement: Measures the change in position of an object, using the starting point and ending point and noting the direction.

Division: Distributes the remaining set of chromosomes in a mitosis-like process.

Domain: Classification category even more general than kingdoms.

Dominance: Occurs when older, more established individuals compete for status within the community.

Dominant Allele: An allele that masks the effect of its partner allele.

Ecology: The study of how organisms interact with other organisms and how they influence or are influenced by their physical environment.

Ecosystem: A group of populations found within a given locality, plus the inanimate environment around those populations.

Egg: Cell Produced by the female gametophyte; also referred to as a female gamete.

Electrical Current: A flow of electrons through a conductor.

Electron Cloud: Three-dimensional space where electrons travel freely; also known as an electron shell or orbital.

Electron Transport: The second step of aerobic respiration that captures the energy created by the release of electrons from the Krebs cycle.

Element: A substance that cannot be broken down into any other substances.

Embryo: What a zygote eventually grown into.

Emigration: Permanent one way movement out of the original range.

Endocytosis: The process whereby large molecules are taken up into a pocket of membrane; the pocket pinches off, delivering the molecules, still inside a membrane sack into the cytoplasm.

Endoderm: The precursor of the gut lining and various accessory structures.

Endoplasmic Reticulum: Large organization of folded membranes; responsible for the delivery of lipids and proteins to certain areas within the cytoplasm.

Endothermic: Reactions that require energy.

Energy Cycle: Supports life throughout the environment.

Enzyme: Protein molecules that act as catalysts for organic reactions.

Epithelial Tissue: Forms the barrier between the environment and the interior of the body.

Eukaryotic Cell: Cells that contain membrane-bound intracellular organelles, including a nucleus.

Evaporation: Escape of individual particles of a substance into gaseous form.

Evolution: The gradual change of characteristics within a population, producing a change in a species over time.

Excretory System: Responsible for collecting waste materials and transporting them to organs that expel them from the body.

Exocytosis: The export of substances from the cell.

Exothermic: Reactions that release energy.

Extinction: When the entire population of a particular species is eliminated.

Facilitated Diffusion: Allows for the transfer of substances across the cell membrane with the help of specialized proteins.

Fermentation: Another name for anaerobic respiration, which breaks down the two pyruvic acid molecules into end products (such as ethyl alcohol, or lactic acid), plus carbon dioxide.

Fertilization: occurs when two haploid cells join to form a diploid cell.

Flower: The primary reproductive organ for a plant.

Food Chain: Energy generally flows through the entire ecosystem in one direction from producers to consumers and on to decomposers.

Force: The push or pull exerted on an object.

Forebrain: Located most anterior, it contains the olfactory lobes and cerebrum as well as the thalamus, hypothalamus, and pituitary gland.

Freezing Point: Temperature at which a substance changes from liquid to solid.

Frequency: The number of wavelengths that pass a point in a second.

Friction: The rubbing force that acts against motion between two touching surfaces.

Gamete : The four haploid cells (egg and sperm) that are found in reproductive organs as a result of meiosis.

Gametophyte: Generated by the reproductive organs of the sporophyte through the process of meiosis.

Gamma Radiation: Consists of gamma rays, which are high-frequency, high-energy, electromagnetic radiation that are usually given off in combination with alpha and beta decay.

Gene: Length of DNA that encodes a particular protein.

Gene Migration: The introduction of new genes from an immigrant, which results in a change of the gene pool.

Gene Pool: The entire collection of genes within a given population.

Genetic Drift: Over time, a gene pool (particularly in a small population) may experience a change in frequency of particular genes simply due to change fluctuations.

Genetic Engineering: The intentional alteration of genetic material of a living organism.

Genome: Sum total of genetic information.

Genotype: The combination of alleles that make a particular trait.

Glycolysis: The breaking down of the six-carbon sugar (glucose) into smaller carbon-containing molecules yielding ATP.

Golgi Apparatus: Instrumental in the storing, packaging, and shipping of proteins; also known as Golgi bodies or the Golgi complex.

Gregor Mendel: Studied the relationships between traits expressed in parents and offspring and the hereditary factors that caused expression of traits.

Gymnosperm: Plants that produce seeds without flowers.

Habitat: The physical place where a species lives.

Habituation: A learned behavior where the organism produces less and less response as a stimulus is repeated, without a subsequent negative or positive action.

Half Life: The time it takes for 50 percent of an isotope to decay.

Haploid: Single unduplicated chromosomes.

Heat: Energy that flows from an object that is warm to an object that is cooler.

Hemoglobin: Component of blood responsible for carrying oxygen.

Heterozygous: When the two alleles for a given gene are different in an individual.

Hindbrain: Consists of the cerebellum and medulla oblongata.

Histone: Short length of DNA wrapped around a core of small proteins.

Homeostasis: A state of dynamic equilibrium, which balances forces tending toward change with forces acceptable for life functions.

Homologous: Structures that exist in two different species because they share a common ancestry.

Homozygous: When both alleles for a given gene are the same in an individual.

Hormones: Chemicals produced in the endocrine glands of an organism which modify metabolic activities.

Hydrogen Bond: Occurs when a hydrogen atom is involved with a polar intermolecular attraction to a more electronegative atom.

Hypothalamus: Involved in hunger, thirst, blood pressure, body temperature, hostility, pain, pleasure, etc.

Immigration: Permanent one-way movement into a new range.

Immune System: Functions to defend the body from infection by bacteria and viruses.

Imprinting: A learned behavior that develops in a critical or sensitive period of the animal's lifespan.

Incomplete Dominance: Some traits have no genes that are dominant and instead produce offspring that are a mix of the two parents.

Independent Assortment: Homologous chromosomes separate and independently sort in gamete formation.

Inheritance: The process by which characteristics pass from one generation to another.

Innate Behaviors: The actions in animals we call instincts; highly stereotyped.

Insulator: Poor conductors of electrical currents.

Interphase: The period when the cell is active in carrying on its functions.

Invertebrate: Those species having no internal backbone structure.

Ion: Charged atom.

Ionic Bond: Bond of attraction between positive and negative ions.

Isotope: Atoms with the same number of protons by different numbers of neutrons.

Kidney: Filter metabolic waste from the blood and excrete them as urine

Krebs Cycle: The first step in aerobic respiration that occurs in the matrix of a cell's mitochondria.

Law of Dominance: One gene is usually dominant over the other.

Law of Inertia: A particle at rest will stay at rest and a particle in motion will stay in motion until acted upon by an outside force.

Law of Segregation: Traits are expressed from a pair of genes in the individual (on homologous chromosomes).

Laws of Thermodynamics: Explain the interaction between heat and work (energy) in the universe.

Learned Behavior: May have some basis in genetics, but they also require learning.

Lymphatic System: The principal infection-fighting component of the immune system.

Lymphocyte: Begin in bone marrow as stem cells and are collected and distributed via the lymph nodes.

Lysosome: Membrane-bound organelles containing digestive enzymes; digest unused material within the cell, damaged organelles, or materials absorbed by the cell for use.

Magnetism: The ability of a substance to produce a magnetic field.

Mass: The amount of matter that is contained by the object.

Mechanics: The study of things in motion.

Medulla Oblongata: Part of the brain that controls involuntary responses such as breathing and heartbeat.

Meiosis: The process of producing four daughter cells, each with single unduplicated chromosomes.

Melting Point: Temperature at which a substance changes from solid to liquid form.

Metaphase: Step two of mitosis; occurs when the spindle fibers pull the chromosomes into alignment along the equatorial plane of the cell, creating the metaphase plate.

Microvilli: Projections of the cell extending from the cell membrane; increase the surface area of the cell membrane, increasing the area available to absorb nutrients.

Midbrain: Located between the forebrain and hindbrain; contains the optic lobes.

Migration: Temporary movement out of one range into another and back.

Mitochondria: Center of cellular respiration

Mitosis: The process by which a cell distributes its duplicated chromosomes so that each daughter cell has a full set of chromosomes.

Molar Mass: The mass in grams of one mole of atoms.

Molecule: Two or more atoms held together by shared electrons (covalent bonds).

Momentum: The product of mass and velocity.

mRNA: RNA strand that migrates form the nucleus to the cytoplasm; also known as messenger RNA.

Musculoskeletal System : Provides the body with structure, stability, and the ability to move.

Mutation: A change of the DNA sequence of a gene, resulting in a change of the trait.

Natural Selection: A feature of population genetics that is the driving force behind evolution.

Nerve Tissue: Carries electrical and chemical impulses to and from organs and limbs to the brain.

Nervous System: A communication network that connects the entire body of an organism and provides control over bodily functions.

Neuron: Carry impulses via electrochemical responses.

Newtons Laws: Three laws that form the basis of most of our understanding of things in motion.

Nuclear Membrane: The boundary between the nucleus and the cytoplasm.

Nucleolus: A rounded area within the nucleus of the cell where ribosomal RNA is synthesized.

Nucleus : An organelle surrounded by two lipid bilayer membranes that is located near the center of the cell and contains chromosomes, nuclear pores, nucleoplasm, and nucleoli.

Olfactory Lobe: Responsible for the sense of smell.

Oogenesis: Formation of egg cells.

Optic Lobe: Visual center connected to the eyes by the optic nerves.

Organelle: Cells components that perform particular functions.

Organic Compound: The building blocks of all living things.

Organism: An individual of a particular species.

Osmosis: A special process of diffusion that occurs when the water concentration inside the cell differs from the concentration outside the cell.

Ovary: The hollow, bulb-shaped structure in the lower interior of the pistil.

Ovules: Small round cases within the ovary that contain one or more egg cells.

Parasympathetic Nervous System: Carries impulses back from organs.

Pascals Principle: The pressure exerted on any point of a confined fluid is transmitted unchanged throughout the fluid.

Passive Transport: Substances freely pass across the membrane without the cell expending any energy.

Periodic Table: Listing of elements by atomic number.

Peripheral Nervous System: A network of nerves throughout the body.

pH: Potential of hydrogen scale, which is a measurement of H+ ions in solutions.

Phenotype: The trait expressed.

Photosynthesis: A crucial set of reactions that convert the light energy of the sun into chemical energy usable by living things.

Pituitary Gland: Releases various hormones.

Polar Molecule: Molecule that has regions of partial change.

Polygenic Trait: Traits produced from integration of multiple sets of genes.

Population: The total number of a single species of organism found in a given ecosystem.

Population Density: The number of individuals of a particular species living in a particular area.

Positron Decay: Occurs when the nucleus emits a particle that degrades into a positron as it passes out of the atom.

Pressure: A measure of the amount of force applied per unit of area.

Prokaryotic Cell: Cells with no nucleus or any other membrane-bound organelles.

Prophase: The first phase in mitosis.

Protein: Present in every living cell, large un-branched chains of amino acids; may also be called polypeptides.

Punctuated Equilibrium: Scientific model that proposes that adaptations of species arise suddenly and rapidly.

Punnett Square: Notation that allows us to easily predict the results of a genetic cross.

Quantum Mechanic: Predicts the probabilities of an electron being in a certain area at a certain time.

Radiation: The transfer of energy via waves.

Reactants: Reacting molecules.

Recessive Allele: The allele that does not produce its trait when present with a dominant allele.

Reflection: The bouncing of a wave of light off an object.

Reflex: An automatic movement of a body part in response to a stimulus.

Refraction: The change in direction of a wave as it passes from one medium to another.

Regulation: Enzyme control that may occur when the product of the reaction is also an inhibitor to the reaction.

Regulatory Genes: Code proteins that determine fictional or physiological events.

Respiratory System: Responsible for the intake and processing of gases required by an organism and for expelling gases produced as waste products.

Ribosome: The site of protein synthesis within cells.

Rough Endoplasmic Reticulum: Has attached ribosomes; instrumental to protein synthesis.

S Phase: The second phase of interphase where cell begins to prepare for cell division by replicating the DNA and proteins necessary to form a new set of chromosomes.

Secretory Vesicle: Carry substances produced within the cell to the cell membrane; packets of material packaged by the Golgi apparatus or endoplasmic reticulum.

Sex Influenced Trait: Requires only one recessive gene to be expressed if there is no counteracting dominant gene.

Sex Limited Trait: Genes located on a gender chromosome.

Skeletal Muscle: Attaches bones of the skeleton to each other and surrounding tissues, which enables voluntary movement.

Skin: An accessory excretory organ that secretes wastes with water from sweat glands.

Smooth Endoplasmic Reticulum: Network of membranous channels; does not have attached ribosomes.

Smooth Muscle    Makes up the walls of internal organs and functions in involuntary movement. (breathing, etc.)

Social Behavior: Behavior patterns that take into account other individuals.

Society: An organization of individuals in a population in which tasks are divided in order for the group to work together.

Somatic Motor Nerve: Carry impulses to skeletal muscle from the CNS.

Somatic Sensory Nerve:    Carry impulses from body surface to the CNS.

Specific Heat: The measure of a substance's ability to retain energy.

Speed: The rate of change of an object's distance traveled.

Sperm: Produced by the male gametophyte; also known as a male gamete.

Stoma: The body of the chloroplast.

Structural Gene    : Code proteins that form organs and structural characteristics.

Substrate: Particular substance of an enzyme that fits within the active site.

Succession: When one community completely replaces another over time in a given area.

Symbiosis: When two species interact with each other within the same range.

Sympathetic Nervous System: Carries impulses that stimulate organs.

Sympatric Speciation: Genetically different members reproduce with each other, producing a population, which is separate from the original species.

Synapse: Point at which homologous chromosomes pair up during meiosis.

T Cell: Mature cells in the thymus gland that patrol the blood for antigens but are also equipped to destroy antigens themselves.

Taxonomy: Study that organizes living things into groups based on morphology or, more recently, genetics.

Telophase: Step four in mitosis; occurs as nuclear membranes form around the chromosomes and disperse through the new nucleoplasm; spindle fibers also disappear.

Temperature: The measure of the average kinetic energy of a substance.

Territory: An area of land that lies within the home range that the individual will defend as his own.

Thymus: A mass of lymph tissue that is active only through the teen years, fighting infection and producing T cells.

Transcription: The formation of an RNA molecule, which corresponds to a gene.

Transduction: The transfer or genetic material (portions of a bacterial chromosome) from one bacteria cell to another.

Transformation: A process in which bacteria absorb and incorporate pieces of DNA from their environment (usually from dead bacterial cells).

Translation: Phase of photosynthesis that requires a second type of RNA.

Transpiration: A process in which some water that has traveled up through the plant to the leaves is evaporated.

tRNA: A chain of about 80 nucleotides that provide the link between the "language" of nucleotides (codon and anticodon) and the "language" of amino acids; also known as transfer RNA.

Valence Shell: The outermost occupied energy level of an element.

Van der Waals Force: Momentary force of attraction that exists between molecules and are much weaker than the forces of chemical bonding.

Vascular: Plants that have tissue organized in such a way as to conduct food and water throughout their structure.

Vector: Mathematical quantities that recognize both the size and direction of the dimension being considered.

Vein: Vessels that carry blood toward the heart.

Velocity: The rate of change of displacement; includes both speed and direction.

Vertebrate: Species that have internal backbones.

Vessel: Arteries, veins, and capillaries.

Villi: Protrusions out into the lumen of the intestine that provide a large surface area for absorption of nutrients.

Viruses: Smaller than even the smallest cells; survive and replicate by invading a living cell.

Visceral Sensory Nerve: Carry impulses from body organs to the CNS.

Voltage: The electromotive force that pushes electrons through the circuit.

Watson Crick Model: Named after scientists who discovered and modeled the structure of DNA.

Wavelength: The distance from one crest (or top) of a wave to the next crest on the same side.

Weight: The force of gravity acting upon that object.

Work: The movement of mass over a distance.

Zygote: Cell that results when a sperm cell fertilizes an egg cell.

Made in the USA
Middletown, DE
28 August 2020